AN INDEPENDENT SPIRIT

*The Quiet, Generous Life of
Helen Daniels Bader*

AN INDEPENDENT SPIRIT

The Quiet, Generous Life of
Helen Daniels Bader

Priscilla Pardini

Bader Philanthropies, Inc.
Milwaukee, Wisconsin

An Independent Spirit: The Quiet, Generous Life of Helen Daniels Bader by Priscilla Pardini
2020 © by Bader Philanthropies, Inc.

ISBN: 978-1-7348309-0-3
Library of Congress Control Number: 2020905794

Design and production: Kate Hawley, Kate Hawley by Design
Copyeditor: Jenny Gavacs
Proofreader: Paula Haubrich
Indexer: Darlene Waterstreet

Publisher:

Bader Philanthropies, Inc.
3300 N. Dr. Martin Luther King Jr. Dr.
Milwaukee, WI 53212

Printed in Canada

To all those who find themselves—during these dark and devastating days of 2020—most in need of the kindness, compassion, empathy, and generosity that defined the life of Helen Daniels Bader.

TABLE OF CONTENTS

Foreword by David Bader vii

Foreword by Daniel Bader ix

Preface xi

1. South Dakota 1

2. Jessie and Lloyd 35

3. A Child of the Depression 63

4. Courtship and Marriage 95

5. Children at Last 119

6. A Complicated Family 149

7. Helen Moves On 161

8. A New Life 183

9. An Insurmountable Challenge 203

Epilogue 221

Bibliography 225

Index 231

THOUGHTS ABOUT MY MOTHER

The first thing that comes to mind when listening for my mother's voice is her telling me, "Stop poking your brother!" I don't remember poking him, but I must have.

DETERMINATION AND PERSISTENCE WERE PART OF WHO SHE WAS.

Even today, I feel my mother's gentle but firm hand pushing me forward in life. She would tell me, "Don't stop trying. You can do it. When you fail at something, get organized and do it again." This attitude got me through engineering school as well as many other experiences in life.

Another saying, coming from her and her parents—"The utmost for the highest," which translates to "You be nice. Don't get dragged into others' ridiculous behavior." I never remember my mother being nasty or manipulative; it just wasn't in her. She was raised well.

Also, she urged me to "Finish what you start." This translates to "Stay focused. Finish your projects in life. Don't get distracted." More specifically, it meant "Finish your education, finish your architecture internship, and pass your architecture boards." I did all of that.

"LET'S GO OUT TO EAT. I'M HUNGRY."

My mother had a great palate and was a wonderful cook. Her good friend Rita Gordy taught her a lot about cooking and going to the Gordys' was a big part of our life back then. We ate very well, and things were well seasoned. When my father was home, my mother—with our help—would prepare formal dinners served on antique china. My brother and I spent a lot of time in the kitchen helping her prepare, serve, and clean up meals. To this day I enjoy cooking dinner and serving it, but not cleaning up. However, I will clean up, if necessary.

When I was in Philadelphia working as an architectural intern, she would often come for weekend visits, and bring me brownies still in the 9" x 13" brownie pan. She left me the pans. After a while I had quite a few brownie pans. When she and I would go out to eat and dessert options were offered, she would tell the waiter, "No, I'm not having dessert," and then nodding in my direction, "But he is having dessert, and please bring an extra fork."

HELPING WAS PART OF WHO SHE WAS.

"I want to help them."

"I want to help this organization."

"Help the lady carry her meat home from the kosher butcher." (And the butcher saying, "That's a Bader.")

"After work, take Millie out and help her find a car. Make sure it's a good one."

"Go help Mrs. Zupnik set up her apartment and hang her paintings."

"Teach me how to use this camera."

"Help your brother."

"Help your father.

"Help me."

"Help yourself."

"Try harder and get some help."

"Ask for help."

"You and Daniel can help set the table, please."

SHE WASN'T AN ANGEL

When it came to one of her boys getting hurt, my mother could get upset and a little unhinged. As an example, I will tell you the minibike story: A minibike is a motorized scooter with small wheels that goes fast. I bought my minibike with my bar mitzvah money and kept it in good condition. When Daniel was twenty-one, he took my minibike out for a spin. He apparently was going fast, crashed into a street curb, and scraped himself up badly. I was not there to see this happen. After this accident, he visited our mother. When she saw him bloodied, she got upset. When I complained to her that he had wrecked my bike, she yelled at me, "Why did you let him ride it?" Then she hit me. (A loving whack, but she meant it.) I replied, "I didn't let him. He took it out of the garage when I wasn't home and tried to jump a curb with it. The curb won." She responded, "It is your fault for keeping that thing; get rid of it." I got rid of it.

RANDOM HELEN THINGS

"Do you feel the beat, David?" My mother's foot was always tapping to the rhythm of some melody whether it was blues or classical music, or when she was playing her violin. Her foot bobbed up and down constantly.

"David, go practice your instrument."

About her mother, she'd say, "Mother is going to outlive all of us." Her mother outlived her.

She would call her father "Daddy" with great love and admiration.

Feeling patterns between parents and children transfer from one generation to the next. I loved my mother in the same way she loved her father.

She couldn't lie or bend the truth. She couldn't even tell a white lie.

Road rage was expressed by her pumping her fist and yelling, "You farmer!"

"You see that man?" she'd ask. "I bet he doesn't have ten cents to his name."

THE PEOPLE AROUND HER

My mother enjoyed people for who they were, even difficult people. She didn't criticize or demonize them for their shortcomings or who they weren't.

Her philosophy was that people are their best when they feel safe, nurtured, and are encouraged to be themselves. "You be you by being the greatest you that you can be."

She said to me about our beloved dog Charlie, "Of course, Charlie rolled wet dirt all over your newly cleaned runner; he's a dog. If I was a dog, that's exactly what I would do." Charlie was a very happy dog.

About a man at work who (literally) wore many different hats, "Did you see Johnny's hats? They are so much fun."

She was a keen observer of the people around her, and if they had good intentions, she would encourage them to be their best selves. She would find the beauty in people even if it wasn't apparent. She really enjoyed her collection of people. What is life for if you can't enjoy the greatness in people?

—David Bader

The Many Sides of Helen Daniels Bader

My mother, Helen Daniels Bader (Danny), was an extraordinary, multifaceted woman—a citizen of many worlds and cultures, and comfortable in all of them.

She was born in a small town, and thus was a small-town girl. She moved to the big city, and was thus a big-city girl. She traveled throughout Europe, and thus was an international lady. Wherever she was, she was authentic, and she was at home.

She was raised in a Christian Science household, and thus had Christian roots. She converted to Judaism as an adult and was a committed Jew. She loved religion and people of all religions.

She worked in a pharmacy as a teenager, and thus was an experienced retail employee. She helped build one of the most successful chemical companies in the world, and thus was an entrepreneur. She earned a degree in social work, and thus was a professional social worker.

She knew how to interact with people in all kinds of settings and environments. She could meet with the homeless, university presidents, rabbis, pastors, chief executive officers, the elderly, and children—always with a smile on her face and a sense of dignity and compassion.

She was like a Swiss army knife: she had a tool for every situation.

She was kind and empathetic. Yet she was a savvy businessperson.

She could make grilled cheese for lunch and Hungarian goulash for dinner.

She was comfortable in the countryside, small towns, and the big city.

She was a loving and compassionate mother, but yet had a tough side to her.

Whatever the situation, she was at ease and confident.

An Independent Spirit: The Quiet, Generous Life of Helen Daniels Bader, written by Priscilla Pardini and published by Bader Philanthropies, Inc., is a compelling account of my mother's extraordinary life. It traces the journey of a young girl born and raised in Aberdeen, South Dakota, who became an entrepreneur, a social worker, and a philanthropist, and whose incredible legacy has impacted thousands of people over the years.

But most of all, Helen Daniels Bader was my mom, and I am blessed to have been raised by her.

—Daniel Bader

PREFACE

It was the early 1970s and Helen Daniels Bader was two decades into a successful career as a businesswoman. Yet, unbeknownst to most who knew her, Helen saw herself in a much different role. Her sons, David and Daniel, were among the few with whom she shared her long-term plan. They recall driving with their mother past St. Rose Orphanage on Milwaukee's East Side and hearing her remark, "I want to work there someday." As David recounted, "I think that was when we began to realize she was interested in social causes. Of course, now we know that was her calling." Added Daniel, "It seemed like a natural fit for her, given how much she really liked working with and helping people." St. Rose's closed in 1974, but Helen went on to reinvent herself, earning a graduate degree in social work as a nontraditional student, launching a second career, and ultimately leaving behind a legacy as one of Milwaukee's best-known philanthropists.

Helen Bader's story is rooted in an independent spirit that, in turn, can be traced to ancestors engaged in fur trading, dry goods sales, and farming who helped settle the Minnesota and Dakota territories. They interacted with members of the local Sioux and Chippewa tribes, fought in the Civil and Spanish-American wars, and worked on the early American railroads, all while combatting some of the nation's harshest weather and most destructive natural disasters, and struggling through the Great Depression.

A child of the Depression who grew up behind the soda fountain in her father's Aberdeen, South Dakota, pharmacy, Helen began defining her own path early on. As a young girl, she was a bit of a rebel, eschewing the hair bows fashioned for her by her mother and grandmother and the paper dolls that were her older sister's favorites. Instead, it was blue jeans and a bicycle for Helen. As a shy teenager, she found the social scene at Aberdeen High School mostly inconsequential, and her academic classes, tedious. Her favorite activity was playing violin in the school orchestra. As a graduating senior, she was recognized in the school yearbook for having "the best sense of all, common sense." But it was as a young, beautiful college graduate that Helen most notably defied convention, marrying the brilliant Jewish chemist and art collector Alfred Robert Bader. For the next thirty years, Helen's life would be made up of a mix of highs and lows, which is not unusual in and of itself. Yet it was how Helen accepted, coped with, and both celebrated and overcame what she encountered that ultimately defined her remarkable life.

An Independent Spirit: The Quiet, Generous Life of Helen Daniels Bader documents that life. Published by Bader Philanthropies, Inc., its origin can be traced to a conversation spearheaded several years ago by Stan Stojkovic, at the time, dean of what is now the Helen Bader School of Social Welfare at the University of Wisconsin-Milwaukee, with members of Bader Philanthropies' board of directors and staff. Bader Philanthropies is also publishing a companion volume, currently in production, tracing the history of the school. The purpose, of course, is to record for posterity the events that defined the life of Helen Bader and shaped the school that bears her name.

As Helen's biographer, I embarked upon this project well aware of my responsibility to do justice to her story, and I am grateful to everyone who helped me in my efforts to do just that. An early and valuable source of assistance was Robert Russell, director of the Beulah Williams Library at Northern State University in Aberdeen, South Dakota, who arranged access for me to archival editions of Aberdeen's historical newspapers. Among the many reasons to mourn the death of local news coverage in America is the fact that biographers of the future will never have the opportunity I did to pour over lively, detailed—and, yes, sometimes downright intrusive—accounts of the lives of regular citizens living in Aberdeen in the early twentieth century. Scattered across the pages of these newspapers were articles capturing everything from the sublime to the mundane, the humorous to the tragic—all providing the details that helped me bring the stories of Helen and her South Dakota ancestors to life.

I also am indebted to others who helped me access key historical information, including Sue Gates, former director of Aberdeen's Dacotah Prairie Museum, and her successor, Patricia Kendall; Sue Schaefer, executive director of the South Dakota Pharmacists Association; Michael Sattell, president and chief executive officer of Ovation Communities; and Carolyn Bucior, former communications specialist at the Helen Bader School of Social Welfare. I am grateful as well to Jacquelyn N. Coutré, the former Bader Curator and Researcher of European Art at Queen's University, for information on paintings donated to the university by the Bader family.

Archivists Ruby Wilson, at South Dakota State University's Hilton M. Briggs Library; Lina Rosenberg Foley, at Lawrence University's Seeley G. Mudd Library; Abigail Nye, Shiraz Bhathena, and Alison Newman, at the University of Wisconsin-Milwaukee Libraries; Steve Schaffer, at the Milwaukee County Historical Society; and Jay Hyland, at the Jewish Museum Milwaukee, also provided me with key assistance, as did librarians throughout the Milwaukee County Federated Library System and at Chicago's Newberry Library.

Following Helen's death, a number of her relatives and friends—some of whom are now deceased—recorded video interviews in which they recounted their memories of her. Sponsored by what was then the Helen Bader Foundation, Inc. under the direction of Robert Tobon, today a program officer at Bader Philanthropies, this project unearthed a wealth of valuable information. I was also fortunate to be able to interview some of these individuals myself, including the late Nita Corré, Rabbi Peter Mehler, and Peter Baime. Other of Helen's friends and acquaintances who agreed to interviews included Ralph Emanuel, Molly Gordy Drew, Joan Prince, Francie Klitsner Wolff, Nina Holmquist, and David Harvey. Still others, such as Carolyn and Sara Emanuel, assisted with photo research.

At Bader Philanthropies, Vice President Lisa Hiller schooled me in the organization's history, and along with Vice President Maria Lopez Vento and Communications Coordinator Merilou Gonzales helped coordinate the book's publication. I am grateful for all of their assistance and guidance as well as the enthusiasm they brought to this project. They, along with other staffers and board members, also reviewed the manuscript and provided valuable input. Especially helpful in this regard were Margaret Foster, Francie Wolff, and Michelle Berrong Bader.

My deepest thanks to my gifted editor, Jenny Gavacs, who provided not only valuable guidance and encouragement over a number of years as I researched and drafted this book, but also impeccable attention to the text. Thanks as well to proofreader Paula Haubrich for her keen eye. Book designer Kate Hawley brought to the project myriad skills, as well as a keen sense of humor and unlimited patience. Whether she was conducting photo research, fact-checking, laying out book pages, or orchestrating the production process, Kate's talent and wisdom proved to be invaluable. Beyond that, I found in her someone who shared my desire to tell Helen's story with truth and sensitivity. Lastly, of course, it is Kate's stunning design that brings my words, and that story, to life.

This project benefited immeasurably from the support and cooperation of Helen's niece, Deirdre Helen (DeVey) Britt, and her nephews, Allyn, Graham, and Dan DeVey. It was Allyn who several years ago gave me a copy of the Daniels family tree that launched my research; last fall, he met with Kate and me in Richardson, Texas, where together we examined the DeVey family collection of historical photos, letters, and other materials that had been held in safekeeping for years with Dan and his wife, Leanne. All of the DeVeys were generous with their time, and I am especially grateful for their willingness to share recollections of their parents, Marjorie and Dick, and their Aunt Helen. They were also incredibly patient with me, answering myriad questions I raised during the fact-checking process. Special thanks to Deirdre, a member of the board of directors of Bader Philanthropies, who not only shared memories and family photos, but also keen insight into Helen's life, and who challenged me to think deeply about her aunt's legacy.

As for the Baders, I was fortunate to have had the chance to meet with and interview Isabel Overton Bader, Alfred's second wife, whom he married in 1982. She was gracious and forthcoming, and I so appreciate her not only talking with me but also reading a draft of the book, pointing out inaccuracies, and offering up suggestions for improvement. Working with David and Daniel was a pleasure. In our very first conversation about the project, Daniel stressed that he wanted the biography to be a complete and honest account of his mother's life, and he and David spent countless hours with me in thoughtful conversations sharing their personal reminiscences. David arranged for me to join him on a trip to London retracing Helen's footsteps as we visited some of the same places she and Alfred frequented during their numerous trips to Europe. It was on that trip that I had the privilege and pleasure of meeting and interviewing Helen and Alfred's good friend Ralph Emanuel.

Although I never had the chance to meet Helen Bader, it has been a privilege to get to know her through this project. And given what I have learned about her, I find myself wondering, as this book goes to press, how she would have felt about its publication. Along with her independent spirit, Helen will be remembered for her humble and unpretentious nature and a lifelong practice of anonymous philanthropy. And so, I have concluded that she would not be particularly keen on the idea. Yet Helen's rich, compelling story deserves to be told, particularly now in the midst of this turbulent spring of 2020 when the example she set—one of resilience, compassion, empathy, and social justice—needs to be emulated perhaps more than ever.

— Priscilla Pardini

REGISTER OF DANIELS

Allyn

Allyn ~ Gaylord ~ Mabbott ~ Flansburgh ~ Bernard ~ Springthorpe ~

Wilder DeVey
Richard DeVey
Helen DeVey
Leonard DeVey

.0—-88
scripsit:
~Marjorie Daniels DeVey

Names visible on the fan chart:

Daniels ~ Daniels (33.)
Joseph Daniels
Joseph Wilson Daniels (8.)
Lloyd Allyn Daniels
Marjorie Jean Daniels
Jessie Leonia Mabbott

Ann (24.)
Nora (12.)

Wilson Uselton (34.)
Martha Uselton (17.)
Mary Jane Baker (35.)
Pearl Rose Allyn
George A Amos Mabbott (10.)
Leonia Annie Flansburgh (11.)

John Sidney A Allyn (18.)
E Phriam Allyn (36.)
Theresa Gaylord (19.)
Frederick Gaylord (38.)
Edward John Mabbott (20.)
Margaret Stuart Bernard (21.)
Edgar John Flansburgh (22.)
Eliza Sarah Farrington (23.)

George Baker (140.)
Eleanor Litz
Jane Quinn
Robert Allyn (74.)
Deborah Avery

John Allyn
Elizabeth Gage

William Allyn (martyred 155...)
Robert Allyn
James Avery
Deborah Selwood

CHAPTER ONE

SOUTH DAKOTA

Helen Daniels Bader was profoundly affected by her upbringing in South Dakota, one of the thirteen states carved out of the land annexed by the United States in the Louisiana Purchase of 1803. Meriwether Lewis and William Clark traveled through the area the following year on their way west; however, the territory had been explored sixty-one years earlier by French explorers, including brothers Louis-Joseph Gaultier de la Vérendrye and François Gaultier Du Tremblay, who at the time—like Lewis and Clark—were searching for a river route through the Rocky Mountains to the Pacific Ocean.

Just west of the Mississippi River the explorers had encountered a vast expanse of fertile grassland that would eventually become known as the Great Plains and America's Breadbasket; attract folk heroes such as Calamity Jane, Paul Bunyan, General George Armstrong Custer, and Wild Bill Hickok; and serve as the site of the Mount Rushmore National Memorial. The weather was harsh: winters were long, cold, and snowy; the summers, hot and often dry. Huge herds of buffalo roamed free.

Lewis and Clark's first encounter with the area's American Indians occurred at the mouth of the James River near the southeast corner of what is now South Dakota, in 1804. There they would take part in a gathering with the nomadic, peaceful Yankton Sioux, who had been pushed west from present-day Minnesota by the Chippewa Indians, and who would go on to populate that portion of the Great Plains that is today North and South Dakota. In fact, the word "Dakota"—the name of one of three tribes of the Sioux Nation—means "ally" or "friend" in the Sioux language.

Opposite background: *Helen Daniels Bader's sister, Marjorie Jean Daniels DeVey, worked diligently on the Daniels/DeVey family tree.*

Opposite foreground: *Long Fox, pictured here in 1872, was a leader of the Yankton Sioux, a peaceful, nomadic tribe whose members were among the first residents of North and South Dakota.*
NATIONAL ARCHIVES

Above: *Leon Flansburgh, Helen's great uncle, pictured with his dog, Ned, was born in Aberdeen, South Dakota, where his family had moved in 1882 to farm.*

A GREAT PLAINS ANCESTRY

Helen Bader's South Dakota roots can be traced back to great-grandparents on both sides of her family. By 1807 the first trading posts, small log cabins located near American Indian villages and staffed by a single, salaried agent, had been established in the area. Decades of trading by English, French, and Spanish explorers had already established how lucrative it could be to barter a range of relatively cheap goods including mirrors, guns, knives, blankets, salt, and sugar with the American Indians in exchange for highly coveted beaver, deer, and buffalo skins. The fur trade proliferated over the next forty years, along with trading posts such as the one established by one of Helen's paternal great-grandfathers, Joseph Wilson Daniels Sr. Born and raised in Virginia, Daniels traveled west with his brother Nathaniel in the late 1840s. They were among the earliest settlers to migrate from the East Coast to what was then the Minnesota Territory. By 1850, travel writer E. S. Seymour was describing the newly formed territory as the "New England of the West"; indeed, by 1860, nearly 80 percent of its native-born, white residents would hail from New England and New York.

By 1870, Helen's paternal great-grandfather Joseph Wilson Daniels Sr. was operating Levy & Daniels, a dry goods store in Stillwater, Minnesota.

Joseph Wilson Daniels Sr. died in 1889.

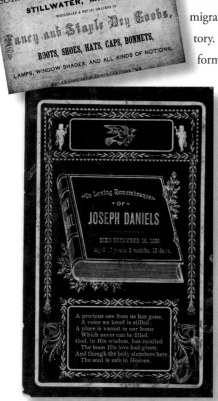

Yet when the Daniels brothers arrived on the scene, it was still largely populated by American Indians. Minnesota Territorial Governor Alexander Ramsey, describing the city of St. Paul when he first saw it in 1849, noted "the motley humanity partially filling these streets and the blankets and printed faces of Indians, and the red sashes and moccasins of French voyageurs and half-breeds, greatly predominating over the less picturesque costume of the Anglo-American race."

Settling in the Lake Pepin area about sixty miles downstream from St. Paul, the Daniels brothers established their trading post, where they bartered with the Chippewa. In 1865, Joseph married Martha Uselton, a Quaker whose family had traveled from Pennsylvania to Stillwater, Minnesota, outside of St. Paul, nine years earlier. Their son (and Helen's paternal grandfather), Joseph Wilson Daniels Jr., was born in 1867. According to family lore, the elder Joseph Daniels may well have been engaged in negotiations between the Chippewa and the US government. By 1870, he was a merchant, operating Levy & Daniels, a "fancy and staple" dry goods store in Stillwater. Martha, he told census takers, was "keeping my house." Their son reportedly recalled his mother wearing her Quaker bonnet, and his father, who spoke Chippewa, sitting along a riverbank smoking and talking with the local American Indians.

Another of Helen's great-grandfathers, John Sidney Allyn, was one of eleven children born in 1832 to a prominent family in Groton, Connecticut. He traveled west to Red Wing, Minnesota, in 1856. Three years later, he married Theresa Gaylord, whose family hailed from New York State, and with whom he would father four children, including Helen's grandmother Pearl Rose Allyn. Helen would be named after another daughter, her great

Helen's paternal great-grandfather John Sidney Allyn married Theresa Gaylord in 1859.

aunt Helen. During the 1860s, John Allyn traveled alone through American Indian territory, carrying supplies from Red Wing to Mankato, Minnesota. As family members attest, his interactions with the Chippewa were less cordial than those Joseph Daniels had experienced, and reportedly included numerous skirmishes. Allyn's life took another dramatic turn some years later when, while working as a petty officer in the US Navy, he was shipwrecked near the Florida Keys while laying cable from Key West to Cuba.

But perhaps the most sensational event of Allyn's life was the way he died on June 4, 1893: murdered with an axe in his own barn, according to the *Red Wing Journal*. At the time, Allyn ran a local hardware store, in downtown Red Wing, and was working as an agent for the United States Express Company, a privately owned company that shipped parcels and freight across the northern states from New England to Colorado. Despite a $1,500 reward put up by Theresa Allyn for information about the murder, the perpetrator was never caught.

Theresa Gaylord Allyn mourned the death of her husband, who was murdered in the family's barn in 1893 by an unknown assailant.

THE MABBOTT BRANCH OF THE FAMILY

Helen's ancestors on her mother's side included her great-grandfathers Edward James Mabbott and Edgar John Flansburgh. Mabbott was born in Lincolnshire, England, in 1843—the seventh of twelve children—and emigrated from there to America with his family at the age of three. By 1850, according to census records, the Mabbotts were living in Arena, Wisconsin, about twenty-five miles northwest of Madison. By the time he was seventeen, Edward had enlisted in the Civil War as a private in the Wisconsin Infantry. Serving for three years, he likely saw action in Arkansas, Louisiana, and at the Battle of Vicksburg, Virginia, and probably crossed paths with Abraham Lincoln in St. Louis. In 1866, Edward married Margaret Bernard, a native of Prince Edward Island, Canada, and settled near Spring Green, Wisconsin. The couple's second of three sons, George Amos Mabbott, Helen's maternal grandfather, was born in 1868 in Richland Center, Wisconsin.

The Flansburghs trace their origins to Flensburg, Germany, near the Danish border. Edgar John Flansburgh moved west from New York in

1847 at the age of seven; what impressed him most was the first leg of the journey on the Erie Canal. The family settled in Michigan, where in 1864 Edgar met and married his wife, Toronto native Eliza Sarah Farrington. Their daughter, Leonia—Helen's maternal grandmother—was born six years later, the eldest of four children. When Leonia was twelve, the family moved to Aberdeen, South Dakota, to farm. There, Edgar made headlines on April 12, 1894: "E. J. Flansburgh has the mumps," reads a short article in the *Aberdeen Daily News*. "A man who lives in this world for fifty-five years before having the mumps, comes very near cheating one disease out of its mission." But Edgar Flansburgh's ultimate claim to fame may have been his invention, in 1895, of what the *Daily News* called "a self-dropping corn planter" fashioned from an old mower. Noted the newspaper, "It works to perfection and beats paying for a planter." After fifteen years in Aberdeen, Edgar and Eliza moved farther west, to Palouse Valley in Washington State, where their descendants still farm.

Left: *Helen's maternal great-grandparents, Edward and Margaret Bernard Mabbott, posed for a formal portrait with Parke, one of their three sons.*

Right: *In 1864, Helen's second set of maternal great-grandparents, Edgar John Flansburgh and Eliza Sarah Farrington, met and married in Michigan.*

LIFE IN THE DAKOTA TERRITORY

By the mid-nineteenth century, with Helen's ancestral roots already well established in the Dakota Territory, three events would take place that set the stage for the widespread, permanent settlement of the area that was to become South Dakota: Under the 1858 Treaty of Washington negotiated by the Yankton Sioux, the tribe ceded fourteen million acres of American Indian land to the US government in return for a four hundred thousand-acre reservation and $1.6 million in annuities. Three years later, the Dakota Territory was created, paving the way for eventual statehood. Named after the Dakota Sioux, the territory was made up of what today constitutes North Dakota, South Dakota, and much of Wyoming and Montana. And in 1862, President Abraham Lincoln signed the Homestead Act, which rewarded settlers with one hundred and sixty acres of land in return for living on it for five years.

In response, another wave of settlers arrived in the Dakota Territory during the 1860s and early 1870s. Like their predecessors, they hailed from New England and Europe, and journeyed west in covered wagons or on boats and rafts traveling up the Missouri River. But many became

Covered wagons bringing settlers to the Dakota Territory had become a familiar site by the mid-nineteenth century.

NATIONAL ARCHIVES

An Independent Spirit: The Quiet, Generous Life of Helen Daniels Bader

discouraged by the harsh landscape and extreme weather—not to mention horrifying experiences unique to prairie life—they encountered. The prairie fires of October 1871, for example, destroyed millions of acres of prairie grass and farmsteads, with flames so fierce they jumped rivers. Adding insult to injury, rattlesnakes found their way into sod shanties and cabins. Historian Helen Graham Rezatto recounted that one woman found a rattlesnake curled around her sewing machine and "killed it with an accurate stab through the head with a long knitting needle." Then there were the grasshoppers, including a particularly devastating infestation in what Rezatto calls the "horrible grasshopper year of 1874." Writes Rezatto, "The hoppers stripped the cornfields, ate potatoes and cabbages right out of the ground, stripped the bark from young willows. The loathsome insects even halted trains with millions of them heaped on the tracks, making the rails so slippery that the tracks had to be sanded before trains could move. The stench of dead grasshoppers over the countryside was sickening."

Meanwhile, the provisions of the Treaty of Washington were proving untenable, with American Indian charges of broken promises and unfair treatment by government agents sparking the 1862 Sioux Uprising. Making

Settlers gathered around their sod house near Aberdeen, South Dakota, in 1882. Sod homes were abundant on the prairie, where wood for log cabins was scarce.

matters worse, once-abundant buffalo and beaver populations were becoming depleted, depriving the American Indians of their most vital source of livelihood. As a result, trading posts evolved: some into large, stockade-enclosed spaces more military than commercial, and others into free-standing general stores. All of these factors—the weather, the critters, the American Indian wars—proved too much for many of the pioneers, thousands of whom returned east or moved farther west.

THE BOOM YEARS AND STATEHOOD

By 1878, however, a third, larger wave of pioneers began pouring into the region, thanks both to the lure of gold in the Black Hills and a network of newly completed railroad lines. In fact, as Rezatto noted, it was an advertising campaign by the Northern Pacific Railroad that promised to transport European immigrants looking for a better life to a "Garden of Eden" with cheap land and giant crops. What's more, according to historian James F. Hamburg, the droughts and locust infestations abated, boosting crop production, as did the introduction of barbed wire and new agricultural methods and equipment.

What these settlers found, however, didn't necessarily live up to what they'd been promised, and like some of those who had come before them, they were profoundly disappointed. According to Rezatto, whose grandfather migrated west in 1882, "When they got off the train at a cluster of shacks beside a railroad track on the Dakota prairies, they were often dumbfounded. Speaking in German or Danish or Norwegian or Swedish, they asked each other, 'Is this a town? Where are we? Where is the tall corn and the waving fields of wheat?'"

The natural disasters kept coming. Thousands of people living near Yankton, in southern Dakota Territory, were forced to flee their homes when an ice dam on the Missouri River burst in the spring of 1881. "For two weeks, large areas of bottom lands, extending many hundreds of miles along each side of the river, have been submerged by water and heavy masses of ice," reads a dispatch sent to the US Secretary of the Interior describing the devastation.

Winter brought some of the most formidable challenges. Consider, for instance, the so-called Children's Blizzard that swept across the upper

Leslie's Weekly published this illustration of the Children's Blizzard, which struck the Dakotas on January 12, 1888, without warning. According to some news accounts, the temperature fell nearly one hundred degrees in just twenty-four hours.
WIKIMEDIA COMMONS

Midwest beginning in the early afternoon of January 12, 1888. It earned its name by trapping thousands of children in their one-room school-houses. According to published reports, temperatures dropped to forty degrees below zero, and wind speeds were clocked at sixty miles per hour. As many as five hundred people may have perished in all, including an estimated two hundred and thirteen students who died attempting to get home. The storm's epicenter was in southeastern Dakota Territory, where in Bon Homme County, it took months to find the bodies of a teacher and nine of her students who died after becoming caught in the wind and freezing to death. In Jerauld County, another teacher was luckier, man-aging to survive the night with her students in a hay mound after failing to reach a farmhouse just one hundred yards from their school. And in Hanson County, two men tied several clotheslines together at the local general store before walking three blocks to the local school and using the line to guide the children into town.

Still, despite any initial disillusionment and the very real hardships Dakota pioneers had to endure, 1878 to 1887 were boom years in the territory. Helen's ancestors and their fellow settlers turned out to be a resilient lot. As Rezatto points out, even as the pioneers beat back the natural elements, they went to work building schools and churches and establishing general stores, saloons, and jails. They bonded with each other over "a long visit at a neighbor's house, an all-night dance with a midnight supper, quilting, and barn-raising, and spelling bees. European immigrants struggled with American Indian tongue-twisters. They argued over plowing methods and fought over the locations of county seats."

Population in the Dakota Territory, which stood at 135,700 in 1880, more than tripled by 1885, with population gains averaging nearly 1,000 new settlers per week during most of the period. Much of that growth can be traced to the arrival of the railroad: the Northern Pacific, through the northern half of the territory beginning in 1871, and the Dakota Southern, through the territory's southern half a year later. Writes historian Shebby Lee, "The influence of the railroads cannot be overemphasized in both the rapid settlement and ultimate success of Dakota Territory. They tended to neutralize the negative weather and conditions by bringing in fuel, food, fencing, and building materials—all unavailable on the treeless plains. And of course, the railroads brought the farmer closer to his marketplace."

With population growth came a push for statehood, which had begun as early as 1871 with calls for dividing the territory into two new states. With the territory's population concentrated in its northeast and southeast corners, and politicians arguing over the location of its capital, the idea of two states was appealing, both to the locals and to Republicans in control of Congress eager to see two new, conservative states join the union. And so, on November 2, 1889, President Benjamin Harrison signed the papers granting both North and South Dakota statehood, reportedly shuffling the documents so it was unclear which he signed first. Based on alphabetical order, however, North Dakota was considered the thirty-ninth state, and South Dakota, the fortieth.

Both North and South Dakota became states on November 2, 1889.
PUBLIC DOMAIN

ABERDEEN, A MAGIC CITY

Helen Bader's paternal and maternal grandparents—Joseph Wilson Daniels Jr. and Pearl Rose Allyn, and George Amos Mabbott and Leonia Annie Flansburgh, respectively—represented different, yet equally valuable, pillars of turn-of-the-century Aberdeen. The Daniels clan embodied the new, pioneer, can-do spirit, with Joseph Jr., commonly known as Joe, growing into a popular figure who reveled first in the life of a trainman, and later, in real estate speculation and auto sales. The Mabbotts were throwbacks: George Mabbott, who had been born in England at the beginning of the Victorian era, would become one of Aberdeen's most highly respected citizens, heading a household that placed high value on social conventions.

Both families settled in Aberdeen, which was incorporated in 1881 to accommodate the westward expansion of the transcontinental railway. The county seat of Brown County, in what is now northeastern South Dakota, Aberdeen was named for Aberdeen, Scotland, birthplace of Alexander Mitchell, founder of the Chicago, Milwaukee, St. Paul, and Pacific Railroad Company. The city soon became known as Hub City, a reference to both its location at the midpoint of nine different railroad lines fanning out in all directions like the spokes of a wheel, and the city's significance as a major distribution center for wholesale goods. According to historian George Washington Kingsbury, the first locomotive—with the Hastings and Dakota Railroad—arrived in Aberdeen on July 6, 1881, paving the way for an influx of homesteaders from New England and New York.

Situated at the midpoint of nine different railroad lines, Aberdeen became known as the Hub City of the Dakotas.

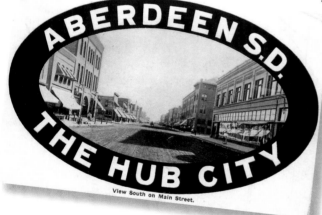

Prior to the arrival of the railroad, Aberdeen's population had stood at just 353, making it one of hundreds of small enclaves dotting the Great Plains that were made up of little more than sod houses and simple frame buildings. However, by July 1882, the city of Aberdeen had no equal in the Great Plains, and according to *History of Dakota Territory,* was "something of a magic city." Population stood at 800 (it would soar to nearly twice that by the end of the year), with 194 buildings, 68 of which were commercial. The city's early settlers, according to historian J. H. McKeever, "were men and women of culture and education," who displayed none of the "pistol-toting wild west rowdyism" often associated with the Dakota Territory. Sue Gates, former director of Aberdeen's Dacotah Prairie Museum, pointed out in an interview that Aberdeen's founders had come west not to farm, but rather to pursue professional lives. "They may have become landowners," she said, "but they weren't farmers . . . they were well educated, economically secure professionals who transferred their professional lives out here."

According to an article in the *Minnesota Farmer* excerpted in *Looking Back,* a publication edited by Gates and published by the Dacotah Prairie Museum Foundation, "There were stores for general sundries, hardware, drugs, lumber, shoes, furniture, meat, and baked goods. Service providers included tailors, barbers, lawyers, doctors, photographers, sign painters, and blacksmiths. There were three restaurants, a cigar manufacturer, a dairy, and four livery barns." The town's first public "enterprise," according to the newspaper, was "the erection of a schoolhouse, rough and cheap it was, but warm, commodious, and well furnished." The Aberdeen Free Library Association was organized in 1884.

Social life was replete with teas, card parties, club meetings, charity balls, book clubs, picnics, amateur theatricals, fashion shows, and musical programs not only common but also well documented in the local press. According to *Brown County History,* Maud Baum, the wife of author L. Frank Baum, "said that she had attended grand parties in the East and even in Europe, but she had the best time in Aberdeen, dancing all night in a red calico gown."

According to *Looking Back,* Aberdeen became the site of the first of several state fairs in 1884, and later, the permanent location of the Brown County Fair. The Ringling Bros. and Barnum & Bailey Circus put on its first shows in Aberdeen in 1892, and would continue to do so annually for more than fifty years. The city's Grain Palace, described as a building designed to "far outshine the existing corn palace in Sioux City," opened to acclaim on September 11, 1893, with a program featuring speakers and exhibits promoting area agriculture. Over the next nine years, until the building was destroyed by fire in 1902, it drew notable speakers, including

Birdseye View in Aberdeen So. Dak
Looking North East from Roof Garben

In 1910, Aberdeen was home to the six-story Citizens Bank Building, the tallest building in the Dakotas.

President William McKinley and famed orator Williams Jennings Bryan. In 1896, the city's Opera House was described as "state-of-the-art," only to be replaced with one declared "the finest show house in the Midwest" just four years later. Future attractions would include an air show in 1919 by the Victory Liberty Loan Flying Circus's World War I ace aviators, a three-day "Tractor Extravaganza" that same year demonstrating the efficiency of a new generation of mechanized farm equipment that drew a reported fifty thousand spectators, and a series of concerts beginning in 1920 by John Philip Sousa.

Meanwhile, Aberdeen pioneer John L. W. Zietlow had organized the Aberdeen Telephone Company in 1896, and soon Aberdeen led the world in the number of telephones per capita: one phone for every 6.5 people. In 1910, the city became home to the six-story Citizens Bank Building, the tallest building in the Dakotas, and the Aberdeen Street Railway, a five-and-a-half-mile-long streetcar route. By 1911, Aberdonians could boast of more than two miles of paved streets—more than in any other city in South Dakota—good news to city residents who had begun buying cars in 1900. Yet, even as Aberdeen embraced modern modes of transportation, as late as 1911 some residents were lobbying for more hitching posts. According to minutes of a town meeting on the subject unearthed by McKeever, "We must have some place to tie our teams or quit coming to your burg. . . . No

man can sit in his rig and do business from his wagon seat." What's more, two of the city's most venerable "employees," mules named Maude and Kate who pulled a wagon that hauled garbage to the city dump, remained on the municipal payroll up until the early 1930s.

To be sure, there were crises: Along with the severe weather and other natural catastrophes that plagued all of the Great Plains came man-made disasters. In 1884, the digging of a city well unleashed water pressure so powerful that the town flooded. Ironically, nine years later, and after several years of severe drought, town leaders hired a Kansas rainmaker who for $1,000 used a secret process to make it rain not once, but twice. Raging fires destroyed not only the Grain Palace, but also the Chicago, Milwaukee, and St. Paul Railroad depot in 1911, and the Sherman and Ward Hotels in 1926. (Ironically, Aberdeen's firemen—world champions in popular firefighting events such as hook and ladder races—were out of town at a competition when, according to *Brown County History*, the city's Farmers Elevator burned to the ground in 1886 in "a spectacular night blaze.") And in 1909, in what likely was the area's most sensational crime of the times, Emil Victor was sentenced to death and hung from a scaffold erected in the yard of the Aberdeen courthouse for murdering four people in a robbery gone bad in nearby Rudolph.

Aberdeen's fortunes were closely linked to the railroad. In 1886, according to Kingsbury, a number of town leaders met and established the short-lived Aberdeen, Fergus Falls & Pierre Railway to open up a route east. The company, eager to earn a $25,000 bonus that the city's citizens had approved for completing the line by the end of the year, arranged for crews to work around-the-clock and in bitter weather conditions. The deadline met, "three hundred members of the track-laying crew were given an Aberdeen banquet on Christmas Eve in recognition of their 'staying qualities' during the heavy snows and frigid temperature[s] which had been characteristic of the fall and winter," wrote Kingsbury.

The railroad not only provided Aberdeen and its residents with hundreds of jobs, but also gave the city's economy a boost that would last for decades. The Chicago, Milwaukee, St. Paul, and Pacific Railroad's huge stockyard just west of town, for example, was deemed "big business for Aberdeen" by the local press. By 1920, thousands of head of livestock being transported east from Montana were fed and watered there in what was described as "the most completely equipped in-transit feed yard in the country." And as early as 1907 the city was home to hundreds of traveling salesmen lured by the Hub City's unparalleled rail access. Train traffic

Trains hauled cattle east from Montana through Aberdeen, where the Chicago, Milwaukee, St. Paul, and Pacific Railroad operated an in-transit feed yard.

An Independent Spirit: The Quiet, Generous Life of Helen Daniels Bader

would continue to grow over the next two decades: by 1928, twenty-six passenger trains were rolling through Aberdeen every day.

L. FRANK BAUM'S ABERDEEN YEARS

No description of Aberdeen at the end of the nineteenth century would be complete without a mention of Aberdeen's most famous (albeit short-term) resident, L. Frank Baum, author of *The Wonderful Wizard of Oz*. The son of a wealthy Pennsylvania oilman, Baum had been born in New York and spent his early years working in dry goods and poultry breeding. His wife, Maud, was the daughter of famed suffragette Matilda Joslyn Gage. Although Baum made an effort to succeed as a merchant, his passion was for the stage, and he toured the country during the early 1880s with his own theatrical company. Giving up show business when Maud became pregnant, Baum tried again to settle into the family business, Baum's Castorine Company, as a traveling salesman hawking axle grease.

Suffragette Matilda Joslyn Gage was the mother-in-law of L. Frank Baum, author of The Wonderful Wizard of Oz, *and was likely the inspiration behind the character of Auntie Em.*
WIKIMEDIA

But Baum soon grew unhappy, and with the company losing money he was lured to Aberdeen in 1888 by his brother-in-law, T. Clarkson Gage, who had established a general store there seven years earlier. Baum opened Baum's Bazaar, a novelty store that stocked everything from glassware, fancy willowware, stationery, and toys, to sporting goods, amateur photography equipment, and high-end leather goods. Literary scholar Michael Patrick Hearn, quoting a press report, describes the store as "an [Aladdin's] Chamber of wonder and beauty," noting that "the rare novelties, Japanese goods, fine China and crockery, books, frames, albums, toys, and candies went like grass before a prairie fire."

In addition to running the store, Baum also indulged his passion for baseball, organizing Aberdeen's first baseball team, the Hub City Nine, and setting up the South Dakota Baseball League. All the time Baum devoted to the team, coupled with a severe drought during the summer of 1889, led to the demise of Baum's Bazaar on January 1, 1890. Explained Hearn, "No one was much interested in buying Japanese umbrellas, bric-a-brac, or fresh-cut flowers during the drought."

L. Frank Baum lived in Aberdeen from 1888 to 1891, operating Baum's Bazaar, a novelty store; running the Aberdeen Sunday Pioneer *newspaper; and organizing the city's first baseball team, the Hub City Nine.*

Undaunted, Baum purchased the *Dakota Pioneer* newspaper, renaming it the *Aberdeen Saturday Pioneer.* He handled everything from writing stories and setting type to selling ads and making deliveries. His "Our Landlady" satirical column was particularly popular. Baum scholar Nancy Tystad Koupal quotes Baum's niece Matilda Jewell Gage asserting that "pithy squibs about politicians and local bigwigs made Baum's personal columns a strong drawing card for his Aberdeen contemporaries, who eagerly bought the paper to discover who was being skewered each week."

Yet, "for all his versatility," writes historian Edwin C. Torrey, Baum "was ahead of the times" and found it difficult to prosper in the West. Deciding it was time to cut his losses, Baum ended his tenure at the paper in April 1891 and relocated to Chicago, armed with lasting impressions and memories that would inform his work. Consider, for example, *The Wonderful Wizard of Oz,* published in 1900. Speculating about the opening scene, which is set in Kansas, Baum biographer Katharine M. Rogers, suggests that Baum may have substituted Kansas for South Dakota, "the grim area he knew intimately," for the sake of his in-laws still living there. Consider, too, the book's main character, Dorothy Gale, reportedly named after Dorothy Louise Gage, Frank and Maud's beloved niece who died as an infant. What's more, Dorothy Gale's Uncle Henry and Auntie Em were likely inspired by Maud's parents, Henry and Matilda. ("Em" apparently drawn from Matilda's practice of signing family letters with her initial, "M.") The influence of Matilda Gage was especially notable. She had traveled to Aberdeen several times during the 1880s, visiting her children and speaking out about women's rights. A Theosophist, she introduced Baum to Spiritualism, the occult, and witchcraft, elements of which would infuse the mystical world of Oz and much of Baum's other fantasy fiction.

On a more concrete note, the "cyclone" that opens the story was no doubt reminiscent of South Dakota tornadoes, and the characters of the Scarecrow and the Tin Woodman likely evoked other Aberdeen memories: scarecrows were extremely popular in the Great Plains during the late nineteenth century, and common on farms outside the Aberdeen city limits. And the Woodman is said to resemble figurines made out of tin scraps that were used in advertising campaigns of the era.

According to Torrey, Baum recalled his Dakota experience "with mingled sighs and smiles," noting that "Hardships that seemed very real then have been hallowed by time, and I am glad now to have had that phase of life." Aberdeen, in turn, continues to remember Baum fondly, in part through the Land of Oz theme park at Storybook Land, a children's theme park located a mile north of Aberdeen. Attractions include a simulated tornado experience, a yellow brick road, and balloon rides.

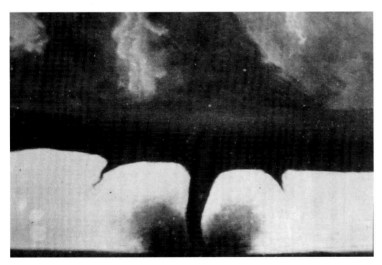

The earliest known photograph of a tornado was taken in 1884, twenty-two miles southwest of Howard, South Dakota. Historians believe that L. Frank Baum drew on his memories of such storms when writing the opening scene in The Wonderful Wizard of Oz *featuring a cyclone.*

NOAA. PHOTO PROVIDED BY NATE MAYES.

THE MABBOTTS

Helen's grandparents George and Leonia Mabbott, who would become two of Aberdeen's most prominent residents, likely frequented Baum's Bazaar and perhaps were fans of the Hub City Nine. Leonia's family had moved to Aberdeen in 1882 from Michigan to farm when she was twelve years old; George arrived four years later from Wisconsin—eighteen years old and reportedly looking for an adventure. They married in 1892, and although they moved back to Wisconsin for two years after their wedding, they returned to Aberdeen in time for the birth of their daughter, Jessie Leonia, in 1894. A son, Leonard, was born in 1902.

The same year Jessie was born, George gave up farming and went to work as a clerk for the Olwin Dry Goods Company, one of the first such stores in the state. By 1900, one of Leonia's cousins—possibly twenty-two-year-old Maudie Farrington, a favorite of Jessie's—was also working at the store and living with the Mabbotts. By all accounts, George did well at Olwin's, which at first sold only carpets, curtains, and piece goods, but by 1903 was offering a full line of merchandise. According to Gates, "some people claimed the interior was the finest in any

Helen's maternal grandmother Leonia Flansburgh, who was born in 1870 in Almont, Michigan, grew up in this house.

An Independent Spirit: The Quiet, Generous Life of Helen Daniels Bader

department store west of Chicago." The store was soon offering delivery and mail order services and featured a state-of-the-art pneumatic tube system to move sales tickets and cash to the store's third-story accounting department. In 1929, Olwin's was purchased by Marshall Field & Company, which operated it for six years. It then returned to local, private ownership until 1969.

It was on "invoice day" in December 1896, while George was still a clerk at Olwin's, that he reportedly "fought his way through a blizzard downtown, shoveled his way to the door of the store, and worked there alone until two o'clock in the afternoon." He also traveled for the company. In late 1898, for example, he was in Hecla, thirty-three miles northeast of Aberdeen, to hold what the *Aberdeen Daily News* described as "a very successful cloak sale."

But George wasn't content selling cloaks, and in 1903 went to work as a district manager for the Aetna Insurance Company. Again, he excelled, and within five years was managing its entire South Dakota operation. By 1910 the family had moved into a new home on Eighth Avenue in one of the best parts of the city, Maudie Farrington had

In 1894, Helen's maternal grandparents Leonia and George Mabbott moved from Wisconsin to Aberdeen and into this house. Posed in front are Leonia and her daughter, Jessie.

Clockwise from top left: *George and Leonia Mabbott; Leonia and baby Jessie; baby Jessie with her grandfather Edgar Flansburgh; and Maudie Farrington, a cousin of Leonia's, with Jessie.*

moved on, and a servant had moved in. Although only in his forties, George had become serious and practical, and in 1914 was appointed to serve as a juror in an inquest into the death of an eight-year-old boy who died after running into the street and being struck by a car.

Before long the *Aberdeen Daily News* was documenting the minutiae of his everyday life, including a complaint he made over children stripping the blooms from a prized lilac bush, a fall from a tree, and nearly every one of his near-constant business trips. The most extravagant by far was a two-week junket to an Aetna convention in San Francisco in 1915 for the company's top one thousand agents and their wives. The trip, mostly by rail, featured stops in Salt Lake City, Los Angeles, San Diego, the Grand Canyon, and Albuquerque. George was also active with the local Kiwanis, YMCA, Aberdeen Auto Club, and the local Methodist church, frequently heading up charitable fundraising drives. His costume for the church's Colonial Social was nothing but the best: a strawberry-colored suit with knee breeches and lace at the wrist and neck, pumps with huge buckles, and a powdered wig.

The theft of George's Chalmers sedan in 1923 made the news when George reported that the last sound he heard, as the thief drove the car away before his eyes, was a "woman's scream." The *Aberdeen Daily News* reported that it was impossible to say if the scream had been emitted "in merriment or fright." Adding insult to injury: when the car was recovered the next morning just southwest of the city, police found the interior strewn with chicken feathers, suggesting that the car thieves "had used it for the transportation of either live or dead poultry. . . ."

Leonia also made the newspapers, mostly for her frequent travels to visit friends and relatives, and for hosting teas and other social and church events at her home. In 1897, while George was still working at Olwin's, she entertained the store's "lady clerks" with a dinner and evening of crokinole, a popular board game of the day in which players tested their dexterity by shooting discs across a tabletop-sized playing surface to score points. In 1933, she made news when the black faille silk gown that

had been part of her trousseau was featured in the "Pageant of the Wedding Gowns" sponsored by her church's Women's Auxiliary. Sometimes, though, the news reports were downright intrusive: "Mrs. G. A. Mabbott, who was quite ill yesterday with an attack of nervous trouble, is better today," reported the *Aberdeen Daily News* on August 31, 1909.

Even the day-to-day lives of the Mabbotts' very young children were fodder for the local papers. The *Aberdeen Daily News* reported in 1907 that Leonard, five years old at the time, was shot in the eye with a bow while playing with another little boy, noting, "It is impossible to tell whether or not he will lose the eye." Readers would learn, a week later from the *Aberdeen Daily American,* that Leonard traveled with his father to Minneapolis "to consult a doctor regarding the serious injury the young man sustained last week to his eye." Leonard seems to have been accident-prone. Three years later, and presumably with his left eye in good working order, he was "injured in the face by an explosion of powder," according to the *Aberdeen Daily News.* "It is hoped and expected that the eyes will not be damaged, and the face will not be permanently scarred." Readers also learned that Jessie contracted measles as a three-year-old and attended a children's lawn party when she was four. And that when Leonia organized a surprise party to celebrate George's fifty-seventh birthday in 1925, "The surprise was complete and for a minute the guest of honor was quite taken aback with consternation and indecision."

A touching snapshot of the Mabbotts' lifestyle can be gleaned from an essay written decades later by their granddaughter Marjorie Daniels DeVey in which she describes their home as "a masterpiece of the golden oak period" where "they always presented a fine and proper appearance, and both appreciated beautiful things." Marjorie was particularly impressed by their kitchen, which "smelled like a mixture of fresh bread, little sour cream cakes, freshly ironed linens and rose geraniums." Likewise, she recalled in great detail the semiannual housecleaning events that Leonia undertook with help from her cleaning lady. "After all the walls were wiped, the woodwork and floors polished, the chandeliers and windows cleaned, the rug aired and beaten and everything smelled like South Dakota sunshine we would all breathe a sigh of relief and enjoy the big house for another six months," wrote Marjorie.

As a child, Helen's sister, Marjorie Daniels DeVey, loved visiting the home of her grandmother Leonia, which she later would describe as "a masterpiece of the golden oak period."

George and Leonia often went shopping together, sometimes at Olwin's, where George's last post had been that of head buyer of what Marjorie described as "domestics"—rugs, linens, and yard goods. However, even after leaving Olwin's to work at Aetna, George continued to insist on "selecting [Leonia's] clothes and especially her hats and he did this with a natural flair for he was truly a buyer of fine things." According to Marjorie, Leonia "loved all the attention to detail; she wore her clothes well—always with her laced corset underneath and very erect posture."

Clockwise from top left: *Pearl Rose Allyn,
Helen's paternal grandmother; Joseph Wilson
Daniels Jr., her paternal grandfather; Lt. Joseph
Wilson Daniels Jr. during his service in the
Spanish-American War; and Pearl Daniels with
her son, Lloyd.*

An Independent Spirit: The Quiet, Generous Life of Helen Daniels Bader

THE DANIELS SIDE OF THE FAMILY

Joe Daniels and Pearl Rose Allyn, Helen's grandparents on her father's side of the family, arrived in Aberdeen in 1906. They had married in Prescott, Wisconsin, in 1893, and their only son, Lloyd Allyn Daniels, was born one year later just across the state line in Lake City, Minnesota. Reportedly, Pearl's father, John Sidney Allyn, did not approve of Joe Daniels's "swinging ways," which included courting Pearl, in part, by driving his buggy—pulled by one black and one white horse—up and down Nicollet Avenue in Minneapolis on Sundays.

By 1900, after serving as a lieutenant in the Spanish-American War, Joe was working in Lake City as a railroad "trimmer," responsible for installing interior fixtures, such as seats, doors, and windows in railway cars. In 1904, when Lloyd was ten years old, the family moved to Mellette, South Dakota, where they lived for two years before settling permanently in Aberdeen, twenty-one miles away.

Over the next twenty years or so, Joe was employed by the Chicago, Milwaukee, and St. Paul Railroad, commonly known as "the Milwaukee," first as a conductor and later as an engineer. Given the prominence of the railroad industry in Aberdeen, the *Aberdeen Daily News* not only published daily timetables listing the arrival and departure times of the city's three major train lines, but also featured regular columns with titles such as "Late Railroad News." On July 19, 1911, the top bit of railroad news was of plans for the laying of thirty-six thousand square feet of concrete flooring for the new sanitary stockyard "which the Milwaukee is erecting at the junction of the Milwaukee and St. Louis tracks." Another item informed readers that conductor Joe Daniels was returning to his regular run after spending two months working on an extension of the railroad's line to Mobridge, one hundred miles west of Aberdeen.

Joseph Wilson Daniels Jr., better known as Joe Daniels, worked for twenty years as a conductor and engineer for the Chicago, Milwaukee, and St. Paul Railroad.

Joe's most dramatic episode as a trainman took place the morning of October 27, 1914, an event reported in a front page story in the *Aberdeen Daily American:*

> Yesterday morning shortly after 9 o'clock, as eastbound freight No. 64 was entering Mina, nine miles west of Aberdeen, conductor Joe Daniels put three hoboes off from the train. One of the men became much incensed at being thus handled, and when he struck the ground whipped out a large revolver and opened fire on the conductor. He was a poor marksman, however, and failed to injure anyone. The police were furnished with a description of the man, but evidently they [sic] did not come into Aberdeen, for a thorough search failed to locate them [sic].

Joe helped organize the Brotherhood of Railway Trainmen's Annual Ball in 1908. The event drew two hundred couples to the local Elks lodge, which was decorated with railroad lanterns, signal flags, and a locomotive headlight. The *Aberdeen Daily American* noted that because so many of Aberdeen's trainmen worked for the Chicago, Milwaukee, and St. Paul, the company "cooperated with the trainmen to enable them to be present by calling in several trains that were on the road and postponing the departure of others." The ball appears to have been the event of the season, signaling the continuing importance of the railroad—and the cachet of being a trainman—in Aberdeen. "This was a remarkably fine affair," reads the newspaper account, "and was very liberally patronized, for the hall was so crowded that it was only with difficulty that anybody could dance. This condition existed until a late hour. The dancing continued until about 4 o'clock this morning."

Joe's descendants would memorialize him in a way that took note of his railroad career, making a donation to Storybook Land to ensure that one of the theme park's miniature train cars would be named after him. The scale model train is pulled by a replica of an 1863 C. P. Huntington locomotive and runs through the park on a one mile track.

Pearl, meanwhile, was active with the Methodist Ladies' Aid Society (no doubt, alongside Leonia Mabbott) and the local Sorosis Club, a

professional women's association created in 1868 by Jane Cunningham Croly when the New York Press Club banned women from attending a dinner featuring Charles Dickens. At a meeting of the club in 1914 held at the Daniels' home, a fellow member gave a paper on "The Intelligence of Plants." Like Leonia Mabbott, Pearl kept up a busy schedule of traveling to visit out-of-town friends and relatives and then playing hostess when they returned the favor.

Both Pearl Rose Allyn Daniels (left), Helen's paternal grandmother, and Leonia Annie Flansburgh Mabbott (right), her maternal grandmother, were born in 1870, and maintained active social lives in Aberdeen.

The local papers also kept track of the days she was "confined to home by illness," and there is evidence to suggest she suffered a stroke—from which she only partially recovered—while in her forties. In fact, in 1917, when Lloyd was twenty-three and required to register for the draft, he claimed an exemption on the grounds of a "sick mother." A news item published in August 1918 not only raised further alarms about Pearl's health, but also about the state of Brown County roads.

By 1918, while still working for the railroad, Joe Daniels was also selling real estate and insurance, and building houses.

Motoring home after a trip to Iowa, Joe and Pearl's car became stuck in a mud hole about thirty miles east of Aberdeen, stranding the couple overnight. According to the *Aberdeen Daily News,* "As Mrs. Daniels is an invalid, they spent a very uncomfortable night on the road and Mr. Daniels expressed himself very forcibly on the condition of the trail at that point. . . ."

By 1918, Joe was working for Draeger Land & Loan Company, a real estate and building construction company that later began handling investment property and selling insurance. Employed as a real estate agent, Joe was also building houses, including two on a piece of property on Sixth Avenue that was described by the *Aberdeen Daily American* as "one of the choicest residence corners in the city." At the site, he built two two-story, craftsman style homes. He and Pearl moved into the first; the second was for Lloyd and Jessie and became the home in which Helen Bader would grow up. As a builder, Joe's vested interests in municipal affairs prompted him to express himself, over the years, on any number of issues, such as local water service (before the Board of

County Commissioners) and the need for sidewalks on Aberdeen's West Side (before the Board of City Commissioners). A 1921 article in the *Aberdeen Sunday American-News* described Joe as "prominent among the city's progressive businessmen . . . having a very extensive acquaintance and wide circle of friends."

According to family lore, Joe went to work for Henry Draeger after being fired from the railroad for refusing to take a train out to Ipswich on the grounds that Pearl, by then wheelchair-bound, was too sick to leave alone. But his granddaughter, Marjorie Daniels DeVey, speculated that the railroad might have been "looking for an excuse to fire him because he had gotten cocky . . . about how much money he was making building houses."

By 1920, Lloyd Daniels was also working at Draeger. A company ad that ran in the *American-News* listed Joe and Lloyd's office and home phone numbers and urged readers to call any time. Ironically, Joe, the former trainman, also loved cars, and went on to sell Durant and Star motorcars for Aberdeen's B & D Motor Company and build boats. In

Joe Daniels built two, two-story, craftsman style homes on what was described as "one of the choicest residence corners in the city." He and Pearl moved into the first; the second was for Lloyd and Jessie, and became the home where Helen grew up.

Although a railroad man for more than two decades, Joe Daniels loved cars.

Joe Daniels pursued a number of careers, and at one point sold Durant and Star motorcars for Aberdeen's B & D Motor Company.

1923, he traveled to Los Angeles with Draeger, and was captivated by the West Coast vibe. "Dear Wife," he wrote to Pearl, who at the time was a patient at St. Luke's Hospital in Aberdeen, "I think this . . . would be a good place for Lloyd as he could open up a drug store . . . and do well. I think I will try and arrange to bring both you and Lloyd out here next fall." There's no record of the family ever taking that trip. And in 1925, Pearl died at the age of fifty-five. Joe lived another twenty-four years, his occupation recorded as "realtor" on the 1930 census rolls.

An Independent Spirit: The Quiet, Generous Life of Helen Daniels Bader

1915 Dodge

Left: *Lloyd Daniels takes to the road behind the wheel of a 1915 Dodge with (clockwise) his father, Joe; a friend, Ethel Granger; and his mother, Pearl.*

Below: *In 1923, while traveling with his boss, Henry Draeger, Joe Daniels kept in touch with his wife, Pearl, who at the time was confined to St. Luke's Hospital.*

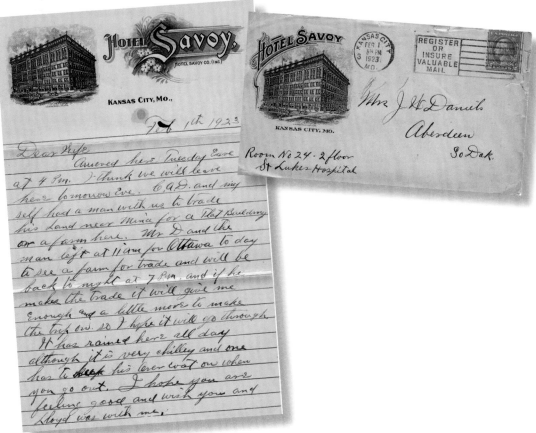

Chapter Two

Jessie and Lloyd

To survive—and thrive—in the harsh, unforgiving South Dakota plains during the turbulent nineteenth and early twentieth centuries, Helen Bader's ancestors were forced to be tough, stoic, resilient, innovative, and optimistic. They were free-spirited, independent thinkers who embraced the unconventional and celebrated bold ideas. These were all qualities Helen herself would exhibit, both early on and throughout her life. Moreover, it was from the Daniels side of the family— and primarily her father, Lloyd Allyn Daniels—that she would inherit her deep compassion for others, and especially those less fortunate than herself, as well as a humble, generous nature that embraced the beauty of simple living. From her Mabbott ancestors, and most notably her mother, Jessie Leonia Mabbott, would come a keen appreciation for both the value of higher education and a deep love of the arts, and a belief in the way art and music can enhance the quality of one's world.

Jessie and her younger brother, Leonard, grew up in a home where education, music, and public speaking were highly valued. Jessie was

Opposite background: *Aberdeen's Central High School opened in January 1912.*

Opposite foreground: *Lloyd Daniels and Jessie Mabbott, who met in school as young teens, became engaged to be married in 1919.*

Below: *Jessie Mabbot was seven years old when this series of photos was taken.*

Jessie Leonia Mabbott was a fashionable daddy's girl.

Lloyd Allyn Daniels was the light of his parents' lives.

five when she gave her first recitation during a Christmas program at the Methodist Episcopalian Church. And by seventh grade, she was one of Lincoln School's debaters, defending the negative side of the proposition "Resolved, that our American statesmen deserve higher praise than our authors." As a sixth-grader at Lincoln School she was awarded an honorable mention for an essay she wrote for the Aberdeen Federation of Women's Club's Arbor Day essay contest. She was also an accomplished pianist, performing often about town for church and social functions, and at her seventh grade graduation.

Jessie was a fashionable daddy's girl, often dressing up and traveling with George in the family buggy when he called on his Aberdeen customers. Yet, even at a young age, Jessie was recognized for her keen intellect. According to family lore, her math skills were such that she and her father often worked together figuring out the risk of insuring potential clients. Jessie inherited her parents' good taste, love of all things formal, and appreciation for the finer things in life. Her social skills emerged early, as evidenced by newspaper reports of a lawn party for friends when she was twelve, and a fourteenth birthday party that included a trip to the Peerless Ice Cream Parlor and the Idle Hour Theatre, deemed by the *Aberdeen Daily American* the "most attractive motion picture house west of Chicago."

As a little boy, Leonard Mabbott performed in a church Christmas pageant and sang a cantata at Aberdeen Opera House. When he wasn't dodging bows and arrows and playing with explosives, Leonard indulged a fascination with electricity, and as a teenager became an amateur wireless operator. To his dismay, on April 9, 1917—three days after the United States entered World War I—he was one of five operators in Aberdeen given forty-eight hours by the War Department to dismantle their stations.

Lloyd Allyn Daniels was the light of his parents' lives, and their move from Mellette to Aberdeen when he was ten years old, was based, in large part, on the idea that it would be good for their son. An only child, Lloyd inherited his father's relaxed, down-to-earth demeanor and keen ability to relate to others. As a young teenager, he made the local newspapers twice: in January 1907, as one of a group of local thirteen-year-olds taking part in a coed sleigh ride, and in the summer of 1908 when he was operated on at St. Luke's Hospital for appendicitis. By the time he was sixteen, Lloyd had a part-time job working as a clerk at the local Goodale Pharmacy.

ABERDEEN HIGH SCHOOL

Lloyd and Jessie likely met in school soon after his family moved to Aberdeen from Mellette and probably were friends when they enrolled at Aberdeen High School. Lloyd was easygoing, friendly, popular, and good-looking: he was slender and of medium height, with hazel eyes and black hair. Jessie was high-spirited, outgoing, and pretty: she was fashionably petite with thick, dark hair, penetrating dark eyes, and a mischievous smile. School life was very much a blend of the social and academic.

According to an article in the school's monthly magazine, the *Blue and Gold,* "In the morning, some pupils arrive early to study, but more come to visit, sit on the radiators, and bother [the janitor] 'Pat.'" One such morning another irritated janitor "attacked the crowd with a broom," continues the article. "No great casualty resulted, however, and soon the assembly room was full of boys, noise, girls, curls, and other things."

According to the Blue and Gold, *Aberdeen High School's monthly magazine, students in 1910 were disciplined for everything from whispering in class to not being able to distinguish the writing of Shakespeare from that of Voltaire.*
PUBLIC DOMAIN

Classes included everything from English, math, history, science, Latin, and German, to debating, stenography, domestic science, music, shop, and bookkeeping. As for discipline, noted the *Blue and Gold,* "Sometimes we are sent to the office for whispering, but usually our disgrace consists of not being able to distinguish between the characteristics of Shakespeare and of Voltaire, or kindred errors." Girls were singled out for "their ability to talk continually for forty minute stretches," while it was the boys—one assumes—who playfully dashed out of their last class of the day, a science lab, "with our apron on, with our little glass pipe in our mouth, with a deflagrating spoon over our left ear, and with various chemical apparatus about our person."

Arrival of President Taft Oct. 23 1911
879 - Aberdeen So. Dak.   © NABrothers

Jessie was elected sophomore class treasurer, a tribute to her math skills; appointed literary editor of the *Blue and Gold*; and cast as one of the fairies in the school's 1910 production of *A Midsummer Night's Dream*. Lloyd also acted in several high school theatrical productions, including *Cupid at Vassar*, in which he played hired hand Hank Gibbon and earned accolades from the *Aberdeen Daily American* for being "one of the most humorous of the cast." He also won a prize at a rather unusual class event. According to the *Aberdeen Daily American,* "The young ladies of the class furnished a collection of untrimmed hats and the boys were asked to show their artistic ability by putting the trimming in place. Lloyd Daniels carried away the prize for producing the best creation."

Jessie and Lloyd were no doubt among the students who gathered on the evening of October 23, 1911, to welcome President William Howard Taft to Aberdeen. According to the Dacotah Prairie Museum Foundation's *Looking Back*, the visit, part of a six-week, thirteen thousand-mile tour of twenty-four western states, included band concerts, exhibitions by the fire department, military drills, and a dinner. Taft spoke both at Aberdeen's Northern Normal and Industrial School (NNIS) and to a massive audience gathered on the courthouse lawn.

Jessie and Lloyd spent their last semester at the new Aberdeen Central High School, which opened in January 1912 at a cost of $180,000. They

Jessie and Lloyd were members of the first class to graduate from Aberdeen's Central High School, which opened the second semester of their senior year.
PUBLIC DOMAIN

graduated that spring, with Jessie completing the school's classical course, and Lloyd, its scientific course. At Class Day exercises the evening before graduation, Jessie played a piano duet with fellow graduate Vera Narregang. Speaking at commencement was Dr. Samuel Smith of the People's Church in St. Paul on the topic "What Society Expects of Education."

At a time when women typically made up 60 percent of high school graduates, Jessie and Lloyd's class included an equal number of men and women, a detail the *Aberdeen Daily American* described as so "unique" that "a black suit alternated with a white dress upon the stage where members were grouped during the exercises." According to the *Aberdeen Daily News,* this "decided increase" in the number of male graduates was a "propitious sign of the times. . . ." In less enlightened reporting, however, the *Daily News* saw a need to call out "the sturdy appearance of the men of tomorrow and the maidenly blushes of the mothers of the next generation." In his speech, Smith revealed his own provincial mindset. Failing to take into account the fact that seventeen of the twenty-six graduates planning to attend college were young women, he proclaimed, "The man who goes to college will have made up in cash value before he is forty the time taken out for his college career."

Smith went on to cite the value of public schooling, which he said was key to solving the "problems of the day." Newspaper accounts of the speech, employing language that exposed the racist attitudes of the day, spelled out those problems as "the danger of unrestricted immigration" and "the Negro problem," issues that would plague the nation for the next one hundred years and beyond. It was "the duty of every true American, the American of American stock," said Smith, "to send his children to the public school, if they are not too bad or too stupid." There, continued Smith, "his children and those of the aliens will be taught the ideas which our forefathers brought over on the Mayflower and which still live through the Americans of today [who] are no longer overwhelmingly an Anglo-Saxon people."

OFF TO COLLEGE

Lloyd, the first in his family to attend college, entered the South Dakota State College of Agriculture and Mechanic Arts at Brookings, about one hundred and fifty miles southeast of Aberdeen. The school had been established in 1881 under the guidelines of the 1862 Morrill Act passed by Congress and signed by President Abraham Lincoln. Lloyd had been encouraged by his employers at Goodale's to pursue a degree in pharmacy, and in 1912 when Lloyd matriculated at South Dakota State, the school was offering two- and four-year pharmacy programs. The former, which Lloyd

Lloyd Daniels, the first in his family to attend college, enrolled at the South Dakota State College of Agriculture and Mechanic Arts at Brookings, South Dakota, in 1912.

PHOTO POSTCARD, PUBLIC DOMAIN

An Independent Spirit: The Quiet, Generous Life of Helen Daniels Bader

would receive in 1914, led to a PhG degree, which prepared students to work as licensed pharmacists. The latter led to a bachelor of science degree, which was required for students planning to pursue medicine or dentistry.

While at South Dakota State, Lloyd took classes in German, chemistry, botany, physics, English literature, and mathematics. His second-year science courses included work in pharmacy-specific skills such as the weighing, measuring, and distilling of compounds. Lloyd spent his time outside of class as chair of the Bible Study Committee of the college's chapter of the YMCA; according to the 1915 edition of the *Jack Rabbit,* the school's yearbook, the organization stood for "clean college life, true college spirit, athletics, literary activities, earnest collegiate work and daily Bible study." Lloyd was also a member of the Miltonian Literary Society, and participated in the school's military program, serving as a cadet with the rank of private in Company A.

In a *Jack Rabbit* display ad titled "An Education in the State College is a Paying Investment," the institution tooted its own horn: "Our collegiate graduates are located all over the world as leaders in agriculture, general science, engineers, pharmacists, teachers of home economics, and as useful citizens. The demand for our graduate is much greater than the supply. Doubtless this accounts for the fact that men who have been graduated only one to three years are getting salaries of $1,500 to $2,000 per year as experts."

Jessie's brother, Leonard, was another of the men of the day who would go on to attend college. He graduated from Aberdeen Central High School in 1920, eight years after Jessie and Lloyd. While there he played football, served as head of the *Blue and Gold* editorial staff, worked as a lighting technician for school plays, and organized a team of classmates to raise money for the city's new YMCA. Upon graduation, Leonard promptly headed off to the University of Minnesota at Minneapolis, where in 1924 he earned a degree in electrical engineering from the school's College of Engineering and Architecture.

As a child, Jessie's younger brother, Leonard, shown here with his sister, was fascinated by electricity. After graduating from the University of Minnesota, he went on to work for Northern States Power Company.

Graduating first in his class ("Aberdeen Boy Wins Highest Class Honors in Engineering College," trumpeted the *Aberdeen Evening News*), Leonard was offered several jobs, including one out East at a company where he had worked the previous summer. Opting for a job closer to home, Leonard took a position with Northern States Power Company in Minneapolis.

But if Lloyd and Leonard were congratulated for continuing their educations, it was Jessie and the other sixteen women in her class moving on to college who deserved respect and admiration. Ahead of their time, they enrolled at a variety of institutions, including Northern Normal and Industrial School (NNIS), which had opened ten years earlier in a four-story, twenty-seven-room brick building. According to NNIS President Charles Koehler, quoted in *Looking Back*, the school aimed to "offer the most thorough instruction and training for young men and women for the profession of teaching. . . ." In exchange, students in 1902 paid tuition and fees totaling twelve dollars. Others enrolled at the University of Minnesota, set off for the Lutheran Ladies' Seminary at Red Wing, Minnesota, or matriculated at area music and business schools.

Jessie took a year off after graduating from high school, spending part of the time visiting her Uncle Leon Flansburgh—pictured here with his dog, Ned—in Washington state.

An Independent Spirit: The Quiet, Generous Life of Helen Daniels Bader

Jessie took a year off after graduating from high school, part of which she spent visiting the family of her uncle Leon Flansburgh, Leonia's younger brother, in Washington State. Decades later, at the age of ninety-three, Leon's son Allan would recall his first cousin's visit, which included a tour of nearby Lewiston, Idaho, noting that "When [Jessie] saw the steep, winding road, she refused to go any farther."

Jessie enrolled at NNIS in the fall of 1913, becoming the first person in her family to pursue higher education. As a high school graduate, she was eligible for the school's one-year teacher training course but stayed on for a second year amassing extra credits that allowed her to transfer in the fall of 1915 to Milwaukee-Downer College in Milwaukee, Wisconsin. Ever her mother's daughter, in the weeks leading up to her departure Jessie threw two of her famous parties, this time for friends headed out of town either for college or jobs. Reported the *Aberdeen Daily News* in August 1915, "all were glad to be together once more," noting the Mabbotts' beautifully appointed dining room "where a chafing dish lunch was served," and the centerpiece "of pansies combined with trailing green vines."

At a time when few women were entering college, Jessie enrolled at Northern Normal and Industrial School, where students were offered "the most thorough instruction and training . . . for the profession of teaching."

In 1915, Lloyd was studying pharmacy at South Dakota State College of Agriculture and Mechanic Arts, and Jessie was poised to enter Milwaukee-Downer College to study mathematics.

Jessie's decision to go away to school in Milwaukee was a bold, momentous one for a young woman from South Dakota in 1915, a decision that broadened not only her world, but also her thinking. Her college degree would also give her a practical advantage not all women graduating from college at the time would enjoy: the means to a job. Lastly, and perhaps even more significantly, Jessie's decision would have profound consequences not only for her daughter Helen, but also for Milwaukee, where Helen would make her home.

MILWAUKEE AT THE TURN OF THE CENTURY

Aberdeen may have been a "magic city," but in Jessie's eyes it must have paled in comparison to Milwaukee, which in 1915 was the twelfth-largest metropolis in the country. At the time, according to Milwaukee historian John Gurda, Milwaukee's national reputation was based on three, related hallmarks: Germanism, socialism, and beer. But by 1920, two years after the end of World War I, the city's German culture would be waning as socialism lost support and Prohibition loomed, threatening the brewing industry.

An Independent Spirit: The Quiet, Generous Life of Helen Daniels Bader

Milwaukee's population was swelling (from 20,061 in 1850 to 285,315 in 1900, and on its way to 457,142 in 1920), largely due to the lure of new jobs ushered in by the Industrial Age. But with the new jobs came growing pains as the labor force became less agrarian and more industrial. This rapid shift brought significant social problems: substandard sanitation and housing, public health challenges, disease, poverty, income inequality, inadequate eldercare, racial discrimination, class struggles, child labor, soaring crime, and unequal justice under the law.

Indeed, Jessie had witnessed some of these same problems in Aberdeen. Yet, given its population in 1915—roughly 27,000 versus Milwaukee's 410,000—the challenges presented on a much smaller scale and were more likely to be addressed on a personal level. In big cities such as Milwaukee, the clarion call for services and policies to alleviate social problems and support people in need was not yet loud nor widely heeded. But it had been sounded, heralding a movement that would see individuals and systems dedicated to helping people and their communities reach their full potential make their mark. One of

In 1915, Milwaukee was the twelfth-largest city in the nation, and was struggling with some of the same social ills Jessie had witnessed in Aberdeen—poverty, income inequality, and unequal justice under the law—but on a much larger scale.
HISTORIC PHOTO COLLECTION/
MILWAUKEE PUBLIC LIBRARY.

those people would turn out to be Jessie Mabbott's daughter, Helen Daniels Bader.

MILWAUKEE-DOWNER COLLEGE

Jessie Mabbott, a woman seeking higher education in 1915, was somewhat of an anomaly. She was the first person in her family—Leonard would be the second—to attend college. At the time, according to the US Department of Education, women made up roughly 60 percent of all high school graduates. Yet only 34 percent of college graduates were women, a figure that would change dramatically over the next two generations as attitudes changed and the doors of universities opened to all. Still, Jessie was not among the initial wave of women to go to college in the United States. Oberlin College & Conservatory, in northern Ohio, had begun admitting women in 1837. Thirteen years later, the Women's Medical College of Philadelphia was established, and in 1861, New York's Vassar College, the nation's first all-female, liberal arts institution, opened its doors.

The history of higher education for women in Milwaukee begins with the creation, in 1848, of the Milwaukee Female Seminary, an event that,

One of the earliest institutions of higher education to open its doors to women was the Women's Medical College of Philadelphia, which was established in 1850.

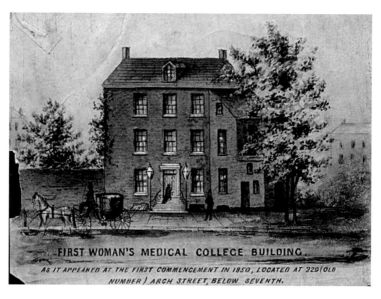

FIRST WOMAN'S MEDICAL COLLEGE BUILDING.

AS IT APPEARED AT THE FIRST COMMENCEMENT IN 1850, LOCATED AT 229 (OLD NUMBER) ARCH STREET, BELOW SEVENTH.

according to *History Just Ahead: A Guide to Wisconsin's Historical Markers,* is said to have "placed Wisconsin in the forefront of education, at a time when colleges for women were almost unknown." Operated out of a house in downtown Milwaukee, the school soon came under the influence of education reformers Mary Mortimer and Catharine Beecher, eldest sister of Harriet Beecher Stowe, who helped reorganize and incorporate it as the Milwaukee Normal Institute and High School. Mortimer's goal, according to historian Minerva Brace Norton, was to make the school's program "equal to that of the best Eastern schools for girls." Its students were to be educated for the so-called women's professions, which according to Beecher included the care and development of children, teaching, and "conservation of the domestic state." The school changed its name in 1853 to Milwaukee Female College, and in 1876, to Milwaukee College.

Meanwhile, Wisconsin Female College had been founded in 1855 under the auspices of the Baptist Church in Fox Lake, Wisconsin, seventy-five miles northwest of Milwaukee. The school's initial mission was to train women for missionary service. However, according to historian Grace Norton Kieckhefer, "the mental discipline was as strong as the moral," with

Milwaukee-Downer College was created in 1895 with the merger of Downer College and Milwaukee College. Two years later, the new institution moved to a ten-acre site on the Northeast Side of Milwaukee, where classes were held in redbrick, Tudor-style buildings still in use today on the campus of the University of Wisconsin-Milwaukee.

ARCHIVES DEPARTMENT, UNIVERSITY OF WISCONSIN-MILWAUKEE LIBRARIES

students expected to master Latin, algebra, geometry, physiology, chemistry, astronomy, and logic. In 1883, Wisconsin Supreme Court Judge Jason Downer, an advocate of women's higher education and a longtime benefactor of the school, died, bequeathing most of his fortune to the college. The move both stabilized the school's finances, and—per Downer's wishes—ensured students would study not only academic subjects, but also domestic economy, hygiene, and religious education. In 1889, the school changed its name to Downer College in his honor.

By 1895, both Downer College and Milwaukee College were struggling with stagnant enrollments, inadequate funding, and poorly defined missions. Yet Downer College President Ellen Clara Sabin had, over the preceding four years, boosted the college's academic standards, and as a result, was offered the presidency of Milwaukee College. She lobbied instead for the two schools to merge, a step that created Milwaukee-Downer College. The new school acquired ten acres on the Northeast Side of Milwaukee between the Milwaukee River and Lake Michigan, and in 1899—after operating for four years out of downtown Milwaukee—moved into its first two buildings, Merrill and Holton halls.

By the time Jessie matriculated at Milwaukee-Downer, another significant development had taken place in terms of higher education in Milwaukee: In 1909, Milwaukee State Normal School, which had been founded in 1885 on the city's West Side, moved into Mitchell Hall on its new Kenwood campus just south of the Milwaukee-Downer buildings. Originally, the school offered only a two-year teacher preparation program, but had broadened its curriculum to include courses in liberal arts and music. After relocating, it expanded its programs yet again, this time adding classes in agriculture, home economics, and journalism. Unbeknownst to Jessie, the school would evolve in ways that would play a big part in the life of her daughter Helen.

JESSIE'S COLLEGIATE YEARS

How did Jessie end up in Milwaukee, and at Milwaukee-Downer College? No doubt, it was her father's doing. George Mabbott had been born in Richland Center, Wisconsin, and he and Leonia had lived there for the first two years of their marriage. Likely he knew of both the Milwaukee Female Seminary, which up until the 1880s was by far the most prestigious college for women in Milwaukee, and Downer College.

By 1915, Sabin had been president of Milwaukee-Downer for twenty years. She would serve in the post until 1921, her tenure spanning "a period of astonishing growth for Milwaukee-Downer and of notable advances in higher education for women," according to Virginia A. Palmer, a historian who graduated from Milwaukee-Downer in 1951. Under Sabin, more than three hundred women received bachelor's degrees, and the campus grew from ten to fifty-three acres occupied by more than a dozen buildings. In her 1920 commencement address, noted Palmer, Sabin sought to dispel the idea "that Milwaukee-Downer was Wisconsin's foremost finishing school" by speaking of the school's dual mission. According to Sabin, "We are not indifferent to academic traditions . . . language and literature, the social

In 1909, Milwaukee State Normal School, founded in 1885 on the city's West Side, moved into Mitchell Hall on land just south of Milwaukee-Downer College. Mitchell Hall is still in use today on the campus of the University of Wisconsin-Milwaukee.

ARCHIVES DEPARTMENT, UNIVERSITY OF WISCONSIN-MILWAUKEE LIBRARIES

sciences, pure science, and philosophy. . . . [Yet] we further believe that woman's education should prepare a woman for women's chief vocation and that the science and art of home-making, which is a business most complex and most significant, should form a recognized part of her training for life."

Truth be told, that "training for life" did not include much, if any, real-world experience. Jessie and her classmates, leading largely sheltered lives at Milwaukee-Downer, rarely ventured far off campus, and thus, likely witnessed little of the social upheaval plaguing Milwaukee. In the fall of 1915, the number of faculty members numbered 37, and the student body stood at 284. The cost of tuition, room, and board totaled $400 per year. Students' days were tightly scheduled and highly regimented, beginning with a "rising bell" at six thirty in the morning and including seven class periods and daily, mandated attendance at chapel. Historian Lynne H. Kleinman noted that it was during chapel sessions that Sabin offered "guidance for students on subjects ranging from their physical appearance

As a young woman, Jessie— shown here behind the wheel —was adventurous and fun loving.

An Independent Spirit: The Quiet, Generous Life of Helen Daniels Bader

to how much credence they should give to fortunetellers, mediums, and psychics." She also valued "character building," and to that end opposed sororities on campus, believing they led to "separations and exclusion." In a far less progressive application of that principle, she also "resisted admitting students of racial minorities" to Milwaukee-Downer, and as was the custom of the day, warned students against the "harmful" nature of developing "crushes" on one another.

An entry from Jessie's diary dated September 25, 1917, reads, "First class under Miss Sabin—was scared to go but I'm not now." In other entries, she describes attending house meetings, hanging pictures in her dormitory room, visiting a local tea shop, and taking long walks with friends. "Dorothy Renner, a freshman, and I went to Grand Avenue Methodist Church," she wrote, adding, "Very nice minister, but not as scholarly as Dr. Beale," presumably referring to her hometown clergyman. A gymnasium had been built on campus in 1908, in large part due to Sabin's belief in physical education for women, and Jessie participated in gym classes wearing a middy

In diary entries from 1917, Jessie revealed that she had initially dreaded taking a class from Milwaukee-Downer President Ellen Sabin, who reportedly set high standards for her students.

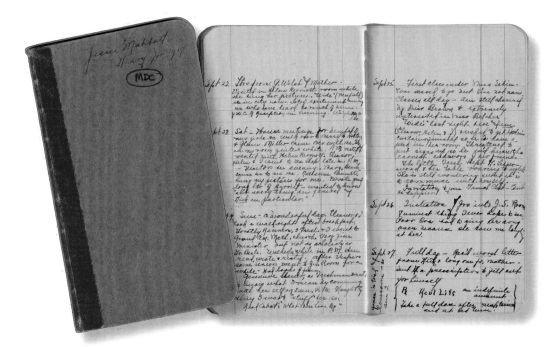

blouse and baggy bloomers. Outside of class, dormitory life was designed to promote student unity. Kleinman noted that, according to a description of life at Milwaukee-Downer in the school's handbook, "Every evening there is dancing in the gymnasium until the study-bell rings. Wednesday evenings we have class tables, and this means singing in the dining rooms. Each class vies with other classes to have the very best songs, and all join in the singing of the regular college songs. Occasionally we have college songs in the chapel or out on the campus."

According to the college yearbook, Jessie was a member of *Le Cercle Français,* ("Invitation to join French Club," she noted in her diary. "Couldn't be happier.") and may have participated in activities sponsored by the Equal Suffrage League, which in 1921 became the League of Women Voters; the Rowing Club; or the Science Club. She also likely took part in or attended the Shakespeare Tercentenary, held in 1916 to commemorate the three hundredth anniversary of William Shakespeare's death. Popular school traditions included the Hat Hunt, in which sophomores hid a vintage top hat somewhere on campus for the freshmen to find. The hunt, according to *Time & Traditions,* a pictorial history of Milwaukee-Downer College and its successor, Lawrence University, sometimes required students "to wade through streams, chisel through rocks, and dig in the earth." Another popular, annual event was Colors Day, when the incoming freshman class was presented with a banner in one of four colors (red, green, purple, or yellow) that would serve as an element of the class's identity over the next four years. (The Colors Day tradition was adopted by Lawrence University and continues today, with not only class banners, but also T-shirts—in the appropriate color—for every incoming freshman.) Students also voted every year for the school's Blue Blazer Girl, a senior recognized for her athletic accomplishments. But by far the most highly anticipated events of the school year were purely social: the cotillions held at one of the city's mansions located along Lake Michigan on North Prospect Avenue to which Jessie and her friends were taken via horse and buggy.

Just two months before Jessie graduated from Milwaukee-Downer, in April 1917, America entered World War I. She may well have been among the students who presented a flag to Troop A of the 1st Wisconsin Cavalry, which was being deployed for France, or one of the Downer Girls who took up patriotic knitting during chapel. According to historian Kieckhefer, the students also "cheered their favorite janitor, Oscar, off to military service, and welcomed him back vociferously, not too many months later."

Jessie was one of the thirty-three members of Milwaukee-Downer's class of 1917, graduating with a bachelor's degree in mathematics. She returned home to Aberdeen and immediately landed a job as an assistant math teacher at NNIS, a post she would hold for the next two years. The *Aberdeen Daily News* noted that Jessie had planned her first two years of coursework at NNIS so that her classes there counted as credit toward her degree at Milwaukee-Downer.

Milwaukee-Downer students, up through the 1940s, were instructed to bring with them to campus a white dress "for college functions." Jessie brought this dress with her in 1917.

"The fact that she took major work in mathematics especially qualifies her for the new position," reported the paper. Jessie maintained her ties with Milwaukee-Downer and her college classmates, holding a house party for three of her college friends the summer following her graduation, and returning to Milwaukee to attend the school's 1918 graduation ceremony.

WORLD WAR I

Meanwhile, back in Aberdeen following his graduation from South Dakota State in the spring of 1914, Lloyd Daniels was working full-time at Goodale Pharmacy. It was there, as a high school student, that he had acquired the nickname he would carry for the rest of his life. As the story goes, when Lloyd first went to work at the store and the pharmacist asked his name, he replied without hesitation, "Lloyd Allyn Daniels." Responded the pharmacist, "Oh, I'll never remember all of that. I'll just call you Dick." And from then on, he came to be widely known as Dick Daniels.

Lloyd began working as a part-time clerk at Goodale Pharmacy in Aberdeen when he was sixteen. His employers not only encouraged him to pursue a college degree in pharmacy, they also nicknamed him Dick.

By early 1916, Lloyd had passed the South Dakota Board of Pharmacy's state examinations, earning an assistant pharmacist license and launching a career that would last for more than fifty years. In the summer of 1917, while working at Goodale's and with World War I raging in Europe, Lloyd registered for the draft. At the time, the *Aberdeen Daily American* published

the names of all registrants "for the information of the public so that the slackers may be ascertained," and urged readers to report "anyone of military age whose name fails to appear in print." Although Lloyd noted on his draft registration form that he believed he was eligible for an exemption on the grounds of a "sick mother," he either enlisted or was drafted. The following summer he was one of one hundred and fifty young men who left Aberdeen for military training at Camp Dodge, Iowa. He was sent to officer's training school at Camp Taylor, Kentucky. His grandson David Bader recalled family stories of additional training his grandfather completed with a cavalry unit in Texas on wooden horses, a tactic imported from England. According to "Wooden Horses for Training Recruits," published in 1917 in the *Field Artillery Journal*, "It has been found that a recruit will learn the proper method of standing to horse, holding the reins, mounting and dismounting, and of executing many of the mounted exercises as well with the wooden horses as with real animals." World War I ended in November 1918, with Lloyd, by then a lieutenant, never seeing combat. He returned to Aberdeen—where his service was celebrated by friends and the local American Legion post—and to Goodale's.

During the summer of 1918, Jessie—who by then had completed a year of teaching at NNIS—was also touched by the war. Taking part in a letter-writing campaign organized by a fellow faculty member in the French Department, she began corresponding with a French peasant soldier. According to the *Aberdeen Daily News,* "For two years his family were lost from him. They lived in northern France in the invaded district." However, noted the paper, "Through the efforts of Miss Mabbott the Red Cross was able to help a brother of his who has been in a German prison camp since 1914."

But even as Aberdonians were rejoicing in the end of the war, late 1918 saw South Dakota, like much of the rest of the country, hit by an outbreak of Spanish influenza that between October and December killed 1,847 state residents—28 percent of all those who died in South Dakota that year. Ultimately, the flu led to an estimated 25 million deaths worldwide, including about 550,000 in the United States. The headline on one article published in a South Dakota newspaper in late 1918 read, "600 Cases of 'Flu' in Aberdeen," a situation that filled St. Luke's Hospital. According to *Brown County History*, "Christmas day of 1918 was a black Christmas—more people died on that day than any other."

POPULAR COUPLE MARRIES

Jessie also had been writing Lloyd throughout his military service. The two had frequently crossed paths while Jessie was enrolled at NNIS before transferring to Milwaukee-Downer College, attending small dinner parties and other social gatherings with friends. Both Jessie and Lloyd were fun loving, gregarious, and well-liked, and had kept in touch the two years Jessie was away at school. It was shortly after Lloyd returned home to Aberdeen, and during Jessie's second year of teaching, that he proposed. They married on September 10, 1919, one week after a four-course luncheon and bridal shower organized for Jessie and another September bride-to-be by a mutual friend. Jessie and Lloyd's wedding, though a relatively simple affair, was nonetheless "of much interest to society," according to an article in the *Aberdeen Daily American* headlined "Popular Young People Married Here Wednesday." It took place at the Mabbott home, with the rector of the Methodist Episcopal Church officiating. Music and flowers were featured prominently. Jessie entered on her father's arm to a piano rendition of the "Wedding March," from *Lohengrin* with selections by Chopin and Rubenstein performed as well. The couple exchanged their vows in front of a display of palms, ferns, gladioli, asters, and daisies. Jessie's silk wedding gown was of white georgette crepe, trimmed with white, moiré ribbons; she carried a bouquet of roses and daisies. Following the ceremony, a wedding breakfast was served in the dining room for fifteen family members and friends. According to a newspaper report, Jessie and Lloyd left that afternoon to honeymoon in Minneapolis, with Jessie wearing a navy suit and

Oscar Melgaard and Ethel Granger (from left to right), *join their friends Lloyd and Jessie for an indoor picnic.*

An Independent Spirit: The Quiet, Generous Life of Helen Daniels Bader

a "smart little velvet hat trimmed with a band of ostrich." Continued the story, "They will be at home after October 15, at 319 Sixth Avenue Southeast in a bungalow which was a gift from the groom's parents."

Life soon became busy: Their first child, Marjorie Jean, was born on July 3, 1921, followed by a son, Kenneth Mabbott, on September 17, 1923. An impeccable housekeeper, accomplished seamstress renowned for her delicate hand stitching, and one of Aberdeen's most celebrated hostesses, Jessie appeared to be in her element as a young wife and mother. Yet, even with a home to run and two small children to raise, Jessie found ways to use what her granddaughter, Deirdre Britt, called her "formidable intellect" and "a mind that wouldn't quit." She filled the family home with classical music and books. Jessie also somehow found time to participate in a range of educational, social, and community activities. By 1922, she was active with the YMCA, the Missionary Society of the Methodist Episcopal Church, and a member of the local chapters of two national study groups—the Clio Circle, organized in 1897 and named after the Greek

Jessie and Lloyd's first child, Marjorie Jean, shown here with her mother, was born on July 3, 1921.

goddess of history; and the Zetetic Club, founded in 1922 with Jessie as its first president. Over the years, Jessie would host numerous meetings of both groups and present papers on topics ranging from the history of French dramas and Galileo to architecture. In one paper she prepared for a Clio Circle meeting in 1924 on the topic of "Methods of Telling Time and Old Time Pieces," she talked about and displayed Lloyd's 118-year-old, eighteen-karat gold watch. A family heirloom, it had been made in Liverpool, England, in 1809 for Lloyd's great-grandfather whose name on a copy of the family tree is recorded as Daniels Daniells. Three years later, the watch, likely the oldest watch in Aberdeen, was the subject of a feature story in the *Aberdeen American-News*. It was put on display at a local jewelry store, with the newspaper noting, it "exhibits no signs of the usual infirmities of old age, [and] still keeps excellent time. . . ."

Jessie also joined the Young Peoples Brown County Republican Club; the Aberdeen Branch of the American Association of University Women (AAUW); and the local affiliate of the Wesley Guild, a youth group affiliated with the Wesleyan Methodist Church. A natural leader, she served several terms as president of the AAUW branch and treasurer of the guild. Jessie also had an active social life, regularly hosting luncheons with and in honor of her mother and mother-in-law, and entertaining out-of-town guests. In May of 1922, she was a guest of honor at a banquet sponsored by the Mathematics Club at NNIS. In fact, Jessie was so busy that in March 1924 she advertised in the *Aberdeen Evening News* for a "Girl for general housework from 9 to 5."

Meanwhile, in April 1920, the *Aberdeen Daily News* announced that Lloyd, "the pleasant and obliging young man who has been in Goodale's Pharmacy for the past eight years," was making a career change "to go into business for himself." Lloyd would, in fact, go to work with his father-in-law as an Aetna Life Insurance agent, and with his father in the city real estate division of Draeger Land & Loan Company. By 1923, however, he was again engaged in pharmacy work, helping to organize the three-day convention of the South Dakota State Pharmaceutical Association in Aberdeen.

(Jessie somehow managed to find time to help plan one of the sessions of its Ladies' Auxiliary.) Outside of work, Lloyd had become active in the American Legion, working on local projects and attending that group's 1926 state convention in Pierre. He also volunteered on behalf of the local Boy Scouts, and the Men's Brotherhood of the Methodist Episcopal Church. And in 1927, he got back into the drug business full-time, going to work at Aberdeen's Buttz Drug Store.

Although life was good for Jessie and Lloyd during the first few years of their marriage, tragedy struck on Friday morning, April 11, 1924, when seven-month-old Kenneth died five days after coming down with measles. "His health has been so perfect in the past that his sudden demise brings a shadow of sorrow that clouds his home and that of his grandparents," reads the *Aberdeen Evening News* account of Kenneth's death. Funeral services, held at Jessie and Lloyd's home, "brought together a large group of sorrowing friends of the young couple," reported the paper. In "A Card of Thanks" published on April 14, Jessie and Lloyd, Leonard Mabbott, and Kenneth's grandparents wrote of their "deep and sincere appreciation of the sympathy and acts of kindness shown us. . . ."

Jessie and Lloyd's second child, Kenneth, shown here with his mother and older sister, Marjorie, was born on September 17, 1923, but died from measles when he was seven months old. Jessie sought comfort in the writings of Mary Baker Eddy, founder of the Christian Science movement.

Devastated by Kenneth's death, Jessie turned to the First Church of Christ, Scientist, taking a course on its teachings in Minneapolis. Mary Baker Eddy had founded the movement in the mid-1800s after recovering from a spinal injury—a recovery she attributed to the power of prayer. Regarding the church's belief in divine healing, Eddy wrote in *Science and Health with Key to the Scriptures*, "It is plain that God does not employ drugs or hygiene, nor provide them for human use; else Jesus would have recommended and employed them in his healing. The sick are more deplorably lost than the sinning, if the sick cannot rely on God for help and the sinning can." Profoundly impacted by Eddy's writing, Jessie joined the Christian Science Society of Aberdeen, which had been organized in 1903; began attending Christian Science services; and immersed herself in church activities. Clearly, her espousal of Eddy's teachings clashed with Lloyd's training and career as a pharmacist. Yet, ever the devoted husband, he supported and respected her decision, often accompanying her to services.

Although his daughter, Jessie, was worried about his health, George Mabbott lived to see the birth of his second grand-daughter, Helen Ann Daniels.

One year after Kenneth's death, Lloyd's mother, Pearl Daniels, died on April 18, 1925, perhaps due to complications from what was likely a stroke she had suffered years earlier. "She bore her long illness with great fortitude," reads the obituary published in the *Aberdeen American-News.* "She was of a beautiful Christian character, [and] a most devoted wife and mother and her sweet expression of appreciation to her many friends who visited her regularly will long be fresh in their memory." By then, Joe Daniels was working full-time building houses (he reportedly built fifty in Aberdeen), and doing quite well. Recalled Marjorie, "He'd sell a house and then go to Minneapolis and spend money on a girl or something—this was after Grandma passed on. Mother would get upset because Grandpa was spending all the money made on that house, and then he'd have to build another one and sell it. So that was our colorful grandpa."

It was on May 20, 1927, two years after Pearl's death, that joy returned to the Daniels family with the arrival of Lloyd and Jessie's second daughter. Weighing in at seven and a half pounds, she was born at St. Luke's Hospital. "As yet, Mr. and Mrs. Daniels have found no suitable name for the baby," reported the *Aberdeen Evening News* on May 23. They settled on "Helen Ann," naming their new baby after one of Lloyd's aunts—Helen "Nellie" Allyn. Marjorie, who was almost six when Helen was born, recalled that Helen's birth helped the family recover from Kenneth's and Pearl's deaths, and deal with worries over the ill health of Jessie's father, George Mabbott. She also pointed out that Helen was born on the same day Charles Lindbergh took off in the Spirit of St. Louis for what was to become the first solo, transatlantic flight from New York to Paris. Much to Jessie's consternation, Lindbergh's accomplishment apparently was of greater interest to Leonard than the fact that he had a new niece. "That's nice, Jessie," Leonard said when Jessie shared her news the next morning, quickly adding, "The damn fool made it. That damn fool Lindbergh—he made it all the way to Paris!" Protested Jessie, "But I have a new baby girl." Responded Leonard, "Oh, yeah, congratulations, Jessie!" According to Marjorie, "[Jessie] never forgave him."

At the time, Leonard was still in Minneapolis working for Northern States Power and visited his parents and sister frequently. In October 1929, he married Blanche Dusseau, who had graduated from a dietetic school in Battle Creek, Michigan, and was working as a demonstrator for a local utility company. According to the *Aberdeen Evening News*, "Mr. Mabbott, who has always been a great admirer of Thomas A. Edison, and his bride selected for their wedding day the fiftieth anniversary of the invention of the incandescent electric lamp." Leonard and Blanche's daughter, Marilyn, was born in July 1932.

Jessie was never able to forgive her brother, Leonard, for taking more interest in Charles Lindbergh's historic, solo flight across the Atlantic—which began in New York on the day Helen was born—than in the birth of his niece.

CHAPTER THREE

A CHILD OF THE DEPRESSION

I f Helen Bader's life was unquestionably shaped by her South Dakota roots, it was also acutely influenced by the timing of her birth—May 1927, on the eve of the Great Depression—the effects of which would not only devastate Aberdeen, but also severely test the fortitude of her family.

Although deeply cherished by her parents and big sister, Helen was a difficult infant, prone to unrelenting crying that made Jessie—who had already lost one baby—understandably anxious. As time went on, she became agitated by the temper tantrums Helen exhibited as a toddler. Leonia tried to help her daughter cope, telling her, "Now, don't make a big fuss over Helen every time she has a tantrum. Just go about your work quietly and keep an eye on her, and she'll calm down."

Helen outgrew her temper tantrums to become a low-key and easy-going child. Despite their six-year age difference, Marjorie and Helen were close and spent time together, especially when they were young. On hot days, recalled Marjorie, they'd play games in their home's cool basement. One favorite outdoor activity was hopscotch. The girls also derived quite a lot of entertainment just sitting on their front steps. On Saturday nights, for example, the local farmers ventured into town, frequently drag racing along Sixth Avenue in front of the Daniels' home, and sometimes colliding with the battered Stop sign on the corner. This prompted numerous calls from Jessie to the local police. "All right, Mrs. Daniels, we'll send somebody out to check it out," was their

Opposite background: The home where Helen Daniels grew up was built for her family by her grandfather Joe Daniels.

Opposite foreground: Three-year-old Helen posed for this photo with her mother, Jessie, and her Easter basket.

Above: Growing up, long-legged Helen loved being outdoors, and frequently skinned her knees.

Left: As a little girl, Helen wore fancy dresses made by her mother and grandmother Leonia.

Right: Helen, Marjorie, and a friend (from left to right) prepare to go sledding on a snowy winter day.

response. (The skirmishes left their mark on Helen, who decades later when encountering aggressive drivers while at the wheel of her own car, would wave her fist out of the window and yell "Farmer!") When the house across the street was converted to a funeral home, the other main entertainment was watching for the hearse, a sure sign that a funeral procession was imminent.

Jessie also arranged for family picnics in the park, this despite Lloyd's preference, after a long day at the drug store, for going home and putting his feet up rather than sitting on the ground eating potato salad. Jessie always made "three times too much food, as everybody does on picnics," reminisced Marjorie. The girls visited their grandparents regularly, and always on holidays; years later Marjorie would tell her own children that her Grandma Mabbott's house always smelled good: a mix of freshly baked cookies and beeswax. In 1933, when Marjorie was twelve and Helen six, the family took a trip to Rapid City, South Dakota, where according to a caption on the back of a family snapshot,

An Independent Spirit: The Quiet, Generous Life of Helen Daniels Bader

"Helen bought a tin cup so she'd always have one whenever we came to a spring." Sunday mornings found the family at Christian Science services and Sunday school classes.

Both Marjorie and Helen were social, but given their age difference, each had her own circle of friends. As little girls, they attended and celebrated birthday parties that at the time were still publicized in the daily newspapers. In July 1928, Marjorie celebrated her seventh birthday at Aberdeen's Melgaard Park, developed from twenty-five partly wooded acres of land donated to the city by Andrew Melgaard in 1909. There, she and seventeen friends spent the day playing games, scrambling over the playground equipment, and eating lunch. The children were driven to and from the park by several of their mothers and Marjorie's Grandpa Joe. From 1927 to 1929, both girls participated in the *Aberdeen News'* Birthday Club, which held monthly events such as movies to which children were invited. The club was co-sponsored by the Walker Amusement Company and Equity Creamery.

Left: *When Helen was six and Marjorie twelve, the family visited Rapid City, South Dakota. Helen bought a tin cup on the trip so she could sample the mineral water in the local springs.*

Right: *Marjorie and Helen's party dresses often were accessorized with matching taffeta hair bows, which Helen often ripped out once she left home.*

Chapter 3: A Child of the Depression

Left: *As a little girl, Marjorie loved playing with her dolls.*

Right: *Helen was a tomboy who loved taking off on her bike, sometimes to deliver newspapers.*

As Helen grew up, she developed her own interests. Unlike Marjorie, who preferred playing indoors—as a little girl, often with her dolls—Helen was a tomboy. One way her independent spirit played out was in her preference for blue jeans over the fancy dresses and bloomers with matching taffeta hair bows that Jessie and Leonia made for her and her sister. In fact, Helen became notorious for ripping out her hair bows the minute she left the house. (That said, even Marjorie admitted to sometimes coming home from school with her bow in her bloomers.) Helen spent as much time outdoors as possible, throwing a ball against the side of the house, and riding off on her scooter—and later her bike—to play marbles and baseball with the neighborhood boys. One favorite pastime: watching local softball games with her father.

Given her long legs and penchant for outdoor activity, Helen was accident prone, often tripping over her feet and skinning her knees. According to Marjorie, it was not unusual for their father to come home for lunch to find Helen howling. Inspecting her newest injury, he'd try to tease her out of her misery with, "Oh, the poor sidewalk!" only to elicit an anguished cry of "Daaaaaady!" Leonia's response was ahead of her time: "Now, Jessie, let Helen wear overalls. If she wants to play around and be a boy, let her be a boy." In fact, Leonia went so far as to nickname her youngest granddaughter "Tommy." Jessie's response, however, was to take Helen to the doctor, imploring him to "Look at those knees. Watch her walk. Tell me, is there something wrong with her legs? Does she need a different kind of shoes?" The doctor ended up agreeing with Leonia: "Jessie, she's just fine," he said. "Put her in overalls and don't fuss over her."

Despite the fact that Helen was the more physically active, daring, and independent of the two girls, she was also the shyer one. Marjorie had the more outgoing personality and was comfortable interacting with adults. Speculated her daughter, Deirdre, "My mother was brought up to think that women—and I think this was dictated by the era—conformed. You tried to be a model girl, and you didn't get your dress dirty or contradict your elders." Her Aunt Helen, on the other hand, "had a more independent streak and was able to express that. Being the younger one, she maybe didn't have to be the good little girl as much as my mother felt she was required to be." Given that opportunity, Helen found small ways (her blue jeans and bicycle) to assert herself a bit more than Marjorie had, and became a little more rebellious and less compliant than her sister. Still, with her innate disposition toward introspection and

Above: *Helen was close to her father, who loved to tease his younger daughter.*

Below: *Although Helen had an independent streak and could assert herself, she was also shy and introspective.*

quiet reflection, Helen was labeled shy and introverted, traits that would continue to define her throughout her life.

Marjorie took tap dance classes, was a Girl Scout—Jessie had by then become active in the Girl Scout Council—and was one of sixteen young Aberdeen children whose photos were used to illustrate *The Child's Own Word-Work Book* by local educator M. M. Guhin about the "whole word" method of teaching reading. In junior high, she won attendance and scholastic awards. Helen, on the other hand, was not a big fan of school, and would jump on her bike and head out to track down friends to play with whenever she could. According to her sister, "She could show up at anybody's house anytime" and be warmly welcomed. And when she did need to "let off steam," she'd simply "go find somebody to talk to."

DANIELS DRUGS

Marjorie was fond of saying she "grew up behind the soda fountain at the drug store," referring to Daniels Drugs, the store Lloyd and Jessie bought in September 1930. George Mabbott had died two years earlier at age sixty, prompting the *Aberdeen Daily News* to note that he had been "interested in every movement that had for its purpose the betterment of Aberdeen and the surrounding community." While Leonia kept up an active family and social life in Aberdeen, Jessie decided to use her inheritance to purchase Aberdeen's Public Drug Store, a move Marjorie said was intended to get her father "out from under being bossed by the other guy all the time." The store, little more than a dirty, old, hole-in-the-wall, had been the scene of a small fire, likely due to an overheated chimney, just four months before it changed hands. The property's saving grace: it occupied prime real estate at 324 S. Main St.

The first drug store had opened in the Dakota Territory in 1862, offering "drugs, shot guns, hardware and everything else that was salable," according to Harold A. Schuler's *A History of Pharmacy in South Dakota*. Schuler writes that Warren J. Page, of Alpena, told the 1921 convention that when he was in practice in 1881, "there was no Board of Pharmacy,

no State Sheriff, no narcotic laws, and no special taxes." According to Schuler, Page admitted:

> We were simply turned loose to do an unrestricted business. I remember with feelings of pride I placed a gold leaf mortar and pestle on a post in front of my store and how the glass show bottles filled with colored solution placed in the windows were in my mind things of beauty as well as necessary advertisements. The glass, labeled shelf bottles were well placed to the front of the store so that a wayfaring man . . . need have no doubt as to the identity of the place. The cash register was represented by the money till with the bell, and a boy on horseback took the place of a telephone. One of my doctors made many of his calls with a high wheeled bicycle.

According to Schuler, efforts to "restrict the dispensing and the sale of medicines to educated druggists and apothecaries" began in 1886 with the establishment of the Southern District Pharmaceutical Association of the Territory of Dakota and adoption of the US Pharmacopoeia (USP) as its standard for the preparation of prescription medicines. The association's Code of Ethics called upon pharmacists to refrain from making alcohol "a prominent feature of a pharmacy," giving medical advice, or saying

Downtown Aberdeen in the 1930s boasted eight drug stores on Main Street, including Daniels Drugs.

SOUTH DAKOTA STATE HISTORICAL SOCIETY ARCHIVES

detrimental things about doctors. By the time Lloyd Daniels took up the profession, pharmacists had to be licensed, a process that required completing a degree in pharmacy or working for two consecutive years in pharmacy, and passing an examination administered by the state's Board of Pharmacy.

In the early years of the profession, everything from pharmaceuticals—such as they were—to cold creams were formulated on-site. But soon pharmacists found themselves competing both with department stores and traveling peddlers. Schuler noted that C. H. Lohr, president of what was by then the South Dakota Pharmaceutical Association (SDPA), told pharmacists at the group's 1898 convention that department stores were selling goods such as sarsaparilla for less than pharmacies, and that the peddler "pays no taxes, trades worthless remedies for a living, and cuts into the druggist's business." What's more, as early as 1909 drug companies began manufacturing prescription drugs, and as their popularity grew, doctors were less likely to prescribe fluid extracts, ointments, tinctures, or powders once exclusively formulated by pharmacists—a skill described as a "lost art." As a result, pharmacists were encouraged to supplement their prescription drug business with other lines of goods such as jewelry, eyeglasses, wallpaper, cigars, candy, magazines, and soda fountain treats.

Daniels Drugs supplemented its prescription drug business by selling cigars, candy, greeting cards, magazines, and fountain treats.

With the opening of Daniels Drugs, "Dad came into his own," said Marjorie. He immediately recruited two clerks with whom he had worked in the past, clerks who wore white uniforms and knew how to get behind the glass-topped counters and sell. Those were the days when, explained Marjorie, "you needed salespeople to bring things out and show them before [customers] bought." Daniels Drugs was one of numerous drug stores—including eight on Main Street, and Goodale's just across the street—doing business in Aberdeen in the 1930s, so competition was stiff. "Well, one drug store specialized in nice books and had jewelry and a little soda fountain up there with a balcony, and another was down where the doctor's building was, so they were handy for their prescriptions," remembered Marjorie. Daniels benefited, in part, from its proximity to a doctor's office just down the block.

But competition wasn't the only challenge. Opening a business in the wake of the Depression was a highly risky move. The financial crisis had hit South Dakota as hard as anywhere in the country: the stock market crash prompted bank failures and thousands of home and farm foreclosures. According to Ralph J. Brown, professor emeritus of economics at the University of South Dakota, per capita personal income losses averaged 58 percent—the worst in the nation, and more than twice the national average of 23 percent. As Marjorie recalled, "There was no money."

Daniels Drugs did business in Aberdeen for nearly forty years under the slogan "The Name You Can Trust."

In 1934, the SDPA entered into an agreement with the Farmers Aid Corporation, a private relief program, to sell drugs to corporation members—poor farmers—at a 10 percent discount. Still, Schuler reports that over the next five years, and despite the discount, "pharmacies were only paid for about twenty percent of their bills. . . ." The good news: according to 1938 data from the US Department of Commerce, pharmacies fared better than many other businesses.

THE DIRTY THIRTIES

Compounding the financial hardships of the Depression was a series of natural disasters—drought, dust storms, and an infestation of grasshoppers—that created a so-called Dust Bowl in the Great Plains and defined the era as the Dirty Thirties. In his paper "Dusting Off the Dust Bowl: The Historical Geography of the Northern Plains during the 1930s," Donald Berg, emeritus professor at the University of South Dakota, describes the phenomenon as "a region, an era, and an event," and goes on to take issue with conventional wisdom locating it largely in Oklahoma, Texas, Kansas, and other southern plains states. After analyzing the "situation as it existed in the northern Great Plains," Berg concluded that "the economic, social, and environmental disaster of the Dirty '30s was comparable, if not more severe in many of its characteristics, to that of the southern Great Plains, which is perceived popularly as The Dust Bowl." There is plenty of evidence to support Berg's position: By December 1934, South Dakotans ranked first in the country in terms of the percent of residents (39 percent) on relief rolls. And between 1930 and 1940, the state lost 7.2 percent of its population—a greater percentage than any other state in the country.

Although severe weather had long plagued South Dakotans, the lack of rain and high temperatures that settled in during the early 1930s led to catastrophic crop failures. "Light Rains in Vicinity of Aberdeen Too Late for Much Benefit," reads the headline in an *Aberdeen Evening News* story

The Northern Plains were plagued by drought and dust storms during what became known as the Dirty Thirties.

An Independent Spirit: The Quiet, Generous Life of Helen Daniels Bader

published on August 4, 1931, that included the ominous fact that "grasshoppers apparently are spreading." Farmers without the ability to raise feed sold off their livestock at severe losses, exacerbating their already-precarious financial situations. Once-rich farmland turned to dust, churned by high winds into blizzards. According to *Brown County History,* "The dirt became so fine that it penetrated everything, even the well-built homes. By eleven o'clock in the morning, the sun was hidden and lamps had to be lighted. The dirt was so thick that driving was hazardous." Writes Berg, "Dust easily accumulated in peoples' homes, rural and urban, contaminated food and water, and generally made daily living miserable." Health risks included respiratory ailments such as dust pneumonia and brown plague, corneal ulcers, skin issues, and psychological depression.

As for the grasshoppers, although they had damaged local crops in the 1920s, the infestation a decade later would prove disastrous. Berg noted that they showed up in "almost biblical numbers" in Rosebud County in the summer of 1931. Deep spring plowing to combat the pests was ineffective, as was an effort to raise turkeys to prey on the insects. The *Aberdeen Evening News* reported in August 1932 that "Hundreds—possibly thousands—of destructive grasshoppers were drifting high over Aberdeen into the southeast today," and that "many tired of drifting along with a casual wind, have descended into [the] streets of Aberdeen." In cities such as Aberdeen, reported the paper, grasshoppers "in countless numbers swirled and

Cattle turned loose in corn fields already ruined by grasshoppers, such as these in Carson, North Dakota, became a familiar site across the Northern Plains in the 1930s.

swarmed about electric globes on great white ways or danced merrily, sometimes fiendishly about office lights." One year later, the plague continued. "Thousands of migratory, goggle-eyed, hungry, inquisitive grasshoppers dropped out of a starry sky Friday night to startle and puzzle people on Aberdeen streets," reported the *Aberdeen Evening News*. And in 1934, one newspaper headline proclaimed, "So. Dak. Leads in Infestation of 'Hoppers' Eggs." Marjorie would later share with her children the fact that the grasshoppers would "eat the clothes off the clothesline." In the end, poisoned bait provided by the government killed the grasshoppers, but much other wildlife as well, and contaminated groundwater for decades to come.

During the Dirty Thirties, it is said, "Farm women mostly swept up dust." But Marjorie recalled that many Aberdonian women did, too. The first thing every morning, "the grasshoppers were in the front door" of the store, she said, where "everything was covered with dust." In fact, all of Aberdeen's Main Street merchants were struggling. Yet Lloyd refused to give up or give in to the harsh economic realities, routinely working nineteen-hour days to keep the store afloat and build his business. It wasn't unusual for him to go back to the store late at night if someone needed a prescription filled. "If anybody had a sick baby out in the country, he'd take it to them," recalled Marjorie. Lloyd also refused to turn away customers who couldn't afford their prescriptions, including the destitute farmers and local Sioux who lived outside of town and were especially devastated by the economic downturn. According to Deirdre, the American Indians typically came to the back door of the pharmacy, where Lloyd provided whatever they needed. "The American Indians came in off the reservation knowing my grandfather was a decent white man," she said, noting that his actions were guided by a "simple sense of kindness and fairness" with "no fuss about it." Indeed, such actions his young daughters not only noticed, but

Lloyd Daniels, familiarly referred to around town as "Dick," became the most beloved druggist in Aberdeen, known for his compassion, generosity, and strong work ethic.

took to heart. And were in large part the reason why Lloyd Daniels became the most beloved druggist in town.

HARDSHIP OVERCOME

To be sure, there were plenty of good times at Daniels Drugs, where a neon sign touted two of the store's bestsellers, "Sodas-Cigars." On opening day, nine-year-old Marjorie walked her three-year-old sister the seven blocks from their home to the store. "So Helen had a cute little dress on and her cute curls," recalled Marjorie, "and we walked down and walked inside, and I said, 'Now, don't tell Daddy that Mother's making a cake.'" Helen promptly looked up at her father, said "Daddy, get down," and whispered in his ear, "Mother's making a big cake!" Continued Marjorie, "I was mortified! I just felt so bad."

Daniels Drugs, which would continue to do business for nearly forty years touting the slogan "The Name You Can Trust," was by all accounts a family enterprise. Jessie was highly involved in its operation, showing up at the store frequently with ideas on ways to boost sales. At the SDPA's 1933 convention its members were told "A druggist must give full attention to business. Keep alert, with your finger on the community pulse. Endeavor to make your drug store the center of drug purchases in your community, and to make people want to trade with you." It was in that spirit that Jessie began pondering ways to entice "the nice North Side ladies to come in and buy perfume and so forth," said Marjorie. Lloyd's response: a friendly competition. "Alright, Mother," he said, "you put in a perfume window, and I'll put in a general merchandise window and we'll see which one sells the most stuff." Jessie's window was beautiful, replete with dainty perfume bottles, compacts, and packages of dusting powder artfully arranged on gold satin. Lloyd filled his window with blue bottles of milk of magnesia, tubes

Jessie, who loved coming up with ways to boost sales at Daniels Drugs, focused on the needs of Aberdeen's women. As a result, the store promoted a line of perfume.

An Independent Spirit: The Quiet, Generous Life of Helen Daniels Bader

of toothpaste, and other drug store essentials. In the end, recalled Marjorie, "He won, of course. But Mother had her fun."

In fact, a 1933 newspaper story about Christmas shopping noted that "all the grace and vanity and femininity of womankind could find satisfaction in Daniels Corner Drug Store this year if they would get a bottle of the Lentheric Cologne in their favorite scent. . . ." The article also plugged men's leather goods, Shaeffer pen-and-pencil sets priced at $2, and candy. Noted the story, which identified Lloyd by his nickname, "Dick Daniels will help you pick out your gifts. . . ." That same year, when he wasn't assisting customers with their Christmas shopping, Lloyd was helping organize the Lions Club's annual Christmas party for underprivileged children.

Even as Jessie threw her weight behind perfume sales, she failed to come to terms with Lloyd's decision to sell Dr. Jellyn's Hog Medicine. The idea originated with Joe Daniels, who according to Marjorie, "could sell anything." With gallon cans of the vitamin compound in the back of his car, he traveled to farms outside of town, convincing farmers to begin raising hogs "because they reproduce fast." Dr. Jellyn's, he added, would keep the animals healthy and ensure they brought a good price when put on the market. When sales of the concoction took off, Lloyd began selling it out of the store, the big gallon cans lined up in front of the building and used to prop open the screen door. "Did that ever hurt my mother's aesthetic sensitivities," recalled Marjorie. "Oh, she hated to see Dr. Jellyn's Hog Medicine out there."

Another scheme of Lloyd's was designed to lure residents waiting for the city bus into the store. He installed a bare light bulb over the front door that customers could turn on, signaling the bus to stop on its way up and down Main Street. "In cold weather they could come in, put the light on, and stand there and wait for the bus," explained Marjorie. It was no accident that the candy counter and shelves lined with other tempting merchandise were strategically located nearby. Nickel candy bars and cigars flew off the shelves. Over the years, coupons for discounts on purchases and drawings for door prizes also proved effective ways to attract new customers and promote store loyalty.

Opposite above: *In a friendly competition, Jessie and Lloyd each decorated one of the front windows of Daniels Drugs. Jessie's featured Hallmark greeting cards, perfume, compacts, and talcum powder. Lloyd's featured drug store essentials such as toothpaste and milk of magnesia.*

Opposite below: *In 1949, Daniels Drugs moved to a new location on Fourth Avenue just off Main Street. There, open merchandise displays made it easy for customers to self-select the items they wanted to purchase.*

According to Marjorie, Daniels Pharmacy held the first and only Hallmark card franchise in Aberdeen in 1935, at a time when the company granted only one franchise per small city. "The salesman came in off the road with huge sample cases to get our order," she recalled. "He came in hot and dusty and tired in August each year with the Christmas line and spread his sample books all over the RX room for Dad and the salesgirls to pick from." At first, only one small rack of greeting cards sat atop the perfume case in front of the store, later replaced by several larger racks.

But it was the soda fountain that was the most special feature of Daniels Drugs. Marjorie recalled delicious ice cream sodas—in lots of flavors and served in tall, frosted glasses—made from farm-fresh ice cream that sold on Ice Cream Soda Special Day for ten cents each. "Sometimes we'd keep track and we'd have five or six of us behind the counter getting in each other's way, but by the end of the day we would have sold two hundred sodas, which was a lot for an itty-bitty drug store." On blazing hot summer days, it wasn't unusual for one of the local doctors to call in a prescription—and in the process, engage with Lloyd. "Do you have an office full of people?" Lloyd would

Marjorie was fond of saying she "grew up behind the soda fountain" at Daniels Drugs.

An Independent Spirit: The Quiet, Generous Life of Helen Daniels Bader

ask. "Oh, the office is full and I don't see any end to it," was the doctor's weary reply, partly due to a lack of air conditioning. "How would you like some fresh lime freezes . . . or some fresh Cokes?" Lloyd would ask. And a little later, recalled Marjorie, "He'd send me down with a tray with all the Cokes or the fresh lime freezes or whatever to revive the doctor. So that kept the doctor's prescriptions coming." Marjorie also remembers workers from the local telephone company coming into the store with their own trays, on which they'd carry out big soda fountain orders, and employees of the S. S. Kresge Company, the local five-and-dime, making the drug store their after-hours watering hole.

Lloyd likely knew fellow pharmacist Hubert H. Humphrey, the future vice president of the United States who in 1931 dropped out of the University of Minnesota to work with his father at Humphrey's Drug Store in Huron, ninety miles south of Aberdeen. Like Marjorie and Helen, the younger Humphrey grew up behind a soda fountain, claiming later in life that the discussions he heard there eclipsed "some of the great parliamentary debates of our time." Like Lloyd Daniels, Humphrey and his father sold not only prescription drugs, but also hog medicine, which they advertised with a wooden sign in the shape of a pig hung over the door of the store. (Little wonder what Jessie thought of that!) However, Humphrey, who worked at the store until 1937, was not meant to be a pharmacist. He grew depressed—and to hate the job—and yearned to pursue an academic career in political science. Living in the Dust Bowl didn't help. In a 1992 article published in the *Seattle Times*, William Ecenbarger quotes a twenty-two-year-old Humphrey: "God, it was terrible! So hot, so terribly hot. The dust, it was everywhere. There was a desolation, a drabbiness. The sky and horizon—dull and bleak. Hope would leave. You didn't want to stay, but there was no way to leave. You felt trapped." According to Ecenbarger, the experience left Humphrey with "a lifelong habit of vigorously dusting everything in sight."

Lloyd Daniels likely crossed paths with Hubert H. Humphrey, the future vice president of the United States, who worked for a while with his father at Humphrey's Drug Store in Huron, ninety miles south of Aberdeen, but ultimately was not meant to be a pharmacist.

WIKIPEDIA

DARKER DAYS

Back in Aberdeen, Daniels Drugs not only survived the Great Depression, but thrived, and Lloyd and Jessie went on to make a mark on the pharmacy profession statewide: At the 1932 convention of the South Dakota State Pharmaceutical Association, which was held in Aberdeen, Jessie was elected vice president of the group's Ladies' Auxiliary for 1933–1934; she went on to serve as president the following year. The auxiliary worked to find ways to support their pharmacist husbands, raised money for scholarships, and organized social events in conjunction with the association's annual conventions. Lloyd served as president of the SDPA in 1935–1936, the year the association celebrated its fiftieth anniversary.

Lloyd served as president of the South Dakota State Pharmaceutical Association in 1935–1936, the year the association celebrated its fiftieth anniversary.

Still, the hardships of the 1930s had taken a toll on Lloyd and Jessie. Jessie was hit particularly hard, emotionally and physically. Still grieving for Kenneth, she became overwhelmed by and unable to cope with the dust, grasshoppers, and poverty that plagued Aberdeen. She grew anxious and depressed, often broke down in tears, and began experiencing migraine headaches that kept her in bed for days at a time. The once carefree, lighthearted, mischievous young woman whose liveliness and spirit had captured Lloyd's heart became intense, dramatic, and high-strung. Perhaps in response, he turned inward and became more self-effacing.

Jessie sought support both from her religious faith—prayer helped combat her migraines—and a few close friends. One of the closest was Matilda Jewell Gage, granddaughter and namesake of suffragette Matilda Joslyn Gage, and niece of L. Frank and Maud Baum. A neighbor of Jessie and Lloyd's, Matilda Jewell Gage was a high school English teacher who later worked in banking; she was also a lover of history, and a founding member of the Aberdeen branch of the American Association of University Women. She is credited with

F. M. Cornwell

Lloyd A. Daniels

Kenneth Jones

SOUTH DAKOTA STATE PHARMACEUTICAL ASSOCIATION

OFFICERS

LLOYD A. DANIELS, Aberdeen · · · · · President
F. M. CORNWELL, Webster · · · · · Vice President
THOMAS K. HAGGAR, Sioux Falls · · · Vice President
    Chairman Educative and Legislative Section
CHAS. A. LOCKE, Brookings · · · · · Vice President
    Chairman Scientific and Practical Section
KENNETH JONES, Gettysburg · · · · · Secretary
FRANK S. BOCKOVEN, Clark · · · · · Treasurer
R. S. WENGERT, Sioux Falls · · · · · Local Secretary

preserving much of the Gage family history, sharing information about her grandmother with Sally Roesch Wagner, author of *The Declaration of Rights of Women: 1876,* a South Dakota bicentennial project. She also opened her home to the public as part of an AAUW Antique Tour in 1959. On display was the mahogany sleigh bed where suffragettes Susan B. Anthony and Elizabeth Stanton had slept while visiting Matilda Joslyn Gage decades earlier in Fayetteville, New York. In 1976, Matilda Jewell Gage helped organize a display at Aberdeen's Dacotah Prairie Museum recreating a typical 1876 Philadelphia "suffragette parlor." Celebrating her Baum roots, she donated her collection of Baum memorabilia to the museum when she died in 1986.

Matilda Jewel Gage— granddaughter and namesake of suffragette Matilda Joslyn Gage and niece of L. Frank and Maud Baum—was one of Jessie's closest friends.
INTERNATIONAL WIZARD OF OZ CLUB

Jessie, eight years younger than Matilda Jewell Gage, admired the older woman's sharp intellect and impressive conversational skills, traits that made her a perfect confidant and mentor. Jessie also found Matilda— whose little sister, Dorothy Louise, had died as an infant—especially empathetic over Kenneth's death. Marjorie and Helen also grew close to Gage. "They called her Aunt Matilda," recalled Marjorie's son Dan DeVey, "and were over at her house as much as their own." His sister, Deirdre, was six years old in the summer of 1961 when she and her mother, during a visit to Aberdeen, had tea with Matilda. "I remember being a bit in awe of her—she was very elegant and a bit formidable," remembered Deirdre. "And her house was full of antiques—a horsehair couch and lamps with fringed lampshades." But what really fascinated Deirdre was a bookcase reserved for the works of L. Frank Baum. "I was so impressed that she had all these books I really loved!" Dan remembered visiting Matilda with his mother in 1978, when she made them chocolate shakes served up in old-fashioned, silver, filigreed goblets with silver straws. "I found her absolutely fascinating—she had a great sense of humor and was always upbeat," he said. "We listened to endless stories."

Still, even with the support of her husband, church, and friends such as Matilda, by the mid-1930s Jessie was taking more and more often to her bed, and it fell to Marjorie—at the time a young teen—to pick up the slack both at home and at the store. She cared for her mother and her Grandmother Leonia, tried to keep an eye on Helen, and often got dinner on the table, all while putting in many hours behind the soda fountain. Helen, still a young girl, found herself with a bit more freedom, which she used to hop on her bike and strike out on her own.

With Jessie struggling physically and emotionally, it increasingly fell to teenaged Marjorie to keep an eye on Helen.

MARJORIE LEAVES HOME

In 1939, when Helen was in junior high school, Marjorie followed in her mother's footsteps, enrolling at Northern State Teachers College (formerly Northern Normal and Industrial School) and then, two years later, transferring to Milwaukee-Downer College. Her years at Aberdeen Central High School had been fun. An accomplished, popular student, she had won attendance and scholastic awards, and was elected multiple times to the homecoming court, reigning as homecoming queen senior year. She especially loved school dances, which she attended wearing formals made by her mother and on the arms of a number of different boys who liked to dance, too. That is, until senior year when she started going steady with the man she would marry, Richard Wilder DeVey.

Dick DeVey, the son of Don and Helen DeVey, had been born in 1922 in Westport, South Dakota, a small town (population, seventy-five) located fourteen miles north of Aberdeen, where his father was owner and president of Farmers State Bank. Dick grew up in Westport, along with his younger sister, Victoria. But in July 1935, when Dick was thirteen years old, his family's home was destroyed by a fire that according to authorities likely was caused by faulty wiring. Although Don DeVey told the local newspaper he contemplated rebuilding, he instead moved the family to Aberdeen, where he continued running the bank and branched out into the insurance business.

It was there, in seventh grade homeroom, that Dick first noticed Marjorie, who was seated nearby thanks to the alphabetical seating arrangement popular at the time. "I was stricken on the spot," he recalled. Happily for Dick, he and Marjorie were thrown together later that year when they were elected king and queen of the school's Rough Rider Day, though he claimed it took him several more years to get her to agree to an actual date. His first impression of Helen is equally touching: Delivering publicity photos for Rough Rider Day to Marjorie's house, Dick encountered Helen at the front door. "Here was this little one with this great big smile," he recalled, "a small edition of my Marjorie." The sisters had "the same bangs that they wore in those days, the same hair color. . . . [Helen] was cute as the dickens and she was really looking me over with her big eyes."

After Dick and Marjorie graduated from high school in 1939, Dick headed to Philadelphia, where he enrolled at the University of Pennsylvania's Wharton School of Finance and Commerce. It was the beginning of a long-distance

Top: *Dick DeVey and his sister, Victoria, were born in the small town of Westport, South Dakota, fourteen miles north of Aberdeen.*

Bottom left: *Dick DeVey* (middle row, white shirt)*, son of the local banker, is the only boy in his class not wearing overalls.*

Bottom right: *According to a local newspaper account, the fire that destroyed the DeVey family home in Westport was caused by faulty wiring.*

$21,000 Westport Fire Lowers Two Buildings

Chapter 3: A Child of the Depression

relationship that would last for seven years, with the couple meeting up back home in Aberdeen, and later in Milwaukee, whenever they could. "We would come home for Christmas," Dick recalled, "It was like an oasis to find her there, and time fell away and all was bliss again."

Although Marjorie's two years at Northern State were relatively uneventful, she enjoyed getting out of the house, even when it meant walking to school during the severe South Dakota winters. It was a respite from years of taking care of her mother, keeping an eye on Helen, and fulfilling her other responsibilities at home. It gave Marjorie her first taste of freedom, a freedom that would expand exponentially when she enrolled at Milwaukee-Downer in 1941. Like their parents, Jessie and Lloyd were strong advocates of higher education for women and approved of Marjorie's move to Milwaukee. After all, Jessie had loved her years there, and she and Lloyd much preferred that Marjorie attend Milwaukee-Downer rather than an East Coast school or a big university.

Just months after Marjorie arrived on campus, the United States entered World War II. As it turned out, Milwaukee was perfectly positioned to aid the war effort: The so-called machine shop of the world, the city was home to a number of factories able to quickly convert their operations to wartime production. Perhaps the most notable was the Allis-Chalmers Manufacturing Company, established in 1901 to produce agricultural and construction machinery. According to the *Milwaukee Journal,* the company in late 1942 began filling more than sixty separate orders related to the production of the atomic bomb, noting that "The contribution of Allis-Chalmers to the bomb may be divided into three sections—first, the equipment especially designed and built for . . . atom sorting;

second, the electromagnetic process and equipment for separating the different kinds of uranium; third, the large power plant equipment which was used to extract plutonium from uranium."

According to the *Encyclopedia of Milwaukee,* women—and for the first time, Black Americans—were brought in to work in the factories. With more children unsupervised, juvenile delinquency spiked. And with corporate profits surging and workers increasingly demanding wage increases, unions grew more powerful. Meanwhile, city residents dealt with housing shortages and blackouts, planted Victory gardens, and contributed to scrap metal and rubber drives. The heaviest toll, of course, came in the number of Milwaukeeans who died in military service: nineteen hundred by the end of the war.

When Marjorie matriculated at Milwaukee-Downer, student enrollment stood at 306 and the number of faculty members at 49. Tuition, room, and board totaled $645. A home economics major, Marjorie was known as "Danny," a derivative of her last name. She recalled Milwaukee as a "wonderful city," and Milwaukee-Downer as a place "we all learned how to be ladies and act properly."

Marjorie arrived on campus just months before Japan bombed Pearl Harbor and the United States entered World War II; Jessie had been there at the beginning of World War I. In the interim, Lucia Russell Briggs had replaced Ellen Sabin as president in 1921. With a bachelor's and a master's degree from Radcliffe College, and teaching experience at Simmons College, a private women's school in Boston, Briggs strongly endorsed the liberal arts model that Sabin had instituted at Milwaukee-Downer. Briggs expanded the school's curriculum, offering bachelor's degrees not only in more academic areas, but also in occupational therapy and nursing. Briggs also led campaigns to grow the college's endowment and oversaw the construction of Ellen Sabin Science Hall in 1927, and Chapman Memorial Library in 1935.

By the time Marjorie and Helen arrived on campus, Lucia Russell Briggs had become president of Milwaukee-Downer College. Briggs would serve in that role until 1951.

ARCHIVES DEPARTMENT, UNIVERSITY OF WISCONSIN-MILWAUKEE LIBRARIES

Chapter 3: A Child of the Depression

In the intervening years, changes had also taken place at the neighboring Milwaukee State Normal School. In an effort by the State Normal School Regents to refocus the school's mission on the instruction of teachers, the school was renamed Milwaukee State Teachers College in 1927. By the 1940s, it had, indeed, become one of the country's top teacher training colleges.

While a student at Milwaukee-Downer College, Marjorie spent a Thanksgiving holiday at the home of her college friend Carol Kirk in Davenport, Iowa. Pictured above are (left to right) *Marjorie; Carol Kirk; and another classmate, Ellen Gut.*

To be sure, Milwaukee-Downer had evolved since the days Jessie had been a coed. "With mother, young ladies did not go down the front steps on their way to a concert without putting on their gloves," Marjorie recalled. "They had their hat and their gloves on before they left the dormitory." By 1941, the rules were far more relaxed. Although skirts and sweaters were required on campus, and dresses were de rigueur at dinner, students successfully petitioned school officials to allow them to wear slacks when traveling at night through the campus's underground tunnels between their dormitory and the library.

By all accounts, Marjorie loved Milwaukee-Downer, making strong friendships that would last the rest of her life. She was active in the Home Economics Club, performed in the school's Christmas and spring plays, and was active in student government. She was also a bit rebellious, confessing years later to her own children that the only time in her life she ever smoked was during her Milwaukee-Downer days when she and her pals—wearing bobby socks and rolling up their dungarees—sneaked off to the basement of their dormitory with their cigarettes. Marjorie graduated in 1943 with a bachelor's of science degree in home economics, but unlike her mother did not return to Aberdeen. She chose instead to fulfill a dream familiar to many who grew up in small towns where, as she put it, "you lived in the same house all your life" and longed to escape. That she did, going to work for Ed. Schuster & Co., owner of Milwaukee's popular Schuster's department store chain, as assistant to the company's personnel director.

BACK IN ABERDEEN

When Marjorie left Aberdeen for Milwaukee in the fall of 1941, Helen—at the time a high school freshman—was forced to step up. "She was the one who got left at home, so she had to take care of Grandma, take care of Mother, and be down at the store with Dad," recalled Marjorie. The next four years were formative ones for Helen, who grew into her new responsibilities with surprising ease. She matured quickly, becoming efficient and dependable. What's more, she came to love spending time helping her father run Daniels Drugs, business experience that would come in handy later in her life.

Given all that was on her plate and a less-than-compelling interest in formal education, high school wasn't as much fun for Helen as it had been for Marjorie. She had taken violin lessons as a child and played through high school, where the orchestra teacher was especially kind and encouraging. Academics, however, came less easily; she had to work hard on her lessons, depending at times on Jessie's math tutoring. She also participated in Spanish Club, and as a senior was lauded in the school yearbook for having "the best sense of all, common sense."

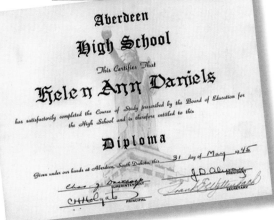

Following graduation in 1945, Helen headed to Milwaukee-Downer, where she majored in botany and played in the school orchestra for four years. Like her sister, Helen was also known on campus as "Danny." Although Marjorie shed the nickname when she graduated, it stuck with Helen the rest of her life. To be sure, school rules had relaxed somewhat in the two years between Marjorie's graduation and Helen's enrollment. According to

Helen graduated from high school in May 1945, and following in the footsteps of her mother and sister, enrolled that fall at Milwaukee-Downer College.

Chapter 3: A Child of the Depression

Opposite top: *Marjorie Daniels and Dick DeVey were married in November 1946 in Minneapolis. Posing for the formal wedding photo were* (left to right): *Dick's father, Don; Dick's sister, Victoria; Dick's mother, Helen; Dick; Marjorie; Helen; Jessie; and Lloyd.*

Opposite bottom: *Helen served as her sister's maid of honor.*

Marjorie, this was especially true regarding the dress code: "By the time Helen got there," she contended, "they could wear anything." Still, as late as 1948, students were told to bring "a white dress for college functions. . . ." Students were awoken every morning by the "rising bell" at 6:45 a.m., with breakfast served from 7:15 to 7:30 a.m. While breakfast and lunch were "informal," students were told to be "prompt" at dinner, which was served in the evenings during the week and at 1:15 p.m. on Sundays.

Helen joined the Spanish and International Relations clubs; participated in Senior Cabaret, a night of class skits; and worked on Christmas Carnival, a bazaar at which money was raised for worthy causes. She also held down a part-time job at a local florist shop. Her best friends were Jerline E. Walfoort, a social studies major from Plymouth, Wisconsin, and a fellow Dakotan, Jane Evelyn Van Houten, from Oakes, North Dakota.

In March of 1946, while Helen was a freshman at Milwaukee-Downer, Leonia died at the age of seventy-five. For a time after George's death, she had rented out a room in her home to a twenty-five-year-old woman who worked as a bookkeeper for the railroad, but by 1940, according to census records, she was living alone. Services were held at the Methodist church, and mourners included friends from her church, the Zetetic Club, and employees of Daniels Drugs.

The following November was marked by a much happier family event when Marjorie left her position with Schuster's to marry Dick, who at the time was living in Chicago and working as an industrial engineer for Marshall Field & Company. The wedding was held in Minneapolis, which Marjorie considered a "happy midpoint" (and, in a tribute to her hometown's railroad heritage, just a day's train ride away) for both the couple's Milwaukee- and Chicago-based friends, and those family members and friends living in Aberdeen. Following the wedding, at which Helen served as maid of honor, Marjorie and Dick honeymooned in New Orleans. Marjorie then joined Dick in Chicago, where for a while they both worked at Marshall Field's. Over the next sixty-one years, Dick's career in industrial management would take the couple to Indiana, Wisconsin, Michigan,

New York, Florida, and Texas. Despite the many moves, Marjorie was good at staying in touch with her friends. She was one of a group of six college classmates who—decades before Facebook—found a way to regularly share the details of their lives. Participating in a snail mail "round robin," they circulated among themselves a package that included written updates of each of their lives. Every time the package would arrive at one of their homes, the recipient would update her portion of the narrative and send it on.

Helen graduated from Milwaukee-Downer in 1949. As it turned out, enrollment at the school had peaked, at 444 students, during 1946–1947, her sophomore year; nine years later, enrollment stood at a dismal 147. John Bockover Johnson, Briggs's successor, cited the Depression era's lower birth rate, increased competition for female students as college-age men enlisted in the Korean War, and a trend toward earlier marriage during

Marjorie, Helen, and Jessie (left to right)—all graduates of Milwaukee-Downer College—celebrated Helen's commencement in 1949.

World War II as some of the reasons for the declining enrollment. Also significant was a move by the state legislature in 1951 authorizing Milwaukee State Teachers College—by then renamed Wisconsin State College, Milwaukee—to begin granting bachelor's degrees. Five years later, it merged with the University of Wisconsin's Milwaukee Extension Center to become the University of Wisconsin-Milwaukee (UWM). According to historian Charles Breunig, "Located literally across the street from Milwaukee-Downer, UWM attracted many day students because its costs were lower than those at Downer (it charged virtually no tuition at this time) and its offerings were more varied." Yet Breunig questioned the prevailing notion that UWM's creation was the reason for Milwaukee-Downer's demise. He noted that Milwaukee-Downer's enrollment decline had begun *before* the state institution began offering bachelor's degrees and stabilized somewhat between 1956 and 1962 when competition with UWM should have had its greatest impact.

Breunig theorizes that Milwaukee-Downer struggled, in part, because it was located in the Midwest and as a result never achieved the status of women's colleges in the East and the South. Furthermore, coeducation became popular in the Midwest earlier than elsewhere in the country, forcing Milwaukee-Downer up against more severe competition from local schools.

An Independent Spirit: The Quiet, Generous Life of Helen Daniels Bader

Despite efforts to draw enrollment from the East Coast and increase the number of students pursuing degrees in the liberal arts—versus occupational therapy and home economics—enrollment stood at only 162 during the 1962–1963 school year, which Breunig said "crippled the school financially." Compounding the school's problems were efforts from UWM, which had been growing rapidly during the 1950s, to acquire some or all of Milwaukee-Downer's forty-three-acre campus. Writes Breunig, "Given these adverse circumstances, it is remarkable that Milwaukee-Downer survived as long as it did."

In July 1963 Milwaukee-Downer's Board of Trustees began merger discussions with Lawrence College, in Appleton, Wisconsin, a liberal arts college that had been established in 1847. The merger deal called for Milwaukee-Downer to sell its campus to the state for $10 million, with the proceeds going to Lawrence and the college's land and buildings transferred to UWM. For its part, Lawrence agreed to absorb Milwaukee-Downer's full-time faculty and students. The Lawrence trustees, however, would not agree to incorporating "Downer" into its school's name (Milwaukee-Downer trustees suggested the consolidated institution be renamed "Downer-Lawrence" or "Lawrence-Downer"). A compromise was worked out: Lawrence College would become Lawrence University, and would include Lawrence College for Men, and Downer College for Women.

The merger was announced at an assembly of faculty and students in October. Reported the *Milwaukee Journal*, "There was a gasp. Then a hysterical giggle. The faculty members had not known. They sat quietly listening. One elderly woman began twisting and untwisting her hands. . . . One girl rose, paused and then ran out of the auditorium doors. Tears began trickling silently down the cheeks of a woman faculty member with twenty-eight years at Downer." A total of twenty-one of Milwaukee-Downer's thirty full-time faculty members, and fifty of the school's ninety students, made the move to Lawrence the following September.

The original Milwaukee-Downer campus remains today as part of UWM's grounds, at the southeast corner of North Downer and East

Hartford avenues in the form of a cluster of red brick Gothic buildings—Holton, Merrill, Johnston, and Greene halls—known as the Milwaukee-Downer Quad. The loveliest and most photographed buildings on campus, they narrowly avoided the wrecking ball in 1973 thanks largely to the efforts of the Committee for the Renovation of Downer Buildings. Subsequently recognized as landmark buildings for their historical significance by the City of Milwaukee Landmarks Commission and added to the National Register of Historic Places, they remain protected. Just north on Downer Avenue stands the beautifully restored Sabin Hall.

Following graduation, Helen returned home to Aberdeen, albeit briefly, to help her parents move Daniels Drugs to a new location located just off Main Street, at 14 Fourth Ave. SE, that Joe Daniels had built for his son. "That was Grandpa's goal, to put up that building for my dad," recalled Marjorie. One week before the store opened, however, Joe was hospitalized. In Marjorie's words, "He had given out." Still, Joe managed one last visit to the store. Then, satisfied, he died on October 2, 1949, at the age of eighty-two. "It was a very sweet story," said Marjorie. "Grandpa Joe was sorely missed."

An avid hunter and fisherman, he had kept the Daniels family in trout and pheasant for years, and after his death a stuffed pheasant encased in glass was displayed in the drug store in his memory. Joe was particularly proud of the fact that because of his good aim the pheasants he brought down were more eatable than most. Explained Marjorie, they weren't "so full of shot." The most interesting fact in Joe Daniels' obituary: that he had learned the art of boat building from the local American Indians while living in Red Wing, Minnesota.

After helping with the move to the new store—where customers for a while had to wait while she and the other clerks dug through still-packed boxes looking for requested merchandise—Helen returned to Milwaukee,

now to work full-time, and begin dating the florist. She had evolved during her college years, widening her worldview and becoming more independent-minded and less likely to embrace the status quo. Veering away from the confines of her white, conservative, Republican upbringing, she identified as a Democrat, made Black friends, and developed an ear for blues music.

Grandpa Joe Daniels was an avid fisherman and hunter who kept his family in trout and pheasant for years.

But according to Marjorie, who at the time was living with Dick and their two little boys, Allyn and Graham, in Hammond, Indiana, even as a young working woman Helen got lonesome for her family, particularly at the holidays. "She would come for Thanksgiving or would want us to come up there or would want to be with Mother and Daddy. . . ." It was on one of her trips to Hammond that Helen introduced Marjorie and Dick to the man she would marry.

Chapter Four

Courtship and Marriage

Helen had met Alfred Robert Bader in June 1950 through Barbara Breslauer, a classmate of hers at Milwaukee-Downer and the daughter of the director of the Sunday school at Congregation Emanu-El B'ne Jeshurun on Milwaukee's East Side where Alfred was teaching. The occasion was a double date at Barbara's home in the Exton Apartments Building, a stunning example of art deco architecture, at 1260 N. Prospect Ave. As Marjorie tells it, Alfred—who at the time was dating Barbara—"took a shine to Helen." The initial appeal? "He thought she was [being] herself and did not put on airs, and she did not wear very much makeup." Alfred had arrived in Milwaukee six months earlier after completing a PhD in organic chemistry at Harvard University to work as a research chemist at the Pittsburgh Plate Glass Company (PPG). By all accounts, he was unlike anyone Helen had ever met.

Alfred Robert Bader had been born in 1924 in Vienna, Austria, to Alfred and Elisabeth Serényi Bader. As he tells the story in *Adventures of a Chemist Collector,* the first volume of his autobiography, Alfred's parents met in a sanatorium, where Elisabeth, the daughter of a Hungarian count, had been sent to recover from an annulled marriage. "When she fell in love with my father, a Jew, her parents objected violently and tried to have her committed to an asylum," he wrote. The two eloped and were married in London in 1912, a move that led Elisabeth's family to disown her.

"By all accounts," wrote Alfred, "Mama was a woman of great physical charm, attractive to men." (Reportedly, she was unfaithful to her husband,

Opposite background:
Alfred Bader launched the Aldrich Chemical Company with his friend Jack Eisendrath out of a garage on the city's East Side. Over the years, it would grow into a highly successful business worth hundreds of millions of dollars.

Opposite foreground:
Helen Daniels and Alfred Bader married on July 6, 1952.

95

and claimed that her first child, Marion, was not his daughter.) According to Alfred, his father was "described as a charming, shiftless gambler, dependent on the kindness of his sister, Gisela Reich." Although Alfred was told that his father had committed suicide two weeks after he was born, rumors persisted that he had, in fact, been murdered.

A DIFFICULT CHILDHOOD

Regardless, following her husband's death, Elisabeth found herself in dire straits: alone and unable to financially support baby Alfred and his two-year-old sister, Marion. According to her son, "What possibility did she have of providing a living for her family? She had been brought up to be a lady but had been cut off from her family, and had no skills whatever with which to earn money." And so, when her wealthy sister-in-law, Gisela Bader Reich, offered to adopt her children, Elisabeth agreed to give up Alfred. That decision, according to Alfred, was based partly on Elisabeth's assertion that Marion was "not in fact a Bader," and partly on "seeing an opportunity to give her son a better chance in life."

Gisela's husband, Sigmund Reich, was a successful businessman who had died in 1922, leaving his widow with considerable wealth, a well-appointed apartment along the Praterstraße in Vienna, and a villa outside the city. Summers were spent in the Alps, on the beaches of the Adriatic Sea, and in the Austrian town of Neuberg an der Mürz, where Gisela and Alfred's father had vacationed as children. By the time Alfred was ten years old, however, Gisela's fortune was gone, the result of her lack of knowledge about Sigmund's business affairs and Depression-era investment failures. The villa was put on the market and the apartment divided, with its antique furniture, carpets, and art sold off piece by piece. Summer vacations were now spent with the family of his governess, Hilda Kozak, in Miroslav, a town in what is now the Czech Republic. Instead of beachcombing or mountain hiking, Alfred worked with Hilda's brother, Robert Hergoz, traveling to nearby villages where they would buy up the skins of slaughtered animals for resale to a local tanner. According to Alfred, his own business acumen can be traced —at least in part—to Hergoz, who excelled at establishing rapport and bargaining with his customers.

Yet despite his family's financial downturn, Alfred remembered life with Gisela, whom he called "Mother," as loving and warm. Fifty years old when she adopted him, Gisela not only worried constantly about Alfred, but also spoiled him—especially when he was a little boy—with "cakes galore." He came to enjoy reading, stamp collecting, and soccer. He credited Gisela, who took him weekly to visit and recite the Kaddish over the graves of his grandparents and father, lit candles on Friday evenings, and never ate pork, for the fact that he grew up a devout Jew. And members of the David Mayer family, who lived upstairs, with immersing him in a religious life that included annual Passover seders he described as the "highpoint of the year."

ENGLAND AND CANADA

In November 1938, in what became known as *Kristallnacht*, or "Night of Broken Glass," Nazi stormtroopers attacked and burned to the ground Jewish synagogues and businesses throughout Nazi Germany and Austria, deeply affecting fourteen-year-old Alfred, a witness to the violence and destruction. One month later, the British government—in response to appeals from British Jewish leaders—began issuing visas to mainly Jewish children of German, Polish, Czechoslovakian, and Austrian descent. Known as the *Kindertransport*, the rescue effort would see ten thousand

Alfred was one of 502 refugee children who left Vienna, Austria, on December 10, 1938, aboard the first Kindertransport, *arriving in England two days later.*

UNITED STATES HOLOCAUST MEMORIAL MUSEUM, FROM INSTYTUT PAMIECI NARODOWEJ children relocated to England over the next two years. On December 10, Alfred boarded the first *Kindertransport* to leave Vienna. Although he did not know it at the time, his view of Gisela, Elisabeth, and Hilda as his train pulled out of the station would be his last. Gisela died at Theresienstadt, a Nazi concentration camp in German-occupied Czechoslovakia in 1942; Hilda, of cancer during the war; and Elisabeth, of a stroke in 1948.

Before Alfred left Vienna, Gisela had reached out to a distant relative living in England, Bessy Emanuel, who with her husband Moritz helped resettle hundreds of Jewish refugees. It was Bessy who arranged for Mrs. Sarah Wolff, an elderly resident of Hove, a small city on England's southern coast just west of Brighton, to underwrite Alfred's living expenses there for the next two years. Alfred lived with Sidney and Ethel Scharff, their two daughters, and two other Jewish refugees. The Scharffs were kind and hard-working members of the Jewish community, and saw to it that Alfred had an opportunity to study Hebrew. He attended the East Hove Senior School for Boys, and—with help again from Bessy Emanuel—was admitted to Brighton Technical College, where he particularly enjoyed his chemistry class.

In 1940, two weeks after his sixteenth birthday, Alfred was moved again, this time as part of a mass deportation of nearly two thousand

Alfred spent fifteen months in an internment camp at Fort Lennox, near Quebec City, as the result of a mass deportation of German and Austrian nationals from England to Canada and Australia in 1940.

PHOTO BY M. ROGER LANGLOIS

An Independent Spirit: The Quiet, Generous Life of Helen Daniels Bader

male German and Austrian nationals to internment camps in Canada and Australia. Under the relocation, which was Britain's response to fears of an imminent invasion by Germany and the potential for German-speaking aliens to be seen as saboteurs, refugees such as Alfred were classified as second-class prisoners of war and deported along with actual German Nazis. Alfred was sent to Quebec City, and for the next fifteen months was held at Fort Lennox on Ile aux Noix. Although conditions during the first few weeks were difficult, he ended up completing his secondary education and earning high marks on his final exams. Looking back, he would describe the experience as "a great time in my life."

QUEEN'S AND HARVARD

On November 2, 1941, Alfred was released from Fort Lennox. By then he had connected with Sarah Wolff's son, Martin, who was living in Montreal and immediately took Alfred in and helped him apply to college. McGill University and the University of Toronto rejected him—McGill because it had filled its quota of Jewish students—but despite the fact that the school year was well underway, he was accepted by Queen's University in Kingston, Ontario, enrolling on November 15. He credits the Wolff family, and the university, with changing his life. "Martin Wolff became the first father figure in my life," wrote Alfred. "In Vienna, there had been no man in the family. In Hove, Mrs. Scharff, rather than her husband, had been the head of the house." Alfred goes on to describe Wolff as "a conservative in the best sense of the word, an introvert, hard-working, totally honest, basically a shy man." As for his six years at Queen's, Alfred worked hard, earning numerous scholarships on his way to completing bachelor's degrees in engineering chemistry and history, and a master's in chemistry.

Alfred graduated from Queen's University in 1947 with a master's degree in chemistry.

Two other events shaped Alfred's life during this period: Sometime during the 1940s, he became a Canadian citizen, an experience that, according to his son David, brought him

Top: *Alfred formally converted to Judaism under the guidance of Rabbi David Shapiro.*

JEWISH MUSEUM MILWAUKEE

Bottom: *For more than thirty years, Alfred taught Sunday School at Temple Emanu-El-B'ne Jeshurun on the city's East Side.*

JEWISH MUSEUM MILWAUKEE

great pride. And during summer vacations while he was at Queen's, Alfred worked as a lab technician at the Murphy Paint Company in Montreal, formulating paints and lacquers. Harry Thorpe, Murphy's president, encouraged him to return to graduate school, offering to help finance his education if he agreed to work for the company after completing his PhD. Alfred agreed, and went on to earn a master's in chemistry and a PhD in organic chemistry from Harvard in 1949 and 1950, respectively. By then, PPG had purchased Murphy Paint, and had established its research labs in Milwaukee.

EARLY YEARS IN MILWAUKEE

Helen met Alfred in the spring of 1950, shortly after he began working in Milwaukee as a PPG research scientist and its first Jewish employee. His research focused on the development of monomers, molecules that can be bonded to other identical molecules to form polymers suitable for a wide variety of consumer products. Alfred was also immersed in the Jewish community. He taught Sunday school at Temple Emanu-El, a Reform congregation, and worshipped at congregation Anshe Sfard, an Orthodox congregation on the city's Northwest Side, under the leadership of Rabbi David Shapiro, a graduate of

Chicago's Hebrew Theological College. It was under the guidance of Rabbi Shapiro that Alfred formally converted to Judaism, a requirement given that his mother had been a Catholic.

Next on Alfred's agenda: settling down. He wanted a wife, children, and a Jewish home and family life, and he began courting Helen—who was interested in the Jewish faith and open to converting—with an eye toward marriage. Yet that spring, on their first real date, Alfred openly talked about another woman, Isabel Overton, to whom he had proposed marriage while abroad the previous summer. Overton, a staunch Protestant, had refused him, certain she could not be the Jewish wife he needed. To Helen's dismay, Alfred couldn't seem to get Isabel out of his mind. Yet, overcoming her doubts, she continued to see him.

Marjorie and Dick DeVey were surprised when Helen brought Alfred to Hammond to meet them. Recalled Dick, "She had never come down with a young man before, so this was mildly interesting, but we hadn't any advance impression that there was anything serious here." They were, however, impressed with Alfred, who by then had already secured a number of patents for PPG. And it didn't take long for Marjorie to realize that Helen was "pretty much in love with Alfred." It was during a Christmas visit to Aberdeen in 1951 that Helen took Alfred home to meet Jessie and Lloyd and get a sense of her background. Jessie turned the tables, writing to one of the deans at Harvard in an attempt to learn more about "the young man who is interested in our daughter." The dean wrote back, noting that although he knew nothing of Alfred's personal life, he could vouch for the fact that "he was one of the finest students we've ever had on campus." Concluded Marjorie, "So Mother, being an educator herself, was sold."

Alfred would confess in his memoir that he compared every young woman he dated in Milwaukee to Isabel. None measured up, but Helen came closest. "She was shy, pretty, and had a background very similar to Isabel's," he wrote, noting that both women had grown up in religious homes in small towns with warm, loving fathers. The one thing that set

An Independent Spirit: The Quiet, Generous Life of Helen Daniels Bader

Helen apart from Isabel: "She wanted to marry me and have a Jewish home and family." As for Helen, she was in love, and dazzled by Alfred's intelligence, experience, and old-world, European charm.

Alfred proposed on Helen's twenty-fifth birthday in May 1952, and they were married less than seven weeks later, on July 6, by Rabbi Shapiro. The wedding took place in the study of his home and the reception was at the Knickerbocker Hotel in downtown Milwaukee. Over the preceding year and a half, Helen had studied Judaism and in an Orthodox ceremony supervised by Shapiro, had converted. Still, the marriage got off to a rocky start, and there were early signs it might not survive. Thoughts of Isabel were never far from Alfred's mind, and one of the places Alfred took Helen on their European honeymoon was to Edinburgh. "We walked where I had last seen Isabel in September 1949," he wrote. "I became physically sick, and Danny knew why, but she remained patiently with me." She did, however, tell him she hadn't thought he would ever marry her because "you care so much for that girl in England."

There were some happy moments on the honeymoon. One stop was in Neuberg an der Mürz in Austria, where Alfred had vacationed as a child. In London, Helen met Alfred's distant cousin Ralph Emanuel, whose mother, Bessy, had helped Alfred relocate to Hove in 1939. Although Alfred and Ralph had known each other as boys—Ralph remembers Alfred as a "serious, conscientious" student "determined to make a life for himself"—they became much closer as adults. Emanuel's first impression of Helen? "Lovely, and very devoted to Alfred." By all accounts, he said, "Alfred was in love."

On their honeymoon, Alfred bought Helen two gifts. One was a fine violin that she played for the rest of her life. While in England, in Burton-on-Trent, Alfred also bought Helen an oil painting that caught her eye: *Musicians* by the Italian artist Pasqualino Rossi. Alfred carried the painting home rolled up in a tube, and then went to a local hardware store to buy lumber that he fashioned into a frame.

Opposite top: *Friends and family pose with Helen and Alfred for a formal wedding photo.* Front row, left to right: *Helen's nephews, Allyn and Graham DeVey.* Back row, left to right: *Helen's sister, Marjorie Daniels DeVey; her aunt, Blanche Mabbott; her uncle, Leonard Mabbott; her cousin, Marilyn Mabbott; Helen; Alfred; her mother, Jessie; her father, Lloyd; and her brother-in-law, Dick DeVey.*

Opposite bottom: *Alfred and Helen on their honeymoon in Neuberg an der Mürz in Austria, where Alfred had vacationed as a child.*

Alfred bought Helen two gifts on their honeymoon: a fine violin and an oil painting by the Italian artist Pasqualino Rossi titled Musicians.

OVATION JEWISH HOME (VIOLIN)

THE LAUNCH OF ALDRICH CHEMICAL COMPANY

Back home in Milwaukee, the couple settled into an apartment on Milwaukee's East Side and Helen got a job as a lab technician at PPG, where Alfred was doing well: one of the patents he secured for the company, on the formulation of diphenolic acid, was sold to Johnson Wax for $1 million. When the company moved its research division to Pittsburgh in 1954, however, Helen and Alfred opted to stay in Milwaukee. They loved the city, which with its German roots reminded Alfred of Austria, and were fans of Milwaukee Mayor Frank Zeidler, a Socialist whose administration was synonymous with frugal, honest government. What's more, a new professional opportunity awaited: Three years earlier, Alfred and Jack Eisendrath, a friend and attorney, had each come up with $250 to start a small company that they were running out of a garage on the city's East Side.

The part-time operation had been set up to produce, secure, store, weigh, label, and ship high-quality research chemicals that met recognized industry standards and made it possible to reproduce experimental results. It was a line of business PPG's head of research had decided not to pursue, believing it would be impossible to compete with Eastman Kodak, the only major fine chemical supplier operating in the United States at the time. Nevertheless, PPG gave Alfred permission to do so, as long as it was on his own time. The new company had been incorporated in August 1951, as the Aldrich Chemical Company, named—following a coin toss that Jack won—after his fiancée, Betty Aldrich. (Had Alfred won, the company would have been named the Daniels Chemical Company.) Its first compound was methylnitrosonitroguanidine, a source of water- rather than acid-based diazomethane, an explosive gas. Its customers included government agencies, universities, medical researchers, and private manufacturers.

In 1954, having left PPG to run Aldrich full-time, Alfred moved the operation out of the garage to a laboratory on the city's North Side. Sales the first year of operation totaled $1,705, jumping to $15,000 in 1954. For a short time, Helen went to work at a local brewery, but soon joined Alfred at Aldrich. Like every other employee in those early years, she sorted and stored incoming stock, packed up orders, and helped get shipments out the door. In 1955, convinced of Aldrich's potential, Alfred and Helen bought out the Eisendraths' share of the company for $15,000.

Early on, Alfred decided that for Aldrich to succeed it would have to offer its customers not only fine chemicals produced on-site, but also more common chemicals available in Europe that could be imported for resale. To that end, he began spending a month or two abroad every year

By 1958, a dozen Aldrich employees were working out of this building in Milwaukee's central city.

visiting small chemical companies. The idea paid off. By 1958, with a dozen employees, the company had moved to a 27,000-sq. ft. building in Milwaukee's central city; two years later it expanded again.

It was 1959 when the company opened a branch office in England. Alfred recruited Ralph Emanuel, who at the time was running his family's business importing and exporting leather, to lead the operation. Emanuel took on the role of agent and assumed a seat on Aldrich's board of directors. His wife, Muriel, became the firm's bookkeeper, and his brother, Alfred, its accountant. Originally known as Ralph N. Emanuel Ltd., and owned jointly by the Baders and Emanuels, it was for a while England's largest supplier of research chemicals.

In 1959, Alfred recruited his distant cousin Ralph Emanuel, a leather importer and exporter, to run Aldrich's new branch office in London. Over the years, Alfred and Ralph would become close friends.

The 1950s found Helen taking on greater responsibility at the company, and the business consuming more and more of her life. At first, she was in charge of invoicing, but before long was heading up importing operations, no small task given the highly regulated nature of chemical importation and the large number of European suppliers—most small companies unknown to US officials—with whom Aldrich dealt. In fact, it was largely because of Alfred's connection to a wide network of European chemists and his love of and ability to "do a deal" that Aldrich grew so quickly. In her role, Helen was required to work closely with US Customs Service officials at the city's port of entry on Milwaukee's South Side. She quickly got up to speed, and was soon demonstrating not only an impressive command of the relevant governmental regulations, but also the ability to work well with sometimes nervous customs officials and postal workers, all of whom loved her. Part politician, part diplomat,

Helen took to the job with composure and levelheadedness, her paperwork always in order and her troubleshooting skills finely tuned. It wasn't unusual for Alfred, anxious over an order not yet received from abroad but already sold to a customer, to repeatedly ask Helen, "Where is it?" Her calm response: "On a boat."

Clearly, Alfred and Helen's management style was rooted, at least in part, in earlier personal struggles. They promised their workers, for example, that should the country be hit with another Depression, no one would be fired. Instead, hours would be cut and their own salaries slashed. Over the years, one of Helen's most significant achievements at Aldrich came in the progressive way she influenced hiring practices. By the 1970s, German and Hungarian chemists who couldn't speak English, some of whom were Holocaust survivors, found themselves working alongside Blacks from Milwaukee's central city sporting big Afros and wearing fedoras. She saw to it—with support from Alfred—that job applicants, regardless of their race and personal histories, were judged against just one standard: their ability to do their jobs. Black females held supervisory positions, something rarely seen in Milwaukee at that time. And mentally challenged workers were hired to wash bottles and complete other tasks in the plant. "The only thing that mattered," recalled their son, David Bader, "was whether people showed up, were sober, and got the job done. And as a result, my brother and I grew up thinking that, of course, Black women were promoted like everyone else."

At Aldrich, Helen was responsible for invoicing and importing operations, and with Alfred introduced a series of progressive hiring practices. She was named a vice president early in her career at the company.

But Helen did more than simply ensure the presence of a diverse work force; she personally related to Aldrich's employees with a measure of understanding and empathy that not only provides a window into her character, values, and beliefs, but also foreshadowed her social work career. Indeed, she was ahead of her time: genuinely comfortable with all kinds of people, a mindset that can be traced to her formative years in South Dakota watching her father interact with the local American Indians. Her travel abroad with Alfred beginning in the 1950s broadened her, and reinforced her innate love of diversity. Beyond that, where Alfred was business oriented, at times gruff and tightfisted, and seldom engaged personally with Aldrich employees, Helen represented the heart of the organization: She made it a point to get to know everyone and came to care about their families, celebrating their successes and commiserating over their problems. When Alfred would ruffle feathers, Helen was there to smooth things out, despite her husband's retort that "You're being too nice." In return, she was universally loved.

Helen's niece, Deirdre Britt, believes it was at Aldrich that Helen discovered her abilities to connect with and motivate others, inspire teamwork, and problem solve—skills she found she enjoyed putting to use to further causes in which she believed. "I think it was an outgrowth of her personality, her genuine interest in and natural ability to work with people, that once given an arena in which to shine forth, blossomed," she said.

One of the beneficiaries of those skills of Helen's that Britt describes was Joan Prince, who as a fifteen-year-old walking around downtown Milwaukee one day in 1970 with her sister came upon the Aldrich Chemical building. "I loved math and science, but I thought the only thing you could do with math and science was become a doctor or nurse," she said. "I remember telling my sister, 'Oh, maybe I could be a chemist.'" Prince decided to come back another day "when I looked better." Although one of her teachers at Wisconsin Lutheran High School urged her to call and make an appointment to talk to someone at Aldrich, she was too nervous, hanging up once the call went through. Instead, she returned to the plant, intending to drop off a letter in which she requested such a meeting. Trying to work up the nerve to go inside, Prince noticed a woman standing in front of the building whom she would come to call Miss Helen. "I told her I was a high school student who wanted to talk to someone about what chemists did and how to become one." Helen took Prince inside and set up an appointment for her to come back and observe one of Aldrich's chemists at work. Recalled Prince, "I was terribly nervous, and she made me feel very, very welcome. She was so nice and genuine and had such a warm smile. When you're fifteen, that means a lot."

Prince did return to talk to one of Aldrich's chemists and went on to major in science at UWM, where she was the first Black student to complete the school's medical technology program and its clinical laboratory master's program. She also earned a PhD in urban education from UWM in 1999. Prince practiced hematology for almost twenty years at Wheaton Franciscan Health Systems, and served as project director of the Professions Partnerships Initiative at the University of Wisconsin Medical School. In 2000, she was appointed UWM's vice-chancellor for Global Inclusion and Engagement, a position she continues to hold today. In 2012, she was named Alternate Representative to the 67th session of the General Assembly of the United Nations by President Barack Obama.

As part of her work at UWM, Prince also came into contact with Alfred. "I remember one day he invited me to lunch at his gallery and I told him about meeting Helen and about some of the students I was working with at UWM," she said. "He had on a plaid shirt, reached into the shirt pocket, took out a checkbook, and wrote me a check to support four of the students so they could study abroad." Yet it is Helen's impact on her own life that Prince recalled most fondly, and which she has tried to emulate, noting, "You never realize the effect you can have on someone's future."

Joan Prince was a fifteen-year-old high school student interested in math and science when she met Helen, who made arrangements for the teenager to observe an Aldrich chemist at work. Today, Prince is vice-chancellor for Global Inclusion and Engagement at the University of Wisconsin-Milwaukee.

JOAN PRINCE

ARCHIVES DEPARTMENT, UNIVERSITY OF WISCONSIN-MILWAUKEE LIBRARIES

Top: *Helen's early married life was dominated by her work at Aldrich and her responsibilities at home.*

Bottom: *Helen remained close to her mother, Jessie Daniels, who regularly visited her daughter in Milwaukee.*

EARLY MARRIED LIFE

The early years of Alfred and Helen's marriage were dominated by business concerns, and evenings would often find them back at the office. To be sure, Alfred clearly appreciated Helen's important contribution to Aldrich's success: He saw to it that she shared equally in the company's profits from the beginning, and named her vice president of customs early on. Yet Helen was also Alfred's wife, and as such, was also expected to keep things running smoothly at home. Although by all accounts Alfred loved and respected Helen, beginning with the early days of their marriage, his wishes clearly came first. For example, and in a disconcerting sign of what was to come, every night at dinnertime he expected food to be on the table—and he wanted it to be good. This, despite the fact that he had little idea how it got there.

In February 1953, Jessie took a ten-day trip to Milwaukee to visit Helen and Alfred, and Helen made a return trip to Aberdeen later that year. The visits would continue for the next two decades, with Jessie and Lloyd coming east to meet their Bader and DeVey grandchildren, and Helen and Marjorie making sure their children got to know Aberdeen. Jessie also corresponded by mail with Helen and Marjorie at least once a week, writing each long, newsy letters that often included newspaper clippings about their friends still living in Aberdeen. Helen and Marjorie responded regularly, as Jessie frequently remarked on news items (from Helen, tales of her travels with Alfred; from Marjorie, funny stories about her children's antics) they had shared in their own letters.

An entertaining writer, Jessie was especially good at setting a scene and telling a story, as exemplified in the opening of this letter to Helen and Alfred:

> Dears: What with crashing into Mr. Foncannon's fence, throwing the wheelbarrow onto the trailer and starting the Ford with a gusto, Father initiated his day—and that of the neighbors, I would say, in good time and at a very early hour. I took it to mean that the master of the household was hungry, which indeed he was. I now have duties done, the table set with a

An Independent Spirit: The Quiet, Generous Life of Helen Daniels Bader

very starched, clean cloth as only Grandmother knew how to starch and iron one, the roast in the oven, Society page scanned, and Puss summoned for her breakfast.

In her letters, Jessie described her shopping trips, social events, study projects, culinary exploits, and news of the neighborhood. "The new family moved in next door yesterday—five children and he travels," she wrote in one letter to Helen in 1955. "Three are under school age. I see the girl . . . out clearing the walk and a little boy. All I hope is that they stay in their own yard." In another letter, she reports that although she did not win a contest to name the newest Coty perfume, she approved of the winning entry: *Accomplice.* "I think it is well chosen—that [it] is in the general trend of the thinking of romance . . . and I am sure mine did not have that angle."

The weather often featured prominently: "It turned very cold during the night and is now like a fall morning," reads a passage describing unseasonal August temperatures. "We have had perfectly terrible heat this week with Wednesday, crowning the record with over a hundred right out here in front. However, that usually brings on one of those bad storms, which seem to characterize this particular season and that it did. We did not receive the moisture so are still like volcanic ash around here, but the nights are cool, and our house stays delightfully so." Fashion was another favorite topic, with Jessie inquiring at one point about the success of Helen's trousseau: "Do you find that you have the proper and adequate things?" she asks in a letter sent to Helen in Vienna during her honeymoon. "I should really like to know how your wardrobe has worked out. And of course, it will depend a great deal upon what the weather has been, but I am sure of one thing—that the old favorite blue cotton dress has come in very handy."

Helen and her mother kept up a lively, frequent correspondence.

Occasionally, Jessie passed on news from Marjorie, including this anecdote about her son Graham that echoed a Dirty Thirties-era memory. "Marjorie said that while she was writing a note Graham came in and dangled a very dead grasshopper in front of her nose," which, according to Jessie, prompted Marjorie to note, "and you know how much I like grasshoppers!"

But Jessie's letters also reveal hints that she was, in some matters, ahead of her time. Take for example, the merits of prepared pie mix: "MJ uses them, I know, and likes them," she wrote. "I think I shall have to give my daughters a lesson on pie crust some time. But the thing is that I had help much of the time when I was making pies, and when I wasn't, we didn't have them. You and MJ have your other very busy business, and anything to make a satisfactory short cut is admissible . . . so if she and you have sense to do what seems right under the circumstances, all power to you, I should say."

Helen and Alfred's closest friends at the time included Jane and Marvin Klitsner, whom they had met in 1954 at Temple Emanu-El when their daughters joined Alfred's Sunday school class. In fact, Alfred considered Klitsner not only his best friend, but also a mentor. A

Marvin Klitsner and his wife, Jane, were among Helen and Alfred's closest friends.

An Independent Spirit: The Quiet, Generous Life of Helen Daniels Bader

prominent, brilliant, and highly respected Milwaukee attorney, Marvin
Klitsner soon began handling Aldrich's legal work, and in 1961 joined
its board. Most Sundays, the families spent time together at the Klitsner
home, where the two men mostly discussed business. Scholarly, religious, and dignified, Klitsner served as president of what was then the
Milwaukee Jewish Welfare Fund from 1964 to 1968. A strong supporter
of Israel—where he lived for part of his life—he was a prodigious fund-
raiser during the Israeli Six-Day War in 1967. According to the *Wisconsin Jewish Chronicle*, Klitsner was "an outstanding architect of the best in
the community," and "a humanist who cared about people and deemed
it his religious and moral duty to improve the world."

As president of the Milwaukee Jewish Welfare Fund, Marvin Klitsner spearheaded the group's fundraising for Israel during the 1967 Six-Day War.

JEWISH MUSEUM MILWAUKEE AND WISCONSIN JEWISH CHRONICLE

Klitsner's daughter Francie Wolff recalls that no matter how often
Alfred was in the Klitsner home, she and her siblings never felt comfortable with him. She notes, nonetheless, that her father respected Bader's
"intellect and extraordinary capabilities," attributes Helen also recognized
early on and likely found captivating. By all accounts, Alfred was a genius
who commanded an extraordinary depth of knowledge, in not just one,
but three distinct areas: chemistry, art, and the Old Testament. A brilliant
chemist, he would grow Aldrich into a highly successful business turning

Alfred grew Aldrich into a company eventually worth several hundred million dollars, in part by prioritizing customer service. Here he is pictured in a company ad campaign in which he encourages customers to "Please Bother Us" with their questions.

his original $250 stake in the company into hundreds of millions of dollars. He would amass what has been called an "unparalleled collection" of old master paintings. And he dedicated himself to a lifetime of extensive religious study. His knowledge in all three areas was narrow, but at the same time, deep, focused, and intense.

According to Daniel Bader, his father lived much of his life in "a different reality—a bubble characterized by European values, a world of Nobel laureates." To be sure, marrying Alfred brought Helen into that world, opening up opportunities that she would take full advantage of over the years. Still, Deirdre describes Helen's marriage as "courageous," noting how significant it was "in those days, to marry someone who had grown up in a different country, in a different faith." Not to mention, someone who would go on to break her heart.

Early 1957 found Helen and Alfred still living in their East Side apartment, where the landlord hadn't raised the rent in four years because, as Alfred put it, "They were so charmed by Danny." But hoping to start a family—and with Aldrich doing well—Helen and Alfred decided to buy a house. They settled on a beautiful, three-story, provincial style mansion at 2961 N. Shepard Ave. At $27,500, Alfred deemed the East Side property "a lot of house for the money." Built in 1909, the five-bedroom, brick home featured built-in bookshelves, a fireplace in the living room, a barrel ceiling in the dining room, and leaded glass windows and copper fittings throughout. An ornate, dark bronze, eight-foot-high menorah stood in the front window.

The Bader home soon became a de facto art museum. Alfred was particularly pleased with the mahogany paneling on the first floor, the perfect background for the couple's growing art collection, and where paintings hung in several tiers. Others marched up the staircase walls and hung in

the vestibule and bathrooms. Whenever a new painting was acquired, it typically would rest for a time on a chair in the living room opposite the sofa, where Alfred—sitting with the family dog—would spend hours studying it and taking in its beauty. In the winter, to ensure that the home's humidity remained at the optimum level, Alfred would regularly boil water in big soup pots and then dampen the edges of the Oriental rugs along the walls, allowing the rising steam to humidify the paintings. As a boy in Vienna, Alfred had

The provincial style mansion Helen and Alfred bought on Milwaukee's East Side in 1957 quickly became a de facto art gallery.

collected stamps, and had grown up in a house full of paintings. The very first painting he bought was a portrait painted by an inmate with whom he was interned in Canada, but by the early 1950s he had already purchased his first old master, *Man Surprised*. Painted by Joos van Craesbeeck, it is believed to be a portrait of Flemish painter Adriaen Brouwer. It was also the only painting Alfred ever bought in installments: sixteen payments of $50. At the time, writes Alfred in his autobiography, "I preferred to acquire dirty, old paintings in antique stores and at auctions,

Above: *The first old master painting Alfred bought was* Man Surprised *by Joos van Craesbeeck.*

Opposite, top: *On their trips to Europe, Helen and Alfred regularly visited art galleries and auction houses such as Christie's and Sotheby's in London. In this photo, they are standing in front of Alfred's favorite painting,* Joseph and the Baker, *attributed to the Dutch painter Carel Fabritius, a student of Rembrandt. It hangs today in the home of Michelle and David Bader.*

Opposite, bottom: *Aldrich Chemical Company's catalogs featured reproductions of fine art paintings.*

hoping that cleaning would reveal great works." But even genuine old masters, he noted, cost much less than today.

On his trips abroad, often accompanied by Helen, Alfred made the rounds of Europe's finest art galleries and auction houses. When in London, for example, where the couple stayed with Ralph and Muriel Emanuel, a typical day would include visits to Christie's and Sotheby's, as well as a number of other auction houses and dealers. (At times, when Alfred could not be in London to attend auctions, he would send Muriel to bid for him.) Wrote Alfred about these excursions, "As I wander from art dealer to art dealer in London, I realize that this is not very different from my [stamp] dealing in 1938, except that paintings are more fun, and the stakes are higher." Helen gamely tagged along, often carrying Alfred's catalogues. Clearly, Alfred was the art authority in the family; he continued collecting for more than six decades and was considered one of the world's leading experts on and dealers in Dutch old masters. Yet Helen also developed a deep interest in fine art and didn't mind Alfred filling their home with paintings. Her favorite painting was a seventeenth century portrait attributed to the French painter Simon Vouet. According to David, she especially liked its "expression of spirituality."

In 1961, with Klitsner, Alfred founded Alfred Bader Fine Arts, which dealt in commercial real estate and artwork. (In 1992, after leaving Aldrich and needing space to hang the many paintings that for years had been on display in the Aldrich offices, Alfred would move the company into a gallery at the Astor Hotel.) And in 1967, Alfred combined his two passions—chemistry and art—when the cover of Aldrich's annual catalog began featuring reproductions of fine art paintings. According to Jacquelyn N. Coutré, the former Bader Curator and Researcher of

An Independent Spirit: The Quiet, Generous Life of Helen Daniels Bader

European Art at Queen's University, Alfred amassed a personal collection of more than 250 paintings over his lifetime, more than 200 of which he donated to Queen's. Among the donated paintings were three Rembrandt character studies from the collection— including one Alfred had given to Daniel, who with his wife, Linda, donated it to Queen's in 2019— and the master's grand *Portrait of a Man with Arms Akimbo*. Alfred told the *Milwaukee Journal Sentinel* in 2016 that the donations aimed to repay Queen's for having been "very good to me when I came out of the internment camp."

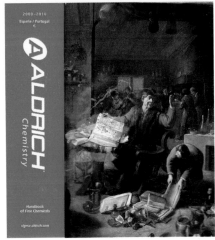

CHAPTER FIVE

CHILDREN AT LAST

By the time they purchased their Shepard Avenue home, Alfred and Helen had been married for five years and were eager to have children. They had no sooner filed paperwork to begin the adoption process when, to their delight, Helen became pregnant, giving birth to David Martin Bader on August 17, 1958. Named in honor of his father's early mentors, David Mayer and Martin Wolff, David Bader was apparently every bit as difficult an infant as his mother had been, complete with temper tantrums. And in an example of history repeating itself, Helen found herself calling Jessie to say, "I don't know what to do. David won't eat." Replied Jessie, echoing Leonia's advice to her decades earlier, "Now listen, Dear . . ." According to Alfred, David was a "rather bashful boy with a beautiful singing voice."

Daniel Joseph Bader, named after Helen's side of the family, was born on January 24, 1961, apparently a much easier baby (according to Alfred, "chubby" and "noisy") who grew up to be more adventurous than his older brother. "I hope you don't mind, but I'm going to name my second boy Daniel also," Helen said to Marjorie, who at the time was living in Milwaukee with Dick and their four children, Allyn, Graham, Deirdre, and two-year-old Dan. Marjorie didn't mind at all. She had named her youngest son after their father as a way of carrying on the family name and was happy to see Helen do so as well.

In 1959, just after Dan DeVey's birth, Jessie and Lloyd visited Milwaukee to meet their newest grandson. Helen and Alfred, just back from

Opposite: On trips to Aberdeen, Helen, David, and Daniel played in Jessie's garden.

Above: In 1958, with the birth of their son David, Helen and Alfred started a family. Two and a half years later, with the birth of Daniel, it was complete.

119

Right: *Lloyd and Jessie regularly visited Helen and her family in Milwaukee.*

Below: *Trips Marjorie and Helen made to Aberdeen with their children were documented in these charming photographs published in the* Aberdeen American-News. *Marjorie and her daughter, Deirdre, visited in 1961, and Helen, with David and Daniel, the following year.*

a trip to Europe, hosted a family party to celebrate the Daniels' fortieth wedding anniversary. Two trips Marjorie and Helen made to Aberdeen around that time were documented in charming photos published by the *Aberdeen American-News.* In July 1961, Marjorie took six-year-old Deirdre to visit her grandparents, where they were photographed having a tea party. Deirdre recalls being so excited by the prospect of traveling

to Aberdeen by train—in a sleeper car, no less—that she was awake the entire night before the trip. The following June, Helen made the same trip with three-and-a-half-year-old David, and sixteen-month-old Daniel. "Mr. Bader, who is a chemist, is in Europe at present," reported the *American-News*. "The couple's hobby is collecting Dutch paintings."

The DeVeys remained in Milwaukee until 1963, living a few blocks from the Baders at 2706 N. Farwell Ave., and the two families visited back and forth often. The DeVey children's memories of those years include the Bader's beautiful but "spooky" house. With all the dark paneling, heavy draperies, and giant paintings on the walls ("portraits of people staring at you," according to Dan DeVey) it reminded them of a museum. Graham remembers a suit of armor and a table radio on which he was unable to tune in his favorite radio station, WOKY. "I wondered who would buy a radio that only played classical music," he recalls. Both boys remembered their Aunt Helen dropping in at the DeVey home with their cousins David and Daniel, sometimes to ask for Marjorie's child-raising advice. Recalls Graham, "She'd come and visit looking so casual—she had on boys' clothes—and I thought she looked like a smaller version of my mother." Allyn DeVey recalls babysitting for his two young cousins on nights when Alfred and Helen went out.

Above left: The DeVeys lived in Milwaukee from 1956 to 1963, and frequently spent time with the Baders. Here, Graham (left) and Allyn (right) DeVey entertain their baby sister, Deirdre.

Above right: The DeVey cousins remember their Aunt Helen as being somewhat unusual in her day for wearing casual clothes. Here she is playing with David.

In 1959, the DeVeys had four children and the Baders, one. On a visit to the Bader home, Alfred holds his son, David, and Dick holds his son, Dan. Seated in front (left to right) *are Deirdre, Allyn, and Graham DeVey.*

AUNT HELEN

Over the years, and even while raising her own children, Helen managed to develop special relationships with her niece and each of her nephews. Most Thanksgivings found the Baders and the DeVeys celebrating together, even after 1963, when the DeVeys moved from Milwaukee to Michigan, and later, to Fayetteville, New York. Marjorie remembered one year when a very young Daniel Bader "stood in front of me at the stove trying to make the gravy." Graham DeVey recalls visiting the Baders several times during the mid-1960s while he was in college at Northwestern University in Evanston, Illinois. He found Helen warm, welcoming, "motherly," and a good cook, making everything from scratch. "I was a little surprised by that," he says, "because I always thought of Mom as the more domestic of the two. And I felt guilty, as a college student, about how much I ate there."

Graham recalls Helen as enamored with and impressed by Alfred, and often thinking about work and her boys. Although he remembers

her as "not one for small talk," she was easy to confide in. "She was very straightforward, looked you straight in the eye, and wouldn't judge you at all. Anything you wanted to talk about was fine with her. She'd smile and nod her head, and let you keep going. And you never had to worry about her inserting her own opinions." And underneath it all, he adds, was "a twinkle, a spark—evidence of her own mischievous streak."

On those visits, Graham also remembers playing with Daniel Bader, who at the time was a little boy. One favorite game was building a snake with plastic bricks. When it wouldn't bend, they took it apart and put it back together with a kink in the middle. "I remember Daniel thought that was hilarious and couldn't stop laughing," recalls Graham. "He was just a wonderful little kid, but based on how he reacted, I wondered, didn't anyone ever play with him?" Dan DeVey recalls once asking Daniel Bader if he ever went fishing with his father. "No, my dad isn't like that," replied his cousin, a response that no

Left: *Graham and Allyn DeVey* (left to right) *attended Riverside High School.*

Right: *As a college student at Northwestern University, Graham* (sitting on couch) *used to visit the Baders.*

Right: Lloyd and Jessie visited Milwaukee regularly to see their grandchildren.

Above: Alfred kept in touch with the daughters of Martin Wolff, his Canadian benefactor: left, Alfred and Helen with Sarah Wolff Orkin; right, Alfred with Rosetta Wolff Elkin and her husband, Victor.

Right: The Baders had less contact with Alfred's relatives than with the DeVeys, but they did see his sister, Marion, pictured here with Helen, from time to time.

doubt contributed to the DeVey children's impressions of Alfred as someone who was intelligent, practical, no-nonsense, and aloof.

Dan's memories of his Aunt Helen: calm and thoughtful, like his grandfather, Lloyd. Her strongest trait, Dan says, was her interest in and empathy for others. Once, when he was eight or nine years old, she gave him what he described as "the perfect book," one on constructing miniature go-karts. "I was into small engines and tinkering with stuff and that book just inspired me."

The early memories of their sister, Deirdre, included dressing up to go visit the Baders, where "I would stare at all the paintings." Grandiose, dramatic, and "a little terrifying" to a young girl, the artwork added to Deirdre's impression that the house came straight out of a fairy tale. Yet Helen took the time to find and share with Deirdre the one or two paintings in the house that were less frightening. Once, coming upon one of a little girl, Deirdre told her aunt, "Well, I like that one." Helen's response: "I like that one, too." Deirdre vividly remembers receiving postcards from Helen whenever her aunt was traveling abroad. "It was very gratifying, as a young girl growing up a little shy and awkward, to realize that my aunt fully understood and appreciated that I had an interest in art. The postcards were always from museums in Europe and featured famous fine art, often old masters. She knew I would collect them, would save them." One special present was a small book on Rembrandt that Deirdre still owns. Helen also encouraged Deirdre's artistic bent by regularly asking her niece how her drawing was going. "I enjoyed talking to her about that," says Deirdre.

Deirdre DeVey Britt has fond memories of Helen, and was particularly touched by the way her aunt cultivated her interest, as a young girl, in art.

The Baders weren't nearly as close to Alfred's relatives, most of whom had been killed during the Holocaust. The family did have some contact with Alfred's sister, Marion, who had remained with their mother when Alfred was adopted, as a child, by his Aunt Gisela. In 1949, Marion married Englishman Cyril Edge, with whom she had a son, Robert. The Baders also saw, from time to time, the daughters of Martin Wolff, his Canadian benefactor and father figure.

Above: *Nita Corré was a friend and mentor of Helen, and the person who launched her on her path to becoming a social worker.*
OVATION JEWISH HOME

Below: *Steffie Zupnik, who sometimes took care of David and Daniel, became a close friend and strong supporter of Helen.*

BUSY YEARS

Among the Baders' closest friends at the time were Fred and Rita Gordy, whom they had met in 1961 when Fred helped them negotiate a real estate transaction. The two couples began socializing together, and the Gordys, who had five children of their own, took care of young Daniel and David when the Baders traveled abroad. Fred recalled the boys as "curious, busy little fellas" whom he and Rita came to love. Helen became especially close to the Gordys; she and Rita would talk on the phone several times a week and Rita considered Helen the sister she never had. Another good friend of Helen's was Nita Corré. The two women connected through their synagogue and later, through their children, all of whom attended the same school. "Helen was a very special lady," recalled Corré. "She was passionate about things she believed in, but she was also sensitive, and shy. And I think that added a special flair to everything she did because although she made sure that everything was done right, she stayed in the background." Decades after they met, Nita Corré would come to play a major role in Helen's life. Over the years, Helen and Ralph Emanuel, who regularly traveled to Milwaukee to attend Aldrich's annual meetings, also grew close. "She was rather amused by my being so very English . . . that stiff upper lip," he recalls.

The 1960s and 1970s were extremely busy years for Helen, who found herself juggling the dual responsibilities of raising children and working outside the home. Given that it would be a full decade before large numbers of women began joining the workforce and the fact that both Jessie and Marjorie had stopped working after they had children, Helen was clearly forging her own way. Even when David and Daniel were babies, she continued working part-time at Aldrich. Having good, reliable, part-time household help and occasional childcare—Alfred deemed hiring a full-time nanny too expensive—made the arrangement possible, even if it meant Helen would sometimes have to take the boys with her on trips to the plant or customs office. (Sometimes helping out was Steffie Zupnik, a Viennese immigrant who had introduced Alfred to members of the Jewish community when he first arrived in Milwaukee, and who over time grew

An Independent Spirit: The Quiet, Generous Life of Helen Daniels Bader

close to Helen.) Alfred described these years as perilous ones for Aldrich, noting "One false step and the company might have gone under." Without a doubt, Helen's efforts were critical to its success. In fact, she briefly served as president of Aldrich in the early 1960s. Recalled David, "Dad was proud of his Canadian citizenship, but it turned out that the company could not get US government contracts because he was Canadian. So, he made my mom president." Eventually, in March 1964, Alfred filed his petition for naturalization as a US citizen.

Once the boys were in school, at Hillel Academy on the city's Northwest Side, Helen took her turn driving in the neighborhood carpool before heading to the Aldrich plant. Late afternoons found her back home, often not only supervising the boys but also entertaining houseguests—the European chemists, art dealers, and art historians visiting Milwaukee to do business with Alfred. He saw the Bader home as the perfect place to entertain them. According to David Harvey, one of those visitors, that was because "Alfred was very careful with his money, so rather than put you up in a hotel, you'd stay with Alfred." As a result, in addition to working at the plant and raising her children, Helen was called upon to put into practice lessons learned from Jessie on how to plan and pull off the perfect dinner party and entertain overnight guests. Recalled Harvey, who at the time was living abroad and running Aldrich's European operations, "Helen looked after us very nicely." According to Marjorie, "It was just remarkable how she could do the work in the office and come home and get ready for a dinner party. She managed to keep everything on an even keel." Rita Gordy also marveled at how much Helen took on, how much she accomplished, and how easy she made it all look, noting, "She was always quietly on the move."

According to Ralph Emanuel, Helen was a wonderful hostess, despite the fact that she couldn't convince Alfred to spend money on home improvement projects such as renovating the kitchen, which would have made entertaining in their Shepard Avenue home easier. Emanuel describes Helen as calm and retiring, and more than willing to take a backseat to Alfred. Yet she was the one, he says, who made visitors feel welcome. That

Ralph Emanuel was not only a friend and business partner of Alfred's, but also a huge fan of Helen's, whom he described as warm and welcoming to visitors.

Above: *Helen met Nina Holmquist, with whom she studied German at the Berlitz School of Languages, in 1968. The two women went on to become fast friends.*
NINA HOLMQUIST

Below: *Everyone who knew Helen, pictured here with David, described her as a wonderful mother who not only loved raising her sons, but also assumed the lion's share of their care.*

was the case, for example, when two of Emanuel's grown children traveled through Milwaukee, telling their father that Alfred had been so engrossed in his chemistry and art endeavors that he completely ignored them.

Emanuel's children weren't the only visitors Alfred found it hard to relate to. According to David Bader, Helen's job description included "explaining to my dad what other people were feeling." He recalls that often, when his parents were entertaining chemists or art dealers, Alfred's mind "would go somewhere else and he'd simply walk out of a room, unaware that he was being rude." Helen learned to gloss over his behavior, telling the bewildered guest, "Don't mind him. Talk to me." Beyond that, Alfred's business associates often arrived in Milwaukee with their wives, and it fell to Helen to entertain them—often at local museums or the Mitchell Park Domes—during the business day.

Given the steady stream of European visitors coming and going—Alfred, David, and Daniel all described the house as a hotel—Helen decided to learn German, telling Rita Gordy she wanted to be able to communicate with her houseguests when Alfred wasn't around, if only to ask them how they liked their coffee or tea. She studied informally with Zupnik, and later enrolled in a University of Wisconsin–Madison correspondence course in conversational German, getting up at five o'clock in the morning to study. "That was her time," explained Rita. Helen also studied German for a year at the Berlitz School of Languages in downtown Milwaukee with Nina Holmquist. According to Alfred, the effort paid off, and Helen learned to speak German quite well. Holmquist agreed, noting that Helen "used her German to support Alfred in his socializing, but also . . . [in her] customs dealings."

MOTHERHOOD

As successful as Helen was at Aldrich, Alfred considered her an even better mother. Consumed by business and art interests, he abdicated his parenting duties, something he would later come to regret. Yet, "I could always console myself that Danny was succeeding wonderfully in being a good parent," he writes. Everyone who knew Helen agreed with his assessment.

David and Daniel were close as children and spent a lot of time playing together. Helen nurtured their interests, including David's penchant for building things such as the backyard fort.

Ralph Emanuel saw her as a "selfless" mother who enjoyed the considerable time she spent with Daniel and David. Francie Wolff vividly recalls Helen's close relationship with her sons, noting that she "took over the lion's share of raising those boys and did a marvelous job of providing them with support and warmth." According to Marvin Klitsner, Helen "loved being a mother and enjoyed watching her sons grow up more than anything else." Corré recalled Helen's pride in David and Daniel, and how hard she worked to ensure that they were part of the community and attuned to its needs.

Just two and a half years apart—and quite different in some respects—David and Daniel were close as children. Daniel remembers being the "tag-along" brother David "sometimes tried to get rid of." Lively and rambunctious, they played together in the basement, the backyard, and nearby Lake Park. David loved to build things, "And so we had a new tree house or a new go-kart every week," he recalls. Dick DeVey recalls Daniel as an extremely curious little boy who once peppered him with questions about a variety of subjects when helping his uncle wash his car. "He was a little dickens who was always doing something unexpected." Helen's approach to child-rearing in those early years? "She was always nurturing our interests," says David.

The boys grew up with two dogs, a cocker spaniel named Sam and a terrier named Charlie, but without a television. In fact, Alfred was so anti-TV that he returned a television set the Klitsners gave the Baders for Hanukkah and instead got a tape recorder. With their mother, they regularly attended

Growing up, the Bader brothers kept busy. Clockwise from upper left: *Although David studied violin, he preferred playing soldier in the family's living room and cavorting with his younger brother and their dog, Sam, in the backyard.*

Chicago and Milwaukee Symphony Orchestra concerts, and at her insistence, took music lessons: David studied violin and trumpet, and Daniel, the flute. Helen, meanwhile, was still studying violin and over the years played in local quartets and with the Jewish Community Center's orchestra. Like most children, "We whined a lot about practicing," says Daniel.

With all that classical music permeating the house, and all the fine art adorning its walls, the Bader home "was pretty intense," recalls David. "It didn't take me long to realize that we were kind of different." He remembers his friends walking into the house, looking around, and asking, "What is all this stuff?" He'd try to explain, but "You didn't quite understand it yourself, or all the ramifications of what you were talking about. It was kind of weird."

Far more conventional was the Baders' dedication to their Jewish faith. "We had many religious experiences as a family," recalled Daniel. "Every Saturday, every holiday. Hanukkah was a particularly big deal." Like Alfred, Helen—who kept a kosher kitchen—was determined that the boys be brought up in a Jewish home. At the age of thirteen, each became a bar mitzvah, working with tutors to learn the Torah portions they would be called on to recite at their bar mitzvah ceremonies. Helen also took her own practice of Judaism seriously, taking special comfort from its ritualistic, emotional aspects. Francie Wolff was struck by Helen's commitment to Judaism, noting, "I remember sitting next to Helen at

Saturday morning synagogue services and being impressed by her sincerity." Yet David contends that his mother was interested in a wide variety of religions and remembers her occasionally pulling out and studying material on the Church of Christ, Scientist. Indeed, the reason she became a Jew was because of his father, says David. "But if he'd been a Buddhist, she would have become a Buddhist, and she would have liked that, too." Nita Corré described Helen as very spiritual, noting that she read widely about different religions. And even though she accepted those of all faiths, she was not a bit interested in instilling her beliefs in others.

The Baders were strongly committed to their Jewish faith, evidenced in part by Alfred's thirty-two years as a Sunday school teacher. Even before their children were born, Helen and Alfred (center back) *included his students in a seder at their home in 1956.*

WHEN THE CAT'S AWAY . . .

During the many weeks every year that Alfred was in Europe (or occasionally, in Japan) on business, life at the Bader home was turned on its head, reflecting just how much Helen's parenting style differed from Alfred's. When Alfred (the boys called him "King Alfred" behind his back) was home, he was engrossed in work, and Helen, with entertaining their business associates. David and Daniel, especially as teenagers, were increasingly left on their own. When Alfred did engage with the boys he could be somewhat distant, strict, and sometimes quick to anger. Daniel was expected to shine Alfred's shoes, while David was required to sing for his father and answer questions Alfred would pose about the paintings on

The mood in the Bader home was serious when Alfred was home.

the walls. "The fact was, everything revolved around him," says David. As a result, it wasn't unusual for the boys to retreat to the kitchen, where Alfred never ventured, and where they felt safe and comfortable.

Alfred was aware of his shortcomings as a father, writing, "I cannot have been as good a father as I should, and probably could, have been." And in his defense, it needs to be noted that major events in Alfred's early life—losing his parents as a child, being forced to emigrate from Europe, living in an internment camp—made for a chaotic childhood. What's more, there was no father figure in his life, no one from whom he could learn how to effectively and compassionately parent.

While abroad, Alfred wrote home regularly of long, hectic days spent racing from small chemical companies to art dealers and galleries. In Milan, Italy, he visited five new companies before heading to Rome the next day to call on more chemists and meet with a Dutch restorer. In Munich, he was offered interesting products from a new supplier; in Japan, terrible inflation made buying chemicals"exceedingly complicated." The art ranged from "a very fine Jacob Ruisdael" to"junky paintings," disappointing auctions, and "prices totally out of control." Alfred described dishonest suppliers, a brutal bout of the flu, and an altercation with a French border agent that nearly landed him in jail. By 1978, the travel was taking its toll. "Perhaps I am just getting too old, but five or six weeks away from home is getting to be too much for me, and I am counting the days to get home.The letters usually began "My dearest Danny," and ended "All my love, Alfred."

According to David and Daniel, the minute their father left town, the entire atmosphere in the house changed dramatically. "It was like two different families," recalls David. The first thing that happened was that Helen, although a good cook, stopped making meals. "We went out to dinner almost every night," says Daniel. Recalls David, "We'd drive to Kentucky Fried Chicken, with my mom banging her hand on the steering wheel and tapping her foot on the floor to keep time with the Black soul music she'd play on the radio." In general, he says, "Life was way more fun when my dad was gone—so much more relaxed. It wasn't as much a business venture as

An Independent Spirit: The Quiet, Generous Life of Helen Daniels Bader

When Alfred left town on business trips to Europe, life for David and Daniel became more fun.

just a household." Helen and the boys went on outings to local museums, concerts, and other events. And by the time the boys were teenagers, they were finally able to sit around watching television, often with their mother by their side. There was also more laughter in the house, something Deirdre Britt attributes to Helen's sense of humor. "She used to, on a regular basis, crack up my older brothers. And to crack up teenaged boys with a quick comment or a witty comeback is pretty hard to do."

Helen also learned to take advantage of Alfred's travels to accomplish projects of her own. After years of unsuccessfully trying to convince her husband of the need to replace the threadbare carpet throughout their house, she took matters into her own hands. Using her own money, she arranged for new carpeting to be installed while he was out of town. Ironically, it was months after he returned that Alfred even noticed the upgrade. When sixteen-year-old Daniel became upset after accidentally scraping the side of Alfred's car when pulling into their home's narrow driveway, Helen told him not to worry. "He'll never notice," she said. "He never did," recalled Daniel. "He was focused on the company, his art, and Judaism. That was his focus. The rest of the world didn't matter."

Chapter 5: Children at Last

That included creature comforts. Averse to spending money on anything other than chemicals and art, he had little interest in, or awareness of, the trappings of day-to-day life. According to Ralph Emanuel, the one reason Alfred purchased the house on Shepard Avenue was to have a place to hang his paintings. "Otherwise," says Emanuel, "he would have been content to live in a hovel." Yet, had one of those paintings gone missing, Alfred would have noticed it instantly. "But other than that, material things didn't matter to him at all," Emanuel says. To be sure, David recalls the day his father, en route to pick up his car at the repair shop, had to call Helen to ask, "What color and make of car do we have?" Another time, a day after Alfred left on a six-week European trip in a pair of shoes he'd just had resoled, the cobbler called to tell Helen he had inadvertently sent Alfred a mismatched pair. Frantic to correct his mistake, the cobbler was aghast when Helen told him that Alfred had worn the shoes to Europe.

ISRAELI SUMMERS

Like most mothers, Helen worried about her children. And David and Daniel are the first to admit that they gave their mother plenty to worry about. The boys were among the first students to attend Hillel Academy, which Alfred had founded with Rabbi David Shapiro and Marvin Klitsner in hopes of providing his sons with the Jewish education he never received. Neither was a great student, and David's early report cards revealed serious problems with reading. (He was later diagnosed with dyslexia.) Alfred's first response was to blame their teachers, but he and Helen also arranged for both boys to see specialists and to get private tutoring in the hope of boosting their progress. Eventually, Alfred concluded that his sons learned less at Hillel than he had hoped they would.

Alfred and Helen found ways to supplement David and Daniel's education. Twice, as young boys, they traveled to Europe with their parents, visiting places such as Vienna and London, where they met the Emanuels. Alfred made sure the boys spent part of each trip in Neuberg an der Mürz,

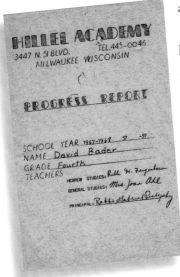

David and Daniel were among the first students to attend Hillel Academy, co-founded by their father. Neither was a strong student, which Alfred blamed on their teachers.

An Independent Spirit: The Quiet, Generous Life of Helen Daniels Bader

as had three generations of Baders before them, including Alfred and Helen on their honeymoon. Again, said David, the trips were a kind of Tale of Two Families: "My father would be there doing business and so when we were with him it would be an exhausting day. He wouldn't eat and we'd be running constantly from this chemical company to that art gallery." When the boys and Helen took off on their own, the fun began. Some of David's favorite European memories include riding on the cable cars in Switzerland and spending part of a day in Neuberg an der Mürz not only hiking in the Alps, but also "listening to early Beatles songs while bowling." When they were older, both boys spent time living with families in Germany, with David working for a while in an Aldrich plant there.

During the summers of 1968 and 1969, much to Helen's dismay, Alfred insisted on sending David and Daniel to Israel for several weeks to improve their Hebrew and "get a feel for what Israel was really like." Helen believed that the boys—David not yet ten, and Daniel, just seven and a half the first year—were too young for such trips, something Alfred would later concede was probably true. While in Israel, the boys were under the care of Ruth Meir, a cousin of David Mayer's, who had lived upstairs from Alfred in Vienna when Alfred was a boy and with whom Alfred, during his formative years, had celebrated Passover. Meir and her family lived in Rehovot, a city about twelve miles south of Tel Aviv and thirty-one miles west of Jerusalem in west-central Israel near the Mediterranean Sea.

Left: *As young boys, Daniel* (standing) *and David* (middle, front row) *spent time during the summers of 1968 and 1969 in Israel where they made friends with the local children.*

Right: *Daniel, who was just seven and a half, had fun playing in the sea near Haifa.*

Helen must have been comforted by Meir's letters, including one in July 1968 in which she wrote, "I can't believe that it is true that we have already for two weeks your dear children with us. I can truly tell you that they are fine and behave so nice. . . . They are interested in everything and they like to do things, buildt [sic], and to work with tools. I think that they are really happy with us. They play also with my children and other boys." Meir added that plans called for visiting the sea near Haifa, "among trees and fresh air." There, Meir would later write, "Daniel begins to swim."

Learning to swim didn't come quite soon enough for Daniel, judging by David's recollection of an incident that took place on a quiet Saturday morning at the beach. The boys' babysitter hoisted Daniel up onto her shoulders and walked into the Mediterranean only to have the sea floor suddenly drop off. "Neither could swim, and they began struggling," recalled David, noting, "That was almost the end of my brother." Coming to the rescue, however, was "a guy on the beach who ran into the water and rescued them both."

In a letter that same summer to his parents, David wrote that he and Daniel had spent two days building an elaborate sandcastle featuring numerous tunnels and which was surrounded by roads. "It looked so nice and looked so much like Jerusalem that we called it Jerusalem," he wrote. On an actual trip to Jerusalem, the boys visited the Western Wall. "At the wall, we prayed *Mincha* and *Maariv*," David wrote, referring to the afternoon and evening prayers, respectively.

Meir wrote that David "likes sometimes to act up and to make us laugh," and that Daniel "was a very good boy" during the few days when he was sick and had to take his pills. In a letter to Jessie and Lloyd, Meir reported that the boys "are very fine and behave so nice that we all are very fond of them." In the same letter, David added a note, telling his grandparents that he and Daniel had been climbing trees, looking at history books, going to movies, and visiting Tel Aviv, where they took an elevator to the top of the city's tallest building. There, from the thirty-ninth story, "we saw the whole city and a lot of the sea."

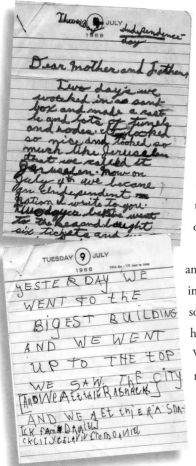

Found among Helen's keepsakes were these letters that David and Daniel wrote to their parents in July 1968 while in Israel.

The following summer, Meir wrote that David "is very good in Hebrew and is a very wise boy." And that "Dany [sic] tries to speak [Hebrew] this year more and understands better than last year." She explained that she gave Daniel several short Hebrew lessons a day "because I don't want him to lose his interest in the language." She also noted that Daniel "is very proud of himself when I let him help me in the kitchen."

Helen and Alfred's letters to the boys in July 1968 are quite touching. Helen, who had made a stop in Salzburg on her way home after taking the boys to Israel, wrote that she had stayed in a small, old castle. In news of home she noted that Charlie, the dog, looked "very handsome with his new, fresh bath," and that "Daddy thinks your club house is very nice. It will be here when you get home." She ends with "I wish I could have seen your city of Jerusalem. Have a wonderful time! Love, Mother."

In his first letter to his sons that summer, Alfred echoed Helen's sentiment, but added his own take on the subject. "I wish I could be with you in Jerusalem," he wrote. "Remember that it is the most important city in the world, where [the Lord] said to Abraham, 'Look northward and southward, eastward and westward, for all the land that you see, to you will I give it and to your children forever.' You, David and Daniel, are Abraham's children, and this is your land." Alfred also asked the boys if, at the Western Wall, they had seen the oversized menorah in front of the Knesset made by Benno Elkan, "the man who made David's menorah at home." In the letter, which he signed "All my love, Your Father, Alfred," he enclosed ten Israeli lira—the local currency at the time—for Daniel and David to share. In a postscript to Alfred's letter, Helen told the boys that "All your neighborhood friends have been asking every day when you are coming back. You will have many stories to tell them."

While in Israel, David and Daniel received letters from Alfred and Helen.

In later letters, both Alfred and Helen wished David a happy tenth birthday, noting that his big day would take place three days before he and his brother returned to Milwaukee. "We will have a large wiener roast for all the neighborhood children when you come home," wrote Helen. She assured the boys, who were flying from Tel Aviv to New York City without their parents, that they would "have a wonderful flight and [that] the stewardess will look after you and give you a lot of attention." Alfred, who planned to meet the boys' plane in New York, told his sons, "Don't worry. God will guard you."

Their grandmother, Jessie, wrote as well. Ever the teacher, she urged David and Daniel to "write down in a little notebook . . . the dates of things you did and saw. Then you will have a very interesting diary and later on in school you can write little themes in your class work." Another idea she floated: "Remember how I made the tapes when you were here to tell of my childhood? It would be nice if you could make some tapes, too, when you get home."

Daniel and David recall those two summers with great affection. "I was really young, but I remember Tel Aviv, the beach, Mrs. Meir, the day care center next door, and pulling fruit off the fig trees," said Daniel. "It was peaceful, the air was clean, and the people were all so accepting. It was a very nurturing place." He admits that the experience, for a seven-year-old, may have been "pushing the envelope a bit." Yet, he noted, "It had a profound impact on the way I view Israel today—a bit romantically and with great fondness." What's more, those first trips laid the foundation for what became a deep, lifelong connection to Israel for both Daniel and David that has helped shape the work of the Helen Bader Foundation, Inc.—and later, Bader Philanthropies, Inc.—in Israel. "There is definitely a very personal element to our giving, which is not political and funds all kinds of programs for people regardless of their backgrounds," said Daniel, who has traveled more than fifty times to Israel over his lifetime. "And it all goes back to those first experiences."

Their grandmother Jessie, also wrote to the boys.

For his part, Alfred took comfort in the fact that although his sons might have gotten more out of their Israeli summers had they been older, they indeed grew to love Israel and returned, on their own, so many times over the years.

BACK TO ABERDEEN

But the boys' favorite trips were the ones they made by train to visit their grandparents in Aberdeen. Early in the morning they and their mother would board the Twin Cities Hiawatha operated by the Chicago, Milwaukee, and St. Paul Railroad (by then commonly known as the Milwaukee Road), travel to Minneapolis, and then transfer to a second, one-car train headed for Aberdeen. "I'm sure my mother probably had better days in her life than spending all day on a train with two small boys," said Daniel, admitting that he and his brother were indeed troublemakers. He and David recall the hours they spent sitting in the train's upper-level dome car. There, they'd make paper airplanes out of the flyers that had been set out on the headrests encouraging passengers to "Come to the Dining Car," and send them swooping down to the lower level, aiming for the conductor and other passengers. David also recalled "stabbing" the conductor with a collapsible toy sword he'd take apart and fill with water. "I still remember that conductor—it was the same guy every year," he said. "Man, I loved that train."

Even though it would be one o'clock in the morning when their train arrived in Aberdeen, Grandpa Lloyd always met their train, and then

Daniel (pictured above) and David especially loved taking trips by train to visit their grandparents in Aberdeen.

Left: *Visits to see Jessie and Lloyd often included side trips to their cottage on Richmond Lake, a manmade lake ten miles northwest of Aberdeen, where the children would swim and go out in a boat built by their great-grandfather Joe Daniels. Pictured here on the cottage's dock are (left to right) Jessie, Marjorie, Deirdre, and Dick DeVey.*

slowly—never faster than 15 miles per hour, the boys insist—drove them home. David and Daniel recall Lloyd as gentle, laid back, and calm, "the quietest man I ever met," said David. Jessie, on the other hand, was talkative, high-strung and intense. "I'd say she probably was worrying about every detail of our arrival hours before we'd even left Milwaukee," speculates Daniel. "She was sort of hovering and buzzing around all the time."

Still, despite Jessie's determination to make everything perfect, the boys recall the Daniels' home as quaint and relaxed, and Aberdeen as a sleepy, small town. They loved spending time with their grandfather at Daniels Drugs, their favorite spot in Aberdeen. They hung out with the local children, and passed many a hot afternoon swimming. Many hours were spent in Lloyd's basement workshop. "My brother and I would go down in the basement and grandfather would make me a sailboat or something and then we'd build and build and build," recalled David. "That's how I got into my building craze." And on every trip to Aberdeen, they would visit the cemetery where Helen's baby brother, their Uncle Kenneth, had been buried.

In later years, the boys would travel to Jessie and Lloyd's small cottage on Richmond Lake, a manmade lake ten miles northwest of Aberdeen,

David Bader (left, with his mother and brother) *recalled the South Dakota landscape as a "sea of cornfields."*

An Independent Spirit: The Quiet, Generous Life of Helen Daniels Bader

where the children would swim and go out in the boat their great-grandfather Joe Daniels had built years earlier. There, Jessie picked wildflowers, enjoyed the prairie grasses, and picked plums for jelly.

David and Daniel remember being struck, even as young boys, by how different Aberdeen was from Milwaukee, and by the extremely different lifestyles the two cities offered. "Out there, it's just cornfields, like a sea of cornfields, like an ocean of cornfields," said David. "Instead of Lake Michigan, you'd see the sky meet the corn." Adds Daniel, "It was a lot different from home—much more relaxed. You had that little town feeling, which is nice." Then, at the end of each trip, said David, "We'd get back on the train to Milwaukee, and go back to living in our museum with our paintings."

Daniel said that it was years of visits to Aberdeen that revealed to him just how much his mother took after his grandfather. Unlike Jessie, whom he describes as "wired, running around in many different directions, and worrying about all kinds of things," Helen was less apt to get too excited when things went wrong. "Our mother wasn't a hyper person to any extent," said Daniel. "She was very intelligent, and very cognizant of what

According to Deirdre DeVey Britt (second from left with her grandparents and siblings), *visiting South Dakota helped her relate to the pride her mother and Aunt Helen had in their Great Plains heritage.*

was happening around her, but I think she was capable of taking it all in and kind of going with the punches. So, that was probably a characteristic that came from her father."

The DeVey cousins also have fond memories of Aberdeen, about which they'd heard scores of stories as they were growing up. Graham remembers imagining it as "a huge, mystical place," and was somewhat surprised to discover it was a "really small town." Graham also remembers his pride, the first time he laid eyes on Daniels Drugs, that "my grandfather's name was on the store." His brother Allyn remembers spending a summer during the 1960s in Aberdeen while he was in high school. "It was great fun to stay with our grandparents," he said. "I helped out in the back room at the pharmacy, and—as a special treat—got to make deliveries around town driving their 1940s-era Plymouth." At the time, the store still had a soda fountain, and Lloyd was still dispensing drugs, though he was in the process of turning the management of the store over to his longtime assistant Clyde Mork.

In 1968, after thirty-eight years in business, Lloyd Daniels sold Daniels Drugs. One of his contemporaries was convinced that Lloyd did not "have an enemy in all of South Dakota."

Dan DeVey vividly remembered one night he spent as a little boy in town with his grandparents while the rest of his family was at the cottage. "I had a wonderful time," he said, recalling Jessie reading him bedtime stories. Now a builder, he has fond memories of Lloyd's basement workshop, and of his grandfather's strong sense of empathy. "He could walk into a room and read the mood. He just sensed what people needed and gave it to them. He really was a living saint kind of guy." Their sister, Deirdre Britt, recalled the trips as occasions that revealed the origins of the pride her mother and aunt found in their Great Plains heritage. "You could just see where their strength came from," she said. "Clearly, they were from pioneer stock that required one to have grit," she said. "You didn't whine, you didn't complain."

In August 1969, one year after Lloyd retired and sold Daniels Drugs to Mork, he and Jessie celebrated their fiftieth wedding anniversary at an open house hosted by the Baders and the DeVeys in Aberdeen. Graham DeVey recalled being pulled aside by a contemporary of Lloyd's, who said to him, "I have to tell you, Dick Daniels does not have an enemy in all of South Dakota." Recalled Graham, "At the time, it didn't mean anything to me, even though the way the guy said it made it sound pretty remarkable. But now, now I realize just how remarkable that was. Here was my grandfather, someone who would talk to anyone or put a sheltering wing around anyone, a very caring and genuinely nice guy. And over time, that's made a heck of an impression on me." Another fond memory of Deirdre's is her grandfather's devotion to Jessie. "I loved his gentle sense of humor, especially with her," she said. "He called her 'Mother,' and could calm her down with a little joke."

If Lloyd was beloved, Jessie was respected. "She was brilliant," said Deirdre. "Her mind was always working; in fact, she would wake up nearly every morning talking about new projects." During the summers when her grandchildren were visiting, Jessie would regularly revert into "teacher mode," even though, Deirdre said, "We were on vacation and not always that interested." Nevertheless, Graham, who went on to become a navy pilot, still gratefully credits her with introducing him to astronomy. And even late in life, said Deirdre, Jessie remained a "strong, formidable, independent woman and feminist icon."

In 1969, Jessie and Lloyd celebrated their fiftieth wedding anniversary. They spent much of their later lives traveling in the United States and abroad.

Alfred wasn't a big fan of the few Aberdeen trips he made with Helen and the boys. To be sure, he genuinely loved Lloyd, noting "You couldn't find a better father." He described him as "a wonderful, quiet, giving person," and pointed out that Helen was much more like him than her mother. Many in the family thought that Alfred had met his match in Jessie, given how authoritative they both were. Alfred admitted that he found her fussy and bossy, although he got along well with her friends, who were impressed with his credentials. Beyond that, "I found the town very dull," he wrote of Aberdeen. "There were no academic chemists and no art." During a family visit in 1977, however, Alfred presented a free, public lecture on "The Bible Through Dutch Eyes" that featured slides of paintings he and Helen owned that had been exhibited at the Milwaukee Art Museum the previous year. According to a newspaper account announcing the program, it was to focus on clues in the works of art that aided in their interpretation, "a kind of super-eyed detective work in which Bader ranks with professionals." Two weeks before Alfred's visit, Jessie previewed her son-in-law's lecture at a luncheon meeting of the Zetetic Club with a program on the Baders' art collection. No doubt her efforts helped boost turnout at his lecture.

According to David (above) *and Daniel* (below), *Helen took an "easy-going approach" to raising teenagers, but found it difficult to abide the rock music they loved.*

THE TEENAGED YEARS

Back in Milwaukee, Helen found that raising teenagers posed new challenges. Of great concern was the fact that neither David nor Daniel was doing well academically at Riverside High School, where in the 1970s the educational standards were subpar and the school's culture rife with racial unrest, risky behavior, and lack of respect for authority. With Alfred either out of town or distracted by business affairs, Helen was thrust into the role of single-handedly raising two teenaged boys who today admit to being wild and somewhat out of control. "I think in general the high school years were the toughest for my mom," said Daniel, noting that over time Helen eventually assumed a rather "easy-going approach" to raising teens. "I think she tolerated all that and let us get through our growing pains, but she wasn't thrilled about the music and the alcohol and everything else that

An Independent Spirit: The Quiet, Generous Life of Helen Daniels Bader

went along with high school in those days." The music that set Helen's teeth on edge included hits by Aerosmith and Led Zeppelin (played with the volume turned way up). No doubt she was relieved when their musical tastes later turned toward jazz and the blues.

Yet if Helen and Alfred at times found the environment at Riverside less than ideal, they appreciated the fact that the school—with a student body that was about half Black—gave David and Daniel the chance to interact with a cross section of the city's population. "I think [Helen] valued the fact that her boys were in contact with all elements of the community and were becoming aware of the difficulties that some people lived under," noted Klitsner. As for Daniel and David, they count their high school years as some of the most valuable and enjoyable of their lives. "People were thrown together, which turned out to be a fabulous experience," recalled Daniel. "Being immersed in so much Black culture—the music, the art—was incredible and life-changing. At school assemblies you'd hear all this funk, R&B, and soul music. We loved that. It was so much fun." Adds David, "And as a result, today we're comfortable talking with anyone."

For Daniel and David (left to right), *attending the racially diverse Riverside High School was a valuable, life-changing experience that left them able to relate and talk to anyone.*

Above left: In an essay she wrote about her sons, Helen noted that David loved cars. Here, he (on the left) *posed with Daniel in front of his beloved 1968 Ford Torino at their mother's Oostburg cottage.*

Above right: Helen described Daniel as likeable and outgoing, and able to interact well with people.

Another lesson learned during those formative years came by way of a mother's example, with Helen urging her sons to refrain from judging others, accepting people despite their backgrounds, and giving everyone the benefit of the doubt. The boys remember, for example, being out to dinner with their mother and getting upset when a Black man seated nearby began yelling at his wife. "My mom told us, 'It's okay,'" recalled David. "And she explained that he'd probably just had a bad day or something, and that they'd work it out." Helen's nonjudgmental approach to life was apparent even in the way she related to the family dog, Charlie. Rather than get upset when he'd roll in the sand and then head for the house, she'd tell the boys, "If I was a dog, I'd roll in the sand, too."

Despite years of worry about David and Daniel, Helen also very much loved and enjoyed her sons, and appreciated their fine qualities, feelings revealed in a rare piece of personal writing:

> Life with two teenaged sons as different as mine can be both hilariously frustrating and rewarding.
> My older son is a car nut. I was rather shaken up one day after returning home from work to find two huge wheels sitting

in my living room looking as if they owned the place. My son's car, a 1968 Ford Torino which he almost never drives for fear of rust, is a black, shiny, rustless automobile with inside carpeting, an eight-track player, and bucket seats. All his necessary errands are done with his mother's beat-up station wagon.

However, this same son is very hard working and conscientious both in his school and regular work. He amazed his boss by being his only employee that refused to take a break.

My younger son is a very likeable, outgoing young man. He has a great interest in people, working with them, talking with them, or just being with them. He is a very enterprising young fellow; he is what my husband calls a wheeler-dealer.

In his first week of high school, he got a job in the school office and became friendly with all the school administrators and teachers. He loves work. Since he was fifteen, he has been working with the audio-visual department of the Milwaukee Board of Jewish Education and is now an apprentice with the stage crew of the Milwaukee Repertory Theater.

He could, however, do without schoolwork. He is not what you would call a bad student, but very little effort goes into actual studying. Withal, both boys are very thoughtful and kind and a delight to be with.

By way of example, Helen taught her sons (Daniel, on the left, and David, on the right in both photos) to refrain from judging others, accept people despite their background, and give everyone the benefit of the doubt.

CHAPTER SIX

A COMPLICATED FAMILY

Looking back, David and Daniel recall that even after Aldrich began thriving financially and their parents had access to considerable wealth, they chose a relatively simple lifestyle. "They weren't zipping all over the world in a Lear jet, driving luxury cars, or spending an extravagant amount of money," said David. Instead, they plowed most of Aldrich's profits back into the company. They credit Alfred for ensuring that their mother, who oversaw the household accounts, also owned half of the business. In fact, Daniel remembered his father asserting that "wives should have their own money." It's a belief no doubt rooted in the financial problems experienced by his Aunt Gisela, which Alfred had observed as a youth and a subsequent promise he reportedly made that no woman with whom he was associated would ever be cheated out of what was hers.

In other ways, however, Alfred was far less enlightened; in fact, in terms of social–emotional development, his skills were woefully inadequate. He was brilliant, but easily bored, and often unaware of how his behavior affected others. And it wasn't just visiting chemists or art dealers with whom he could be off-putting. Marvin Klitsner's daughter Francie Wolff recalled that as a teenager she once pointed to a small painting in a cabinet at the Bader home, telling Alfred, "I really like that." Alfred lost no time informing her that the painting was, in fact, a Rembrandt, and in the process, made her feel "stupid" for not realizing its significance. Again, it fell to Helen to smooth things over. Looking back, Wolff believes her

Opposite background: *By the late 1970s, David and Daniel* (far left and far right) *were out of high school and Helen was finding Alfred* (center) *increasingly difficult to live with.*

Opposite foreground: *In middle age, Helen's independent spirit made her more adept at picking her battles and holding her ground.*

Above: *Despite their wealth, the Baders maintained a relatively simple lifestyle, exemplified by Helen mowing the lawn.*

discomfort in the Bader home likely stemmed from Alfred's "domineering personality and how he treated Danny, who was unfailingly gentle, warm, and accommodating."

By all accounts, Helen was a wonderful mother, devoted wife, caring friend, gracious hostess, and accomplished, hardworking businesswoman. She was compassionate, tolerant, and empathetic. She was humble. But she wasn't a saint. The little girl who refused to wear dresses grew up strong and resolute, knowing her own mind and more than willing to break the rules. Despite her conservative rearing, she married an Austrian Jew, converted to Judaism, became a Democrat (her favorite expletive was "Ronald Reagan !*&#?!"), and would go on to forge not one, but two successful careers. Over what would be her thirty-year marriage to Alfred, Helen learned to pick her battles, stand her ground, and at times, simply walk away. Often, when they'd argue, he'd tune her out, and over time she became less bothered by his behavior, noting, "Alfred will be Alfred." And after years of letting him dictate her schedule, especially when abroad, Helen started holding her own. Alfred wanted to be out and about at seven o'clock in the morning? "Fine, you go along without me," she'd tell

After years of letting Alfred dictate the schedule on their European trips, Helen began making her own plans. On one such trip, she met up with her friend Fran Weis in Austria to attend the Salzburg Festival.

An Independent Spirit: The Quiet, Generous Life of Helen Daniels Bader

him. London again? "Not this time," she'd say. "I'm going to the Salzburg Festival." And off she went, meeting up with friends in Austria in much the same way she had jumped on her bike and tracked down her pals as a young girl growing up in Aberdeen.

As for his sons, Alfred had long counted on them to follow in his footsteps and take over Aldrich, and so he arranged for both of them, as teenagers, to work several summers at the plant. Although David would much rather have been working on cars, he ended up sorting chemical samples while listening to his father conduct business over the phone. "He'd turn the charm on and off, praising one person, then reaming someone out, then lowering someone else's salary," he recalled. Daniel, whose summer jobs were in the shipping department, did go on to work for Aldrich as a computer technician for two years after high school. But like his brother, he never planned to pursue a career at the company. Instead, both boys, despite having struggled academically in high school, went to college— David to study engineering and architecture and Daniel, computer technology and business. To be sure, all their lives they had repeatedly been reminded that their parents were college educated and that their father

Alfred long imagined that his sons would take over Aldrich Chemical. David and Daniel did work at the company summers during high school, and Daniel for two years between high school and college. However, both chose other careers.

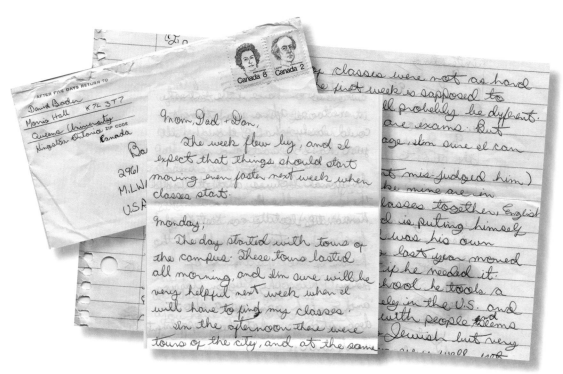

Bowing to the wishes of his father, David enrolled at Queen's University, Alfred's alma mater, in 1976. Writing home, he noted that he found his classes less difficult than expected.

held a degree from no less than Harvard University. "There was always that pressure," recalled David. "Going to college was expected."

Thus, in 1976, and at his father's insistence, David enrolled at Queen's University. In two letters written shortly after arriving on campus, he provided a day-by-day rundown of orientation, noting the week "flew by," and describing his roommate as "a very nice fellow" who "gets on well with people and seems very straight-forward." Classes, at least the first week of the term, "were not as hard as I had expected." Yet Queen's proved not to be a good fit, and after one semester, David transferred to the University of Wisconsin-Milwaukee, where he spent a year before transferring to the University of Wisconsin–Madison. There, in 1982, he graduated with a degree in ciivil engineering. After a short stint working at a small inks and dyes chemical company in Philadelphia ("I came home a different color every day!"), he returned to Milwaukee and UWM's School of Architecture & Urban Planning, where in 1986 he earned a master's degree in architecture.

Daniel went east for college in 1981, first spending a year at Eisenhower College, a liberal arts school in Seneca Falls, New York, affiliated

with the Rochester Institute of Technology (RIT) in nearby Rochester, and then transferring to RIT to earn an associate's degree in computer technology and, in 1987, a bachelor's degree in business. One of the advantages RIT offered was its proximity to the DeVeys, who were living about ninety miles away in Syracuse at the time, and Daniel spent a lot of time with his aunt, uncle, and cousins. "My mom wanted me to be close to her sister. It was her way of making sure I was nurtured while away from home."

Helen attended Daniel's graduation from Rochester Institute of Technology in 1987.

THE END OF A MARRIAGE

By the time David Bader left for Queen's University in 1976, his parents' marriage, which for decades had been undermined by the torch Alfred carried for Isabel Overton, was beginning to collapse. The year before, and twenty-three years after marrying Helen, Alfred had begun having nightmares in which Isabel's aged father appeared, berating him and demanding to know, "Why are you not with Isabel?" The first love of Alfred's life, Isabel had been born in 1926 and grew up in the gold

Below: *Isabel grew up poor, but attended Victoria College in Toronto as a scholarship student.*

mining town of Kirkland Lake in northern Ontario. She was the middle of three children of Herbert and Stella Sirr Overton. Herbert, a cabinetmaker, had emigrated to Kirkland Lake from England in 1906 and found work as a carpenter in the town's mines. Stella, from nearby New Liskeard, had left school at thirteen to help raise her six younger siblings. Kirkland Lake was a rough town, and although the main industry was gold mining, miners' wagers were low, and the Overtons' lives, difficult. "Isabel has told me," Alfred writes in his autobiography, "how happy she was one day when she found a dime under a davenport pillow; it enabled her mother to buy vegetables for the next meal."

Herbert and Stella were devout, highly moral Protestants. Herbert was a student of the Bible and a part-time, lay preacher. Both he and Stella loved music, and sang in the church choir. Isabel played the piano and her sister, Marion, the violin. Despite never having attended college, Herbert and Stella were also strong proponents of higher education, a sentiment they passed on to their children. Isabel was a scholarship student at Victoria College, part of Victoria University, in Toronto. There she earned an Honours BA degree in the arts and went on to teach school. Her brother, Clifford, earned an Honours BA degree in chemistry, mathematics, and physics from Queen's and became a metallurgist.

Isabel and Alfred met aboard the RMS Franconia *during the summer of 1949. They would marry thirty-three years later.*
PUBLIC DOMAIN

A EUROPEAN ADVENTURE

The summer after receiving her degree in 1949, Isabel sailed for England aboard the RMS *Franconia,* realizing a long-held dream to visit England. She was traveling with a young woman named Ruth Hunt, taking the place of a friend of Ruth's who was unable to make the trip. Their plan was to spend the summer cycling around England before securing one-year teaching positions. Five days into the voyage, on July 14, 1949, Isabel met Alfred, who was going abroad for the first time since his deportation to Canada in 1940. Nine days later, in London, Alfred asked her to marry him.

Alfred's proposal came despite a major complication: the fact that he was Jewish, wanted children, and wanted to raise them in the Jewish faith. According to Jewish law, that could not happen unless their mother was Jewish. It was something Alfred and Isabel debated as they toured London before Alfred left for the Continent. He ultimately cut that trip short, returning to Burton-on-Trent in central England, ostensibly to meet the man whom his sister, Marion, planned to marry, but mostly in hopes of reconnecting with Isabel. Visiting Lichfield Cathedral not far from Burton-on-Trent, Alfred was touring the cathedral "without much interest, until I saw the one woman who had been on my mind so constantly. . . ." He and Isabel spent the next two weeks together. They toured Sussex, Brighton, and Hastings, visiting friends and looking for

Isabel lived and taught school in Bexhill-on-Sea, a resort town in southeast England, for more than thirty years. Here, she can be seen in 1950 (far right) *bicycling on the beach with friends* (left to right) *Yvonne, Harry, Stephen, and Christine Portch.*

a teaching job for Isabel. They also traveled to the Edinburgh International Festival in Scotland, which had been established in 1947 to celebrate emerging theater, music, opera, and dance in postwar Scotland, England, and Europe.

By then, with Alfred poised to return to Harvard in mid-September, Isabel had been offered a job teaching English and history at St. Francis School, a private girls' school in Bexhill-on-Sea, a resort town in southeast England. Writes Alfred, "I paid little attention to Bexhill, because it was to be just an interlude, one year in her life. Little did I know. . . ." Indeed, Isabel had come to Europe to have an adventure—marriage wasn't on her radar—and she would go on to teach in Bexhill not for one year, but instead, for thirty-two.

LONG-DISTANCE COURTSHIP

Isabel and Alfred kept in touch for the next two years. Her letters, published in 2000 as *A Canadian in Love,* are full of affection for Alfred. Clearly, she loved him. Yet she grew increasingly anxious, at first about her decision to stay in England, and then about her inability to accept his proposal. In the end, it came down to a quandary over how they would raise their children. "It would not be a question of shame, Alf," she wrote on June 5, 1950, "but to have a child of mine in my arms and not to have pledged myself to guide him into a way of life I believe the best, would be impossible."

An Independent Spirit: The Quiet, Generous Life of Helen Daniels Bader

Back in Kirkland Lake one year later for the wedding of her sister, Isabel wrote Alfred the last in a series of eighty-two letters, concluding, "I'm sorry Alf that I've incurred your wrath because of my inability to face a situation. It probably sounds silly to you. But I beg you to forgive me." Ultimately, Isabel's parents did not see the issue of religion as insurmountable, something her mother revealed to Alfred in a letter in October 1951. "I told her we would be happy for her to raise the children in the Jewish Faith," she wrote. "Whatever we may not understand of God's plan or purpose . . . one thing is clear. The Jews are God's people, and all the families of the earth will be blessed, through God's promise to Abraham."

As for Alfred, he eventually accepted the fact that he and Isabel would never marry; he wanted—and needed—a Jewish wife, something she could not be. "When my many letters and notes to her went unanswered," he wrote, "I suspected that she had found another man and was now smiling about that interlude in her life with a Jew." Moreover, he was growing desperate to get married and start a family of his own, in part to compensate for the lack of one growing up. Over the next few years, he would write Isabel sporadically, with the last few cards signed "Alf and Danny." That was how Isabel came to know that he had, indeed, gotten married.

RECONNECTION

The nightmares in 1975 prompted Alfred to track Isabel down, discovering she had never married and was still teaching in Bexhill. He wrote her and visited her the following spring on his next trip to Europe. Their visit was strained, with Isabel pointing out the obvious: Alfred was a married man with two children. "Go away," she told him.

Alfred's behavior over the next five years—driven by his love for Isabel and lack of empathy for Helen—was inexcusable. Despite Isabel's objections, he traveled to Kirkland Lake to see her that August. She managed to elude him on two subsequent trips he made to England, but Alfred simply would not give up, finally convincing Isabel to spend a day with him in Bexhill in April 1977. For a while—defying Isabel's wishes—Alfred wrote

By the late 1970s, Alfred was confiding in David, at the time still a teenager, about his love for Isabel.

to her daily, sometimes in front of Helen; over the next few years, Isabel and Alfred met occasionally in Kirkland Lake and when he traveled abroad. Helen was devastated, all too aware of what was going on: Alfred was, in effect, leading a double life. He would return from visiting Isabel captivated, oblivious to Helen's feelings.

David Bader was only a young teenager when, much to his dismay, his father began confiding in him about his feelings for Isabel. "I didn't want to hear about it," said David, recalling the conversations that continued with greater frequency once Alfred began traveling back to Europe to see her. Alfred would literally be reduced to tears, telling David how much he loved and missed Isabel, oblivious to the distress—and later, the anger—these conversations were causing his son. Ironically, years later and equally passionate, Alfred would remorsefully confess to David that, "I was mean to Danny; what I did to her was horrible." Concludes David, "He loved my mom, but in the end, was too much in love with Isabel to let her go."

Yet, strangely, Alfred wasn't seriously contemplating divorce, seemingly content to maintain the status quo. In October 1978, for example, Alfred attended Lloyd Daniels's funeral in Aberdeen with Helen and the boys. Life at Aldrich, and at home, went on much as always. Looking back, Ralph Emanuel said he believes Alfred had lost "all sense of proportion and was quite simply obsessed" with Isabel. "I think he believed he could have both of them," he said. As for Isabel, "I don't think she had a chance," he said. "Alfred was just too persistent." Emanuel is quick to note that Alfred had many wonderful qualities. "He was extremely generous, deeply concerned about the world, intelligent, focused and a hard worker. And he could be enormously charming when he wanted to be." Yet, he adds, "Alfred saw only what he wanted to see, related only to people who were useful to him. And he had no comprehension of how hurtful his words and actions could be. It wasn't malicious. It was a defect, an illness."

Francie Wolff describes the way Alfred conducted himself as simply "odd," noting that he couldn't seem to differentiate between appropriate and inappropriate behavior. Looking back, Fred and Rita Gordy's daughter Molly Gordy Drew believes Alfred's behavior was grounded in a profound "lack of empathy," noting that "Although he could feel great affection for those within his world, once you no longer fit or were not part of his plan, he simply didn't care how badly he hurt you."

Various members of the family, however, suspect that Alfred may have been exhibiting characteristics of undiagnosed Asperger's Syndrome, citing as evidence his apparent incapacity to understand the effect his actions were having on Helen and his sons. They also take note of his social awkwardness; a near-obsession with art and chemistry; and his relentless, single-minded pursuit of Isabel, who became aware of what she also described as Alfred's "odd" behavior only after they married. "It must have been very difficult for Helen to cope all those years," she said. Meanwhile, David speculated on one possible trigger for his father's symptoms, pointing out that "We don't know how the trauma of having witnessed Nazi brutality in his Vienna neighborhood, especially on *Kristallnacht*, and then having been a child refugee might have affected his relational development."

By reconnecting with Isabel without seriously contemplating a divorce from Helen, Alfred was, in effect, leading a double life.

CHAPTER SEVEN

HELEN MOVES ON

For her part, Helen was trying to keep things on an even keel as long as Daniel was still living at home. She continued working at Aldrich, which in 1975 had merged with the St. Louis-based Sigma Chemical Company, to become the Sigma-Aldrich Corporation. Although Aldrich was half the size of Sigma, it had a lot to offer. In 1974, according to a *Milwaukee Sentinel* story headlined "Aldrich Firing Up All Burners," the company's catalogues offered up 18,000 chemical compounds and rare research chemicals, sales of which totaled $11 million. The merger also was practical: Sigma would provide research-grade biochemicals, and Aldrich, research-grade organic compounds. Alfred became president of the new company, which over the next four years reported annual sales increases of 15 percent and increased its share of the $100 million research chemical market to somewhere between 30 and 40 percent. By 1979, annual sales totaled $68 million. With Alfred at the helm—as president until 1980, and then as chairman of the board of directors for another eleven years—Sigma-Aldrich continued to thrive financially. By 1986, for example, sales had reached $215 million. The merger, however, put in place a corporate structure that gradually eroded the power and control Alfred had long enjoyed at Aldrich, a situation he found increasingly frustrating. More and more often, he found himself unable to put his ideas into action; instead he was forced to work with top executives "convinced they were right about everything." Compounding the problem was the fact that the new company's culture

Opposite background: *By the late 1970s, even with her marriage failing, Helen tried to keep daily life running smoothly, mostly for the sake of Daniel, who was still living at home.*

Opposite foreground: *In 1981, Helen entered graduate school. She was often up early doing homework in the kitchen.*

Above: *Helen continued to play her violin, a wedding gift from Alfred, throughout her life.*

Right: *In 1975, Aldrich merged with the St. Louis-based Sigma Chemical Company to become the Sigma-Aldrich Corporation. Although Alfred* (left) *and longtime Aldrich executive Bernie Edelstein* (right) *were among those who remained at the company, Alfred became increasingly frustrated with his lack of control.*

Opposite, top and bottom: *In 1978, just five years after earning a master's degree in social work from the School of Social Welfare at the University of Wisconsin-Milwaukee, Nita Corré was named executive director of the Milwaukee Jewish Home.*

OVATION JEWISH HOME

proved to be vastly different from that at Aldrich, and riddled with office politics Alfred was ill-equipped to navigate.

Something that hadn't changed at Aldrich was the affection its employees continued to feel for Helen. Marjorie's son, Dan, recalled visiting the plant in late 1978 with his mother. "Helen showed us around and I remember thinking how smart and strong my aunt was," he said. "The company was expanding, and she knew all about the new safety codes that had to be met. And, of course, everyone knew her, and it was obvious how much they loved her." But there was little love at home. Although Helen and Alfred were living under the same roof, they were increasingly living separate lives and the atmosphere was noticeably tense. According to Marvin Klitsner, Helen was strong, and kept her feelings mostly to herself. "You wouldn't have known she was struggling unless she reluctantly confided in you," he said.

In 1979, Helen did turn to her friend Nita Corré, telling her, "I want to get together with you to discuss what's going on in my life." Corré had been born and raised in Gibraltar, a British territory located off the southern tip of Spain, before moving with her husband, Alan, to Philadelphia. They had arrived in Milwaukee in the late 1960s when Alan was named chair of the Hebrew Studies Department at the University of Wisconsin-Milwaukee (UWM). Although Corré had a degree in economics and had worked as an accountant, she was interested in pursuing geriatric social work, motivated by her memories of the way elderly people had been treated in Gibraltar—with affection and reverence. Those memories, however, clashed with what she had seen when visiting Philadelphia nursing homes with Alan: elderly patients sitting listlessly in wheelchairs lined up along the hallways. "I knew this was not right," she said, "and I wanted to bring a piece of Gibraltar to Milwaukee." Corré, by then in her thirties and the mother of four, enrolled in UWM. By 1973, she had earned both a bachelor's and a master's degree from the university's School of Social Welfare. Although there was no such field as geriatric social work at the time, school officials accommodated Corré's interest; she was able to take a number of independent reading courses and complete a field placement at what was then the Milwaukee Jewish Home. By 1978, she had been named executive director of the facility.

Helen's shy nature, penchant for privacy, and reluctance to talk about herself made it painfully difficult to reach out, even to Corré, who immediately suggested they meet for tea at what was then the Coffee Trader on Milwaukee's East Side. Helen revealed the long, humiliating story of Alfred's history with Isabel, and shared her realization that divorce was inevitable. Recalled Corré, "She was hurt, and as angry as she could get in front of someone else. And she said to me, 'My life is ending.'"

Corré reassured Helen that was not the case. Her advice: go back to school, get a degree in social work, and come work with her at the Jewish Home. Responded Helen, "But I work in chemistry." Corré persevered, seeing in Helen someone who was genuine, caring, and generous—exactly the kind of employee she wanted on staff. In the end, she convinced Helen not only that the Jewish Home needed her, but that Helen also needed the home. "This might be a time of opportunities for you, too," she said, noting that Helen had spent years in business and raising a family. "Perhaps this is a time to be fulfilled through a different avenue." Specifically, she suggested that Helen might like working with dementia patients, noting, "They don't have any pretense, they really just take you for who you are, appreciate what you do for them. . . ." In retrospect, Corré admitted that her suggestion may

Above: *It was in 1979 at Milwaukee's Coffee Trader restaurant that Helen revealed to her friend Nita Corré, whom she had met years earlier through their children, that a divorce from Alfred was inevitable. Corré advised Helen to enroll in graduate school, earn a degree in social work, and come work with her at the Milwaukee Jewish Home.*

"I REMEMBER COFFEE TRADER" FACEBOOK PAGE

Right: *The early 1980s was a time of reflection for Helen, who was trying to determine what do with the rest of her life.*

An Independent Spirit: The Quiet, Generous Life of Helen Daniels Bader

have been a bit premature, given that Helen hadn't even decided to return to school. Yet Helen nodded. Clearly, Corré's words had struck a chord. In fact, Helen was already familiar with the Jewish Home, having spent time there both as a volunteer and on visits to her friend Steffie Zupnik, who had moved into the home due to memory loss. Over the years she knew the Baders, according to Nina Holmquist, Zupnik lost all respect for Alfred, and became one of Helen's strongest allies.

Helen also discussed her future with her sons, traveling at one point with David to visit other cities and trying to decide if she wanted to relocate. In the end, Helen decided she belonged in Milwaukee and took Corré's advice: she left her job at Aldrich (where it took three people to replace her), started doing volunteer work at the Jewish Home, and enrolled in UWM's School of Social Welfare in January 1980 to pursue a master's degree in social work (also known as an MSW). Although it was a big step in her life, Helen approached it in her characteristically unassuming and low-key way. "She simply told us she was going back to school to get some training in social work," recalled Klitsner. "I thought that was great and told her so because I thought she was a natural born social worker and getting some professional training would enable her to do great things." Apparently, Alfred felt

As she contemplated her future, Helen discussed her options with her son David.

differently. "He didn't like it," said Holmquist. "He belittled social work and couldn't understand why she was doing it."

But Helen was not to be dissuaded, and her decision to go back to school turned out to be a good one: She was energized by her fellow students, almost all of whom were decades younger than she was. She enjoyed attending classes and undertaking fieldwork. Although the changes in her life couldn't have been more dramatic—and at times challenging—she thrived, grateful for the chance to think about something other than the state of her marriage, and instead to begin forging her own identity. Helen was also incredibly busy: although a full-time student, she continued running the household, catering to Alfred, and watching out for Daniel, who was still living at home and working at Aldrich. Early mornings found Helen up doing her homework.

"She wanted her own identity and was driven to get her degree," recalled Daniel. "It was as if she had jumped off a cliff from the world she knew— her friends, her family life—into one where suddenly in her fifties she was attending classes and writing papers." But even as graduate school proved to be exciting and stimulating, it also induced a measure of anxiety and stress. "She was hesitant," noted Corré, "because social work requires a lot of interacting with people, and she was shy." Beyond that, Helen had never been comfortable confronting thorny issues. Said Corré, "She was much more comfortable in agreeing with people than in challenging [them]."

Years of tension and sadness came to a head in December 1980 when Helen told Alfred she wanted a divorce.

It was in December 1980, on the night of the Baders' annual Christmas party for the Aldrich employees, that Helen told Alfred she wanted a divorce. Only a few days earlier Alfred had returned from visiting Isabel, and that evening following the party had phoned her. Overhearing part of the conversation, Helen decided she'd had

An Independent Spirit: The Quiet, Generous Life of Helen Daniels Bader

enough, telling Alfred, "We can't go on like this. You see Isabel and you are a man entranced." Alfred didn't deny it.

Helen moved out of the family's Shephard Avenue home, using her own money to rent both an apartment at 1570 N. Prospect Ave. and a cottage on Stodyk Ingelse Road in Oostburg, about forty-five miles north of Milwaukee. (She took with her Pasqualino Rossi's *Musicians,* the oil painting Alfred bought for her on their honeymoon, and one painting attributed to Simon Vouet from their collection. Today, the Rossi hangs in the home of Linda and Daniel Bader, and the one attributed to Vouet, in the bedroom of David's daughter Helena.) According to David, it was Helen's friend Marilyn Cooper who convinced his mother to make the move after finding Helen in tears, eventually revealing to her friend that "Alfred is running off with this other woman." Responded Cooper, "That's not right. You have to get out of here." David saw the move as significant. "My mother had the strength to get out of the house," he said, "and in the process, set a good example for me and my brother."

Helen's favorite painting attributed to Vouet now hangs in her granddaughter Helena's bedroom.

Helen was also supported by Holmquist. The two had become fast friends, often bonding over their mutual love of music. "Danny had a subscription to the Chicago Symphony concerts in Milwaukee, and the extra ticket went to me for years," she recalled. Helen also gave Holmquist's son Tom violin lessons as well as her first violin. His brother, Carson, told his mother recently that he remembered Helen as "a good listener who always understood us." Holmquist said she remembered Helen as "the kindest, most compassionate, most generous woman I've ever met."

It was no surprise to anyone that Helen managed on her own much better than Alfred, who according to Ralph Emanuel, needed a wife to look after him. Once Helen moved out, he said, "Alfred lived a clerical life." Daniel recalled the time he spent living with his father before leaving for college as "strange," noting, "One thing I remember is that he didn't cook; what he wanted was for me to take care of him."

GRADUATE SCHOOL

While in school, Helen's confidence grew. Maintaining a demanding schedule, she earned As and Bs over three semesters and two summer sessions. Her courses included Theories of Sociological Development and Change; Personality Theories; Psychopathology; Human Services Systems; Counseling, Poverty, and Urban Culture; and Social Welfare Policy Development. She completed three semesters of Field Instruction, one each at the state public defender's office, the Legal Aid Society of Milwaukee, and what was then the Mount Sinai Green Tree Health Care Center.

Helen's niece, Deirdre Britt, recalled that once when she was in high school in Fayetteville, New York, Helen came to visit. "She had all of these books with her and she was studying, and I thought it was strange because someone her age didn't have to go to school anymore. Then I realized she chose to be in school . . . and found that very interesting and intriguing. I was impressed. It seemed like hard work. And it was only later that I realized why she had gone back to school." Deirdre sees that decision as an example of her Aunt Helen's "constant interest in growing herself, educating herself, and not just in a formal sense, but in all contexts. She was determined to remain a vital part of the world in which she was living."

Helen entered UWM's MSW program interested in working with the homeless and those with mental disabilities. However, as early as her first semester at UWM, she was writing papers on another area of interest: treatment options for the institutionalized aged. In "A Personal Model for Effective Treatment of Grief and Depression in Nursing Homes," she proposed using an individual reinforcement therapy model incorporating behavior modification and group therapy to treat nursing home residents exhibiting social and emotional problems. The goals of such an approach, wrote Helen, include modifying "a grief-stricken resident's behavior so that he may move toward a state of wellness." And in an early nod to what ultimately would become her chief area of interest—working with Alzheimer's patients—she advocated for group therapy sessions in reality orientation, a "systematic attempt to give the patient correct information about his environment."

In a second paper she wrote that semester, "Aging and the Institutionalized Self," Helen shares her vision, writing, "An ideal nursing home is one which would overcome the negative aspects of institutionalization: cold personal environment, loss of family, regimentation, role of dependency, lack of social relations, demoralization and lack of individualization." She goes on to describe how she would reconfigure such institutions:

> The nursing home should be divided into a facility for the confused and forgetful and a facility for the sick but well-oriented elderly. The confused should live in small sheltered households. Effort should be made to keep a quiet atmosphere and selective stimulation should be used to help the confused feel less badly about themselves.

Helen suggested that such residents take part in family-style dining, have access to landscaped outdoor areas, and be allowed to furnish their rooms with furniture from home. Family members, she wrote, "should be contacted regularly and encouraged to visit often and to participate in small family-like activities. Again, the goal, she wrote, was "to encourage the

Helen took social work classes in the modernist, eleven-story Enderis Hall, home to the School of Social Welfare at the University of Wisconsin-Milwaukee. The structure towers over the original, red brick buildings of Milwaukee-Downer College, where Helen earned her bachelor's degree in 1949.

ARCHIVES DEPARTMENT,
UNIVERSITY OF WISCONSIN-
MILWAUKEE LIBRARIES

Even as a student, Helen was advocating for radical changes in elder care that included family-style dining and access to the outdoors.

OVATION JEWISH HOME

confused old person to take a renewed interest in life and focus his attention on everyday happenings."

In other writing, Helen describes her interaction with a twenty-year-old Black client she worked with through a field placement with the Mental Health Division of the Wisconsin State Public Defender's Office. The angry young woman, whose mother had died suddenly three years earlier, was tormented by "spirits" in the form of demonic voices. Diagnosed with paranoid schizophrenia, she had been committed to the Milwaukee County Mental Health Complex after stabbing her father in the hand with a kitchen knife. Working with lawyers who secured the woman's release, Helen helped arrange for her to return home, despite her hostile relationship with family members. Over the next ten weeks, in weekly sessions, Helen met with the client, aiming both to improve her home life and help her "achieve some inner peace and happiness in everyday living."

The paper offers insight into Helen's already considerable social work skills: "The beginning was very slow," she writes. "She was very hostile, never looked at me directly, often sat sideways, snapping her fingernails and answering with a few angry words. She told me I was part of society, and since she hated society, she hated me also." Helen suggested that the young woman keep a journal of things that bothered her, engage in at least one short, friendly conversation and one pleasurable activity with her father and

An Independent Spirit: The Quiet, Generous Life of Helen Daniels Bader

brothers every day, and improve her job-seeking skills. The interventions worked: The client's attitude improved, as did the atmosphere at home. She enrolled in a job training program and told Helen she was "beginning to enjoy life more." Although the client offered no insight on what had brought about the changes, Helen wondered if "having one caring person made the difference." She noted that working with this client required "a great deal of kindness, patience and persistence. . . ." And she cited as her greatest accomplishment the fact that the client "accept[ed] me at all." The turning point came, Helen wrote, "When I told her no one was going to take her spirits away from her—everyone has his own private world. She seemed to relax and from then on, she followed through on every idea I had."

Another paper analyzed the improper implementation of the 1979 Wisconsin Mental Health Act, which Helen argued had led to "frequently inconsistent, ineffectual, and disenfranchising application of the law." She highlighted the need to change public perception that the mentally ill are a threat to the public, provide a system of emergency shelters for the mentally ill, and offer professional development on the subject of mental illness to law enforcement personnel. Helen's master's thesis was a review of the literature on the causes of senile psychoses or deterioration due to life stress factors. Her conclusion called on social workers to "promote human contacts, social participation and meaningful work with the elderly individual in order to maintain optimum function."

In her graduate thesis, Helen explored the connection between stress and behavioral dysfunction in the elderly.
OVATION JEWISH HOME

LEGAL AID SOCIETY

Helen found her field placement work, and particularly the time she spent at the Legal Aid Society of Milwaukee, the most meaningful component of graduate school. At the time, the organization was nationally renowned for advocating for the rights and interests of the mentally disabled, an issue of great interest to Helen. While at Legal Aid, she helped place borderline mentally ill clients—many of whom were homeless and facing involuntary commitment to mental hospitals—in group homes or other less restrictive environments. The work involved not only locating and facilitating such placements, but also ensuring clients' access to additional support services such as outpatient therapy.

Helen excelled at the task, according to Thomas Zander, Legal Aid's executive director, who called her "one of the most remarkably talented and sensitive students we ever had in terms of her ability to relate to the clients, feel comfortable with them, and advocate for their interests." Zander worked closely with Helen, and they both, he said, "really clicked in our professional relationship." They regularly conferred about pending cases, met with clients at the Milwaukee County Mental Health Complex, and testified in court on behalf of clients county officials wanted institutionalized.

At Legal Aid, Helen found herself not only the oldest of the students doing fieldwork, but also older than most of the staff. In fact, she was often the Legal Aid worker closest in age to the agency's clients. That "level of maturity and sophistication," said Zander, was an asset seldom seen in other field placement students. Often, Zander and his staff members found themselves relying on Helen's experience and commitment; her time at Legal Aid, he said, was "as much our learning from her as her learning from us."

Beyond that, Zander remembers Helen as warm and personable. "She treated everyone she worked with like family . . . you felt like she was your mom or your older sister." Those relationships continued even after Helen left Legal Aid, with dinners she hosted at her apartment for Zander and other staff members to both socialize and talk about the Legal Aid's work.

During her field placement at the Legal Aid Society of Milwaukee, Helen succeeded in placing borderline mentally ill clients—many of whom were homeless and facing involuntary commitment to mental hospitals—in less-restrictive environments. Thomas Zander, Legal Aid's executive director, appreciated Helen's ability to relate to the clients, feel comfortable with them, and advocate for their interests.

Helen's interaction with one Legal Aid client named Vivian exemplifies the degree of commitment and compassion she brought to her work. Vivian was a typical Legal Aid client: Although she had been in and out of mental hospitals for more than twenty years, Legal Aid's clinical psychologist believed she was capable of managing safely in the larger community with reasonable support. Nevertheless, county officials were moving to have Vivian permanently institutionalized. Legal Aid took the case to court, pointing out that Helen had set up a placement for Vivian in a care home, and had arranged for additional day care and therapy. The court accepted the arrangements, on a trial basis.

Helen's patience, ability to listen, capacity for empathy, and nonjudgmental nature endeared her to her clients, both as a student and later as a licensed social worker.

As Zander tells it, all was going well until the middle of one night when police found Vivian wandering the streets, disoriented and confused. In her pocket, they found Helen's business card, on which Helen had written her home telephone number. And so it was that at three o'clock in the morning Helen received a phone call from the police describing the situation and the fact that the operator of the care home was refusing to take Vivian back in. Realizing that Vivian was on the brink of being returned to a mental hospital, Helen picked her up from police custody and together they returned to the care facility, where Helen stayed with Vivian until morning, eventually convincing the operator to take Vivian back.

At first, Vivian had been incoherent, but gradually she revealed to Helen the reason behind her breakdown: The preceding day had not only been Mother's Day, but also the twentieth anniversary of the day Vivian had lost custody of her children due to her mental illness. Vivian's sense of loss had been overwhelming. Helen, of course, understood. They spent the early morning hours talking about their experiences as mothers, with Vivian sharing the pain of losing her children. As the sun rose the next morning, Helen took Vivian out for breakfast. By then, with Helen's help, she had come to understand what had happened and was once again stable. According to Zander, "It was really because of the commitment and personal sensitivity of Helen Bader that Vivian was spared an institutionalization that might have lasted a lifetime." Something that did last a lifetime was Helen's ongoing relationship with the Legal Aid Society. Her commitment to the agency's work was so strong that she returned as a volunteer after her field placement ended. "She was willing to drop whatever she was doing to serve a client in need," recalled Zander.

An Independent Spirit: The Quiet, Generous Life of Helen Daniels Bader

LIFE POST DIVORCE

Helen received her MSW on August 15, 1981, a notable achievement and a milestone in her life. The fact that their mother was now a trained social worker made all the sense in the world to David and Daniel. "For years, my mother had heard Dad talk about being discriminated against for being Jewish, had seen the racism in Milwaukee and at Riverside High School, and had advocated for hiring and promoting minorities at Aldrich," recalled David. He also remembers driving down North Lake Drive as a child with Helen, and passing St. Rose Orphanage, run by the Daughters of Charity from 1848 to 1974. "She'd always tell us she wanted to work there someday," he said. "And looking back, I think that was when we began to realize she was interested in social causes. Of course, now we know

According to David and Daniel, social work was their mother's calling. In fact, they vividly recall her telling them that she wanted to work at St. Rose Orphanage on Milwaukee's East Side.

MILWAUKEE COUNTY HISTORICAL SOCIETY

that was her calling." Adds Daniel, "It seemed like a natural fit for her, given how much she really liked working with and helping people."

Meanwhile, Helen's divorce from Alfred had become final in June 1981. Holmquist accompanied her to the final hearing, waiting in her car for Helen until it was over, and then taking her out to lunch. The legal process had gone smoothly, largely because Alfred followed Marvin Klitsner's advice and agreed to divide the couple's assets equally. In fact, the proceedings were so civil that Klitsner represented both Helen and Alfred. Still, the split initially took a heavy emotional toll on Helen, and even Alfred concluded "it must have been, emotionally, unbelievably difficult." He describes the boys as "truly shaken" and initially "quite unbelieving" at news of the divorce, contending they had "no inkling of what was happening between 1975 and 1980, and even thought we were joking." Daniel and David see it differently, not surprising given that Alfred had been talking with them about

Above: *Helen and Alfred's divorce was amicable; in fact, Marvin Klitsner represented both of them in the proceeding, and afterward managed to remain a friend of each.*

Below: *Following Helen's divorce, Rita and Fred Gordy's allegiance went to Helen.*

Isabel for much of that time. "Obviously, we knew there was going to be a divorce," said Daniel.

Most of Helen and Alfred's friends, however, were shocked, finding Alfred's behavior particularly difficult to understand given Helen's years of devotion. "Because she loved him so much and had so much respect for his abilities, she did almost anything he wanted," recalled Ralph Emanuel, stating what many were thinking. "She was selfless, always putting his needs—without resentment—before hers." The Klitsners tried especially hard to remain neutral, and while some in the Jewish community sided with Alfred—by then he had become renowned in the Jewish community for his generosity, business acumen, and scholarship—most of the couple's friends and acquaintances sided strongly with Helen. In fact, many stopped speaking to Alfred.

He recalled Rita and Fred Gordy as "tremendously angry with me," and that Rabbi Shapiro, who had guided Helen during her conversion to Judaism, was the "most hurt and shaken." Helen was especially comforted by the support she received from her sister, Marjorie—who would later describe the divorce as a positive "turning point" for Helen—and

An Independent Spirit: The Quiet, Generous Life of Helen Daniels Bader

brother-in-law, Dick DeVey, who reassured her that the pain she was going through would lead to a happy, independent life.

Back in England, Ralph and Muriel Emanuel were among those surprised and angry. "Up until Alfred rediscovered Isabel, I thought theirs was a normal marriage," said Ralph, noting that Helen and Alfred had celebrated their twenty-fifth anniversary with them in London in 1975. Upon reflection, he recalled, "We made more of a fuss of it than they did." Still, he said, they seemed happy, "as far as we could tell." Although Alfred had mentioned Isabel to Ralph Emanuel over the years, he had always described her as "a friend." Emanuel believed him until, sometime in the late 1970s, he was persuaded by Alfred to visit Isabel in Bexhill-on-Sea. He found her "very emotional," sharing with Emanuel that she was trying to resist Alfred's advances. Later, traveling on business near London, Alfred began baring his soul to Emanuel, who lost his temper over what he saw as his friend's inappropriate and unwarranted behavior. But Ralph Emanuel's anger was mild compared to Muriel's. Intellectual, frank, and highly principled—not to mention a trained writer and editor—Muriel fired off a scathing letter to Alfred, berating him for his despicable conduct. "Few people ever criticized

Muriel Emanuel had known both Alfred and Helen for many years; however, following their divorce, she strongly sided with Helen, refusing to forgive Alfred for the way he had treated her.

Alfred," recalled her husband. "If you did, he never spoke to you again. And certainly no one had ever criticized him the way Muriel did." Alfred never forgave Muriel, whose intelligence and advice he had long respected, and demanded to know why Ralph hadn't stopped her from writing to him. He was so upset he never stayed in the Emanuel home again. Said Ralph, "It's amazing that after that letter my friendship with Alfred survived." Yet Alfred encouraged him to stay in touch with Helen, which he did, continuing to see her whenever he was in Milwaukee.

Over the next twenty years, Alfred kept rehashing the divorce in long letters to and weekly Sunday night phone calls with Emanuel. Finally, in a written response in 2000, Emanuel told his friend, "I do not particularly wish to relive this difficult period. Fortunately, it had a very happy outcome for Isabel and yourself, but I still remain cognizant of the hardships suffered by Danny. Yes, I think you are right that she gained satisfaction from a subsequent, very productive life and being her own person, but the humiliation and hurt remained." He went on to note that he took comfort in knowing that at the time he had been a good friend to Alfred, but added, "Maybe I [would] have acted differently had I not believed your assurance that you did not wish to leave Danny."

Ultimately, Helen rose above the pain of Alfred's betrayal, moving on without resentment.

In the end, as Dick DeVey had predicted, Helen was able to rise above and emerge from the pain Alfred caused her—a feat that did not go unnoticed. Marvin Klitsner credited Helen for the "classy way" she handled the divorce. "She knew and understood that we continued to be friends with her ex-husband, nevertheless she found it in her heart to continue to be close, intimate friends with us," he said. "I don't think she had an ounce of resentment in her system." His daughter, Francie Wolff, noted that although divorce was not unheard of or necessarily frowned upon in the Jewish faith, it was somewhat unusual for a couple to divorce after decades of marriage. "I would say I was proud of her," said Wolff, "for facing a man and saying, 'I want out.'" Rabbi Peter Mehler, rabbi of the synagogue in Sheboygan Helen joined in the early 1980s, noted that unlike the ill will and bitterness that often characterized life after divorce, Helen "wanted to live her life free of anger and animosity and wanted her sons to be engaged by a sense of warmth and love."

Emanuel noted that Helen never felt sorry for herself, and instead found ways to redirect her grief and build a new life. "She may have felt some bitterness, but she never expressed it," he said. "In fact, she never spoke to me about Alfred again." Emanuel is one of many who contend that Helen's marriage had never been easy. "Finding herself on her own for the first time in nearly thirty years," he said, "was likely liberating. I think," he adds, "she was probably much happier."

In early 1981, upon learning that Helen had left Alfred, Isabel burst into tears. "I felt terrible, but what could I do? Danny left him because of me, and there I was telling him I couldn't marry him. When I thought about it, I decided that was kind of dumb." And so, on January 17, 1982, Isabel and her mother, Stella Overton—who was living with her at the time in Bexhill—flew to Milwaukee via Chicago, where Alfred and Daniel met them at O'Hare International Airport. Nine days later, Isabel and Alfred were married in a civil ceremony at the University Club of Milwaukee by Milwaukee County Circuit Court Judge Robert Landry. In attendance were Daniel; David; Stella Overton; Isabel's sister, Marion Overton Dick; and Marvin and Jane Klitsner. Ten years later, Isabel converted to Judaism. Following her conversion ceremony, she and Alfred were remarried in a Jewish wedding.

Because Alfred had failed to tell Helen about the wedding, it was David who broke the news to her shortly before it took place. Isabel, learning that Alfred hadn't been in touch with Helen, tried to make amends, phoning her afterward in what must have been a difficult conversation. The two had met years earlier in England when Isabel was still trying to evade Alfred. Helen, on her own, had come to see Isabel, who

Helen came to see Isabel in England when Isabel was still trying to evade Alfred. She described Helen as "a very lovely person."

confided that she was thinking of moving away. At the time, recalled Isabel, "Danny said to me, 'Don't do that, Isabel. He'll only try to find you.' I thought she was a very lovely person." Years later, Helen and Isabel ran into each other on North Downer Avenue in Milwaukee. Isabel recalled saying, "Good morning," hoping she and Helen would talk and get to know each other a bit. As it turned out, they did not. And Isabel ultimately concluded that "Helen thought Alfred didn't love her. He loved her; he just wasn't in love with her."

Isabel and Alfred would live for nearly thirty years in the Shepard Avenue house (albeit, at Isabel's insistence, with an updated kitchen), and travel extensively together abroad on business and for pleasure. Although Isabel's life, like Helen's, revolved around Alfred, he saw her as more of an advisor than he had Helen. Recalled Ralph Emanuel, "Where Danny had been accepting of everything, Isabel not only knew what she wanted, but also went after it. And Alfred listened to her." Emanuel marvels at the fact that Alfred, despite his many idiosyncrasies, was blessed with two marriages of more than thirty years each to two women who loved him unequivocally. "Life is certainly peculiar sometimes—and not always as planned," he said.

Helen urged David and Daniel not to blame Isabel for their parents' divorce, and they went on to have a positive relationship with their father's second wife. Pictured in Berton-on-Trent, England, the summer after Isabel and Alfred's wedding are (front row, left to right) Daniel, David, and Isabel; (back row, left to right) Alfred's nephew Robert Edge, his brother-in-law Cyril Edge, Alfred, and his sister, Marion Edge.

Neither Daniel nor David recalled ever blaming Isabel for the divorce, and ultimately—largely due to their mother's encouragement—both developed good relationships with her. Any anger they harbored was with their father during the years preceding the divorce, when his unwillingness to give Isabel up had inflicted so much misery on their mother and filled their home with stress and unhappiness. Alfred confessed to taking some comfort in the fact that even after their divorce he tried to be helpful to Helen. He offered advice, for example, when she was audited by the Internal Revenue Service, pointing out to the auditor that she had actually overpaid in a number of areas and was in fact entitled to a small refund. Years later, he would claim that "as marriages go, between 1952 and 1975, it was better than most," something he attributed to "Danny's love, patience, and hard work." And what if he could live his life over? Would he marry Helen? "If I didn't, there would be no Daniel or David, so the answer must be, yes." Still, he added, "On my day of judgment, I'm sure God will ask me how could I treat Danny like this?"

IS THIS OVERLOOKING A
60'-STRETCH OF GRAVEL ROOF

TOO
REMOTE PHYSICALLY AND
PERCEPTUALLY, ALSO ORGANIZAT
FROM THE UNIT.

AOM.+S

IT SEEMS THAT A CONT
POINT IN THIS ZONE WI
SERVE TO SEPARATE EAS
SERVICES, FROM WEST =
ACTUAL UNITS.

IF MOVED/ELIMINATED
THE CONNECTION BETW
UNITS CAN BE MORE
"PERMEABLE".

REVIEW THE NEED FOR
THIS KIND OF SPACE;
(HOW ABOUT REMOTE TV.
OBSERVATION?)

TYPICAL ROOM:
(OOR) ORGANIZATION

Helen _____ Center.   Scheme 3-A (15

MAIN FLOOR: ENTRY SEQUENCE: COMPLICATED

√ OVERAL ORGANIZATION OF PUBLIC SPACES: GOOD BASIC PLAN; SPECIFIC
RESOLUTION SHOULD PROVIDE MORE AND SIMPLER DEFINITION OF SPACES

CHAPTER EIGHT

A NEW LIFE

Following graduation, and armed with a reference from Corré, Helen applied for a job at the Milwaukee Jewish Home, where she was hired and assigned to work as the social worker for the dementia patients living on the fourth floor. Corré was delighted, gratified that the plan she had proposed to Helen just two years earlier had been put into place.

The Milwaukee Jewish Home had been established in 1906 as Beth Moshav Zekanium, or Home for the Aged. Designed to serve elderly Jewish Milwaukeeans in need, it was located in a small house on Galena Street on the city's North Side. In 1930, with the home unable to meet the community's needs, it moved farther west to a new, larger facility on North Fiftieth Street. According to the *Wisconsin Jewish Chronicle*, the $90,000 building incorporated "the very latest and most modern ideas in a home for the aged, and every possible facility for the care and comfort of the old folk has been provided for." That included private rooms for up to fifty-two residents, a yard with a garden and walkways, a synagogue–auditorium, a dining room, sun parlors, and an infirmary. In 1939, the home's name was changed to Jewish Home for the Aged, and ten years later its capacity was doubled with the construction of an addition on adjacent land; it would be expanded once again in 1956.

Over the years, as eldercare models evolved, the home's mission expanded. Psychiatric services, physical and occupational therapy programs, and recreational and social activities were introduced as a way of not only

Opposite background: *Helen dreamed of building a state-of-the-art home for the elderly, and she worked with local architects and national experts in the field on early plans for such a facility.* OVATION JEWISH HOME

Opposite foreground: *By the mid-1980s, Helen was spending as much time as possible at her cottage on the Lake Michigan shore in Sheboygan.*

Above: *The origins of the Milwaukee Jewish Home, where Helen worked as a social worker, can be traced to a small house on the city's North Side that opened in 1906 as Beth Moshav Zekanium, also known as the Home for the Aged.* OVATION JEWISH HOME

Home for Aged Supplement

The Wisconsin Jewish Chronicle
A Weekly Paper for the Jewish Home

MILWAUKEE, WIS., SEPT. 6, 1929

vol. 23 — No. 1

Cornerstone Ceremonies Sunday, Sept. 8

-HOME OF THE AGED JEWS-

providing custodial care, but also improving residents' quality of life. But by the late 1960s, in response to changing demographics, medical advances, and new trends in senior living, it had become clear that the home needed to move again. The new site: Milwaukee's East Side, on land overlooking Lake Michigan and adjacent to what was then the Jewish Community Center at 1414 N. Prospect

HOME FOR AGED JEWS

Above and right: *In 1930, the Home for the Aged moved to a much larger building on the city's West Side.*
OVATION JEWISH HOME

Below: *And in 1973—by then known as the Milwaukee Jewish Home—the facility moved to its present site on North Prospect Avenue.*
OVATION JEWISH HOME

An Independent Spirit: The Quiet, Generous Life of Helen Daniels Bader

Ave. Opened in 1973 with 115 residents, the $2 million facility—renamed the Milwaukee Jewish Home—soon expanded to serve 200 people.

Helen threw herself into her new career, quickly establishing rapport with each of the dementia patients assigned to the home's fourth floor. Her immediate goal, said Corré, was to make sure everyone's needs were met, even if that meant meeting those needs herself. It wasn't unusual, for instance, for Helen to take it upon herself to get a resident's eyeglasses repaired or take home someone's ironing. "It drove us all nuts," Daniel Bader told the *Milwaukee Journal* in 1994, "how she'd always have to fix all those little things, and run all those errands." Yet both David and Daniel were aware that the residents saw their mother as more than a caretaker, and that their bonds with her ran deep. "It was obvious they all had these great relationships with her," said David. Helen's sister, Marjorie, tells the story of the time Helen took three residents with her to a concert at the Pabst Theater in downtown Milwaukee. On the way, her car hit a pothole, abruptly jostling her passengers in the back seat, and sending one of the women's wigs flying. Helen's initial worries that the woman would be upset evaporated when she and her friends burst out laughing, totally comfortable in Helen's company. According to Marjorie, that's how Helen related to the residents: in small, personal episodes. Corré saw Helen's

Some of Helen's most fulfilling years were those she spent as a professional social worker.

level of commitment and dedication to the residents as exemplary. "She wanted to make sure they were taken care of with a lot of compassion, love, and patience," she said.

Before long, Helen was named the home's assistant director of social services and its education coordinator. Clearly ahead of her time, Helen soon realized that she—and the Jewish Home—needed to do more for its dementia patients, and approached Corré about the possibility of attending a conference in Florida on dementia, the term used to describe the loss of mental function common in many older adults. Told the home didn't have the money to send Helen to Florida, Helen assured Corré that was "not a problem." At the conference, Helen first learned about Alzheimer's disease, which by 1976 had been recognized as the most common form of dementia.

It was an autopsy of a female patient that led German physician Alois Alzheimer to link her short-term memory loss to the dramatic and abnormal changes he observed in her brain.

WIKIMEDIA

It was in 1906 that Alois Alzheimer, a German physician, linked a fifty-one-year-old female patient's profound short-term memory loss and deteriorating psychological condition to the dramatic and abnormal changes he observed in her brain during autopsy. Four years later, in recognition of his discovery, the condition was named after Alzheimer. With the invention of the electron microscope in 1931, and the development of a scale for assessing brain function in 1968, scientists began correlating the degree of individuals' cognitive impairment with

An Independent Spirit: The Quiet, Generous Life of Helen Daniels Bader

the volume of damaged brain tissue, which led to greater understanding of the disease.

In response to growing awareness of the disease, the Alzheimer's Association was established in 1980, and its Southeastern Wisconsin Chapter, in 1981. Yet it would be another eight years before the chapter would hold its first Memory Walk to help promote widespread understanding of the disease and raise funds for related research. Meanwhile, it was still common practice to label older adults dealing with the complications of old age as "senile," whether their problems were related to physical infirmities or declining mental acuity. Typically, many of those in nursing homes and other facilities for the aged received little more than custodial care, often confined all day to wheelchairs that lined the hallways—reminiscent of what Corré had witnessed two decades earlier in Philadelphia.

Up through the 1980s, it was not uncommon for elderly nursing home residents to receive little more than custodial care.
ALAMY

Helen found the practice, which was especially difficult for dementia patients to bear, unacceptable. Based on what she had learned in school, as well as her own intuition, she believed that those struggling with profound memory loss or other mental disorders needed and would benefit from specialized programs. In fact, she had wondered during her earlier visits to Steffie Zupnik why her friend wasn't getting the chance to participate in more activities. Helen was inspired by what she was learning about

Alzheimer's—often on vacation days spent at national conferences. In San Francisco in 1985, she attended one titled "Alzheimer's Disease: A Mystery Unravelling," where she attended sessions on the efficacy of cognitive training techniques for Alzheimer patients, recommended strategies for Alzheimer caregivers, and innovations in Alzheimer care units. Back home, she sponsored a visit to the Jewish Home by one of the conference speakers, Rita Nacken Gugel, a national consultant on the disease. In a letter to Gugel setting up the visit, Helen requested that she "assess our program in general and review the design of the individual care plans in particular, and then make recommendations." Corré described the outcome of that visit as the impetus for a major dementia care initiative at the Jewish Home characterized by a series of best practices such as personalized activities and music and art therapy classes. David Bader saw the project as a creative outlet for his mother, empowering and adding meaning to her life.

Meanwhile, Helen was putting in place a number of her own ideas about how to make the home's dementia residents less anxious and more comfortable, and their lives more enjoyable. One initiative begun by Helen was the Resident of the Week program, which sought to boost the self-esteem of the dementia patients on the fourth floor. As she explained

Above: *Helen attended this conference, later arranging for one of its speakers to visit the Milwaukee Jewish Home and review its programs.*

Right: *Music therapy, introduced at the Milwaukee Jewish Home during Helen's tenure, has become one of its most popular and successful programs.*

OVATION JEWISH HOME

An Independent Spirit: The Quiet, Generous Life of Helen Daniels Bader

in a report about the program, "characteristics such as low morale, feelings of insignificance, docility, withdrawal, and negative self-image are common among this nursing home population." What's more, she noted that fourth-floor residents often felt "looked down upon" by those residing on lower floors who were "higher functioning and more cognitively alert."

Based on a similar initiative underway in a Washington, DC nursing home unit, the Jewish Home's Resident of the Week program celebrated the past accomplishments of the fourth-floor residents and acknowledged the contributions each brought to their living unit at a party featuring a photo display and biographical presentation by a social worker. "The featured resident gives little bits of information about his or her past, which adds a delightful touch to the biographical sketch reading," wrote Helen. "Staff members observe confused, disoriented residents become more alert when speaking about past experiences." Again, Helen was ahead of her time: guided conversations with dementia patients that focus on their long-term memories has been shown to be an effective way to boost their self-esteem.

It was about this time that on a lark Helen took advantage of an offer from the local Arthur Murray Dance Studio for a free ballroom dancing lesson. "She'd always loved dancing, and was good at it," recalled Fred Gordy. "And after that free lesson she was hooked." She signed up for

Helen took up ballroom dancing in her fifties, and went on to win awards at regional dance competitions.

more lessons and private coaching, becoming so accomplished that she represented the studio at regional contests and came home with awards, including a first-place trophy for her freestyle cha-cha in 1987. Rita Gordy recalled Helen coming back from the competitions and happily sharing her photos. The appeal was obvious: a temporary escape from the pressures of the day, not to mention a fun way to exercise—to music.

Although dance and movement therapy is now widely recognized as an effective component of Alzheimer's treatment, that wasn't the case in the 1980s when Helen began donning costumes, performing for residents, and then drawing them onto the dance floor with her. Rabbi Peter Mehler, of Beth El Congregation in Sheboygan, recalled that the first time he saw Helen she was dancing with an Alzheimer's patient who was shuffling along with her. "He couldn't dance," Mehler recalled, "but his appearance made it very clear that dancing with Helen Bader was giving him a few moments of comfort and I was very touched. I don't think that's something that anybody can do, and it's certainly not something that can be done as graciously as she did it."

er A Two-Year Wait . . .

Beth El Gets A New Rabbi

Rabbi Peter J. Mehler of Congregation Beth El

Rabbi Peter Mehler became head of Beth El Congregation in Sheboygan in 1984. He would become a friend of Helen's, whom he saw for the first time when she was dancing with a resident at the Milwaukee Jewish Home.
SHEBOYGAN PRESS

Another time, Mehler and an anxious congregant who was moving into the Jewish Home encountered Helen dancing with a group of residents. She reportedly pulled the man into the group and his fears vanished.

But Helen didn't need to be on the dance floor to connect with the home's Alzheimer's patients, many of whom became increasingly agitated and anxious as the disease progressed. Sometimes, patiently sitting down and talking to them was just as effective. Mehler found that particularly admirable, given the devastating effects of Alzheimer's—personality changes, mood swings, and repetitive behavior and speech—that prove especially frustrating to caretakers. "To do that takes a very special kind of person," he said. Helen also had the ability to connect in ways that were

An Independent Spirit: The Quiet, Generous Life of Helen Daniels Bader

helpful to the residents' children—most often their adult daughters—whose distress, in some cases, translated into behavior that was even more challenging than that of their parents. Rita Gordy was well aware of Helen's knack for effectively engaging and empathizing with others. "When she was talking to you, you felt she had all the time in the world to sit down and listen to what you had to say. She was just as wonderful with the patients and their families . . . and her sense of empathy . . . that was one of the reasons she was good at her work."

Helen's willingness to devote herself to some of society's most vulnerable and take steps to do something about their situation can be traced back to her youth in Aberdeen during the depths of the Great Depression. She never forgot her father's middle-of-the-night deliveries to Brown County's drought-ravished farms, or his willingness to fill the prescriptions of local American Indians who'd show up at the back door of Daniels Drugs unable to pay for their medication.

Decades later, Helen found herself in a position to respond to the needs of another group marginalized by society. Corré speculated that the effort Helen made throughout her life to overcome her own shyness helped her identify with those facing hardship. "I don't think she had an easy time herself, not because she was not talented, but because she was so shy," she said. "And I think she wanted to make sure that anyone [experiencing] any kind of difficulty or problem would be taken care of with a lot of compassion and a lot of love and a lot of patience." In return, just as Corré had predicted, Helen was profoundly changed—and her life deeply enriched—by the years she spent working at the Jewish Home. Corré described Helen's evolution as a "blooming flower" whose "beautiful, sterling qualities—her warmth, understanding, and empathy—emerged cautiously over time."

During the 1980s, Helen regularly visited her mother, Jessie, who had moved to Fayetteville, New York, following Lloyd Daniels's death in 1978, to live with the DeVeys. By all accounts, Helen's deep concern for society's most vulnerable citizens could be traced, in large part, to her experiences growing up in Aberdeen during the Great Depression. From her father came her compassion; from her mother, her resilience.

According to Marvin Klitsner, there wasn't any specific reason that Helen adopted Alzheimer's disease as the cause that would shape the last years of her life. "It was just part of her wanting to help people who were in great difficulty," he said. "She saw what a struggle it was and knew they needed better care." Klitsner and his daughter Francie Wolff saw firsthand what a difference Helen could make when his mother-in-law—her grandmother—moved to the Jewish Home and came to treasure Helen as both a friend and social worker. They describe Helen's work with the aged as "inspirational," informed by her kindness, patience, and warmth. Deirdre Britt sees her Aunt Helen's interest in and work on behalf of Alzheimer's patients as "revolutionary," coming as it did at a time when few others were so inclined. "She was a pioneer, someone who simply saw this group of people who were confused and distressed and who weren't getting the help they needed. And she became their champion."

Between 1981 and 1989, Helen not only improved the quality of life for hundreds of Alzheimer's patients at the Jewish Home, but also laid the groundwork for putting in place research-based ways to address the challenges of Alzheimer's care. Despite her shyness, Helen's independent spirit took over, making her more comfortable speaking out about her concerns, challenging the status quo, and suggesting alternative approaches to age-old problems. One area of concern was the physical layout of the home, still a beautiful building, but one designed to deliver relatively short-term nursing home care. Recalled Corré, "It was a question of how to serve this group of people going through a long, difficult journey who seem to be lost in a building that was inappropriate for their needs." That, in fact, was one of Helen's greatest frustrations: making the building work for Alzheimer's patients. By 1986, as the home celebrated its eightieth anniversary—and much to Helen's delight—officials had begun contemplating a separate care center for Alzheimer's patients. David Bader, at the time a graduate student in architecture at UWM, arranged for Helen to meet with Uriel Cohen and Gerald D. Weisman, professors at its School of Architecture & Urban Planning who were researching how best to design living units for dementia patients. She envisioned a state-of-the-art facility designed exclusively for those with Alzheimer's, many of whom—despite being unable to live independently—she believed would benefit from remaining active and engaged. Helen had written about one of her ideas in a graduate school paper: the notion—now universally accepted but at the time untested—that such a facility should have two wings: one for those in the early stages of Alzheimer's and another for those in the later throes of the disease.

That is one of the design principles explored in *Holding on to Home: Designing Environments for People with Dementia* co-authored by Cohen and Weisman and published in 1991. "Facilities for people with dementia must respond to both major variations in needs across individuals and variations within individuals over time," they write, advocating for a "responsive continuum of care." Other design principles they endorsed included small-scale living units that make group living more homelike and less overwhelming, and the use of existing community resources to supplement those offered on-site.

Helen supported the work of UWM Professors Uriel Cohen and Gerald D. Weisman, who incorporated into their architectural designs research-based concepts aimed at improving facilities for dementia patients.

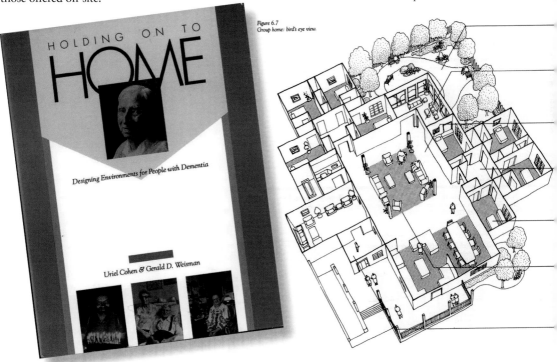

Figure 6.7
Group home: bird's eye view.

SHEBOYGAN LIFE

By the time Helen went to work at the Milwaukee Jewish Home, she was dividing her time between her Milwaukee apartment and her Oostburg cottage. Although the apartment was conveniently close to work, Helen was growing increasingly nervous about the building's parking lot, which was poorly lit at night. When Corré urged her to move into the fifteen-story,

In the mid-1980s, Helen moved to the Newport apartment building where her friend and colleague Nita Corré lived. Corré convinced Helen to make the move, in part, by telling her that if they were neighbors, they would have more opportunities to talk about the future of the Milwaukee Jewish Home.

Russell Barr Williamson-designed Newport apartment building at 1610 N. Prospect Ave. where she lived, Helen first protested that it was "too fancy." In the end, Corré prevailed, having assured Helen that if the Newport wasn't too fancy for her, it wasn't too fancy for Helen. Yet the argument that sealed the deal was Corré's pronouncement that if she and Helen lived in the same building, they'd have even more opportunity to discuss the long-term future of the Jewish Home. Once again, Helen took Corré's advice, moving to the Newport and calling on David to help her remodel her unit. Soon thereafter, she seized on exactly the kind of opportunity Corré had promised. It was a Sunday afternoon and Helen proposed that Corré join her on a shopping trip to Marshall Field's on Milwaukee's West Side to buy lamps for her new apartment. "No sooner had we left the parking lot," recalled Corré, "than she said, 'Now, let's talk about the Jewish Home.'" In fact, nearly every time the two got together, after chatting for a while about their children or a favorite movie, Helen brought the conversation back to how best to serve the Jewish Home's dementia patients. "And we would dream," said Corré, "about a beautiful place designed for [them], a place where the staff would be specially trained."

Helen rented the Oostburg cottage, which was right on Lake Michigan, for about a year before buying her own property on Evergreen Road in Sheboygan's Black River neighborhood. Located a short walk through the woods from the lake, it was one of two small, side-by-side cottages that had been built decades earlier for a pair of sisters. Helen enlarged and renovated the place, adding a deck on which she loved to sit, watch the lake, and think about her day. She used the property, which she called her "doll's house," as a getaway destination. To be sure, Helen loved her work at the Jewish Home. But it was physically challenging and emotionally draining. At the lake, most every weekend year-round and for longer stretches during the summer, she recharged. And, recalled Marjorie, it was the perfect place to blow off steam. "When she got fed up, which she did, she'd bolt," recalled Marjorie. "And she'd bolt out to her Sheboygan house and get her music, and her view, and her roses, and her dog, and put on her overalls and go for a walk, and just relax completely before she'd take on the next phase of whatever she had planned. That's how she coped."

David and Daniel visited whenever they were in town, beginning in their late teens. Daniel remembers Helen getting up early while he and his brother slept in, with all of them then heading off together to go out for lunch or dinner, just the way they had growing up when Alfred was out of town on business. The Gordys visited as well, often on their way to or from Green Bay to spend time with Fred's parents. Their daughter, Molly Gordy Drew, recalled her father's amazement—and delight—when he came upon a Rembrandt etching hanging in the bathroom, "where the humidity was ideal." Helen would also invite other friends up, sometimes suggesting, "Let's go play golf," despite the fact that she considered herself a "terrible golfer." Recalled Marjorie, "They go, play three holes or so, and have some laughs."

Above: *The cottage Helen bought on Evergreen Road in Sheboygan was located just a short walk through the woods from Lake Michigan. According to Helen's sister, Marjorie, spending time at the cottage was the perfect antidote to the emotionally draining aspects of Helen's job.*

Below: *David, along with his brother Daniel, visited his mother at her Sheboygan cottage whenever he could.*

But Helen wasn't one to spend all her free time golfing or sitting on the deck looking out over Lake Michigan. She worked with Corré to plan an annual party at her lake house for her Jewish Home colleagues—everyone from nursing assistants to administrators. Helen knew better than anyone how difficult it was to work with dementia patients, and believed it was important to build up the emotional resources of her fellow workers so they'd be able to do their jobs well. The parties—much anticipated and popular events—were a way for her to acknowledge their hard work, and say, "Hey, we're a team, in this together, both inside and outside the home."

Helen regularly invited her former Aldrich and Milwaukee Jewish Home coworkers to her cottage on Lake Michigan. Here she is pictured with (left to right) Lorraine Hill and Stella Ward, longtime Aldrich employees.

Helen also became deeply engaged in the community, particularly through Mehler's Beth El Congregation, where she attended services beginning in 1984. Mehler, who like all Helen's other close friends knew her as Danny, found her unassuming and very down-to-earth. Despite her wealth and sophisticated appreciation of theater, classical music, and visual arts, she drove a two-year-old Oldsmobile Cutlass and enthusiastically supported Sheboygan's amateur theatrical productions, musical events, and art shows. At the time, Mehler was trying to stabilize the area's Jewish community, which was in decline and mostly made up of older adults. His plan, which Helen helped fund and put in place, was to bring congregants together at weekly free lunches following Saturday services to get to know each other, talk, and perhaps spend the afternoon together. Helen attended regularly, making new friends and organizing many such outings.

Helen reserved some of her time in Sheboygan to develop a new skill: playing the flamenco guitar. She began taking lessons from Peter Baime at the Wisconsin Conservatory of Music in Milwaukee in January 1986,

An Independent Spirit: The Quiet, Generous Life of Helen Daniels Bader

telling Baime she had always wanted to play the guitar, and had become increasingly interested in the musical rhythms she had been introduced to in her Latin dance classes. "It's going to be now or never," she added. Baime found Helen an excellent student: Given her extensive musical background, decades of experience playing the violin, and a passion for her new endeavor that translated into dedicated practice time, Helen made good progress, mastering enough flamenco technique within several months to begin playing traditional dance music in the *farruca* and *verdiales* styles.

Dick DeVey turned out to be right: Helen's post-divorce life was fulfilling and fun, and the years she spent working at the Jewish Home and relaxing in Sheboygan were some of the best of her life. Her work was important and fulfilling. She reconnected with old friends and made new ones. She took long walks in the woods, danced, and learned to play the guitar. And she took in quintessential Wisconsin events such as the state fair and Summerfest. Helen even found time to do a bit of dating after initially asking Rita Gordy if she should accept an invitation that she had received from a man to go out for coffee. Rita's advice: "It's a cup of coffee! Go and see how it turns out." In the end, Helen developed a platonic relationship with a man who lived in the Sheboygan area with whom she went antiquing and out for dinner, and an even closer bond with a cousin of Rita's, a widower living in Chicago. "She had some fantastic years at the end of her life," said David. One of his best memories: meeting up regularly with his mother while he was in graduate school at UWM, often over a steak dinner or glass of Scotch. Noted David, "She actually had quite an amazing palate."

Helen took flamenco guitar lessons at the Wisconsin Conservatory of Music from Peter Baime, who found her an excellent student—in part because of her background as a violinist.

PETER BAIME

SELF-DISCOVERY

A paper Helen wrote in late 1980 while she was in graduate school provides a window into the thinking she was doing about the next—and what would be the last—stage of her life. Exploring the character of Barbara Lavette in Howard Fast's 1978 novel *Second Generation,* she focuses on how one navigates the process of self-actualization as described by psychologist Abraham Maslow. The novel is set mostly in San Francisco in the 1930s, where Lavette, the young adult daughter of a once-wealthy San Francisco businessman, struggles to resist the prevailing social and cultural forces of the day in order to embrace the creative life. Ultimately, Barbara gives away virtually all of her worldly goods and directs her lawyer to set up a charitable foundation as a vehicle for distributing her $14 million inheritance. She then devotes the next stage of her life to the process of self-discovery, something she achieves by writing a novel. In the conclusion to the paper, Helen noted that Lavette becomes an example of the "self-actualizing, creative" individual Maslow describes as "independent, autonomous, and self-directed" as well as "very tolerant and accepting of everyone, [displaying] no racial, religious, or social prejudice."

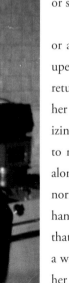

While a graduate student, Helen embarked upon a process of self-discovery that included serious reflection on how best to dispose of her personal fortune.

Did Helen see herself in the character of Barbara Lavette or aspire to be like her? Possibly. Like Barbara, Helen had upended her life. She had left an unfulfilling marriage, returned to school, and was embarking on a new career. In her paper, Helen noted Maslow's point that "the self-actualizing person is extremely healthy and independent . . . free to resist social and cultural pressures to think and behave along certain lines. They do not openly rebel against cultural norms or deliberately flaunt social codes, but on the other hand, they are governed by their own inner nature, not that of [the] culture." Such a message rang true to Helen, a woman who although disinclined to "openly rebel," lived her life according to a set of firmly held inner convictions.

Helen may also have been intrigued by the steps Barbara took, in the process of becoming self-actualized, to divest herself of her fortune. When it came to philanthropy, Helen and Alfred had long, and generously, supported many local causes—religious, cultural, and social. They enjoyed being in a position to give, and saw their philanthropy as both a way to make a difference and as one of the rewards of all the effort they had put into building Aldrich. After their divorce, Helen maintained the practice, using her own funds. In some cases, such as when she and her coworkers were solicited by Milwaukee Community Chest or United Way campaigns, she did so openly, making donations more or less in line with those of colleagues. But because Helen didn't want to find herself in the public eye, much less become known as a rich person, whenever she was inclined to give more substantial gifts she did so anonymously. According to Marvin Klitsner, this sometimes meant she made two donations to the same organization.

EARLY PHILANTHROPY

It was Klitsner who advised Helen on her private philanthropy, setting up a fund in her name at the Jewish Community Foundation in the early to mid-1980s through which many of her larger, anonymous donations were made. He noted that Helen wasn't one to randomly give away money. She targeted her donations to organizations and agencies with good track records whose work she believed in, occasionally sitting down to consult with their representatives on new programs or improvements to those already in place. In a letter to the foundation in January 1986, Klitsner noted that Helen planned to make donations totaling $174,500 over the course of the year. Local recipients, he said, would include the Milwaukee Jewish Federation, the Legal Aid Society of Milwaukee, the United Way, the United Performing Arts Center, the Wisconsin Conservatory of Music, and the Milwaukee Symphony Orchestra, as well as a number of smaller agencies and programs working on behalf of needy children, the handicapped, and the disadvantaged. She established a scholarship in the memory of her close college friend Jerline E. Walfoort at Lawrence

Right up until the end of their marriage, Helen and Alfred supported many religious, cultural, and local causes. Helen would continue that practice for the rest of her life. Helen's philanthropy was rooted in issues that touched her heart, leading her to search for ways, both personally and financially, to solve problems.

University designed to recognize and encourage a junior or senior majoring in English, and made a contribution to what was by then South Dakota State University in memory of her father. She also funded the creation of an Alzheimer's unit in a long-term care facility in Israel.

Helen had great respect for the work of the Legal Aid Society, and became one of the organization's most generous benefactors. Director Tom Zander, in turn, was touched by Helen's genuine compassion for the agency's clients.

Helen's support for the work of the Legal Aid Society of Milwaukee was particularly strong; in fact, she became the organization's most generous donor during the mid-to-late 1980s. Her interest in the organization—which grew out of and was informed by her fieldwork there during graduate school and subsequent volunteer work—evolved into a continuing relationship with the agency and Thomas Zander, its executive director. Over lunches at the Jewish Community Center that sometimes included David and Daniel, Helen and Zander would socialize a bit and then get down to business, talking about the work of the Legal Aid Society. One tangible outcome of those conversations: a fund earmarked for impoverished women embroiled in divorce or child custody cases who needed legal support. Helen also used her lunches with Zander to pick Zander's brain about the needs of the Milwaukee community or seek out his assessment of various agencies and nonprofits. "I felt privileged to sort of be her consultant," he recalled.

Like Klitsner, Zander recognized that Helen's approach to philanthropy encompassed more than merely identifying a problem and making a dona-tion in hopes of solving it. He described Helen as the rare individual not only willing to write Legal Aid a check, but also interested in working directly with its clients. Mehler noted that Helen's philan-thropy began with an issue "touching her heart," which in turn led to finding ways, both personal and financial, to deal with it. Often, that meant using Mehler as the conduit through which she reached out to individuals struggling with illness, economic hardship, or other personal problems, helping them, he said, "in a very considerable way." He found Helen was unique in that despite her wealth, she never forgot where she came from—

Helen's philanthropy was rooted in issues that touched her heart, leading her to search for ways, both personally and financially, to solve problems.

small-town America in the heart of farm country populated with vulnerable people. To be sure, during the prime of her life she had grown wealthy, trav-eled extensively, and immersed herself in the arts. Yet she had also, at times, found it difficult to deal with her wealth, which Mehler described as both a blessing and a curse. "The blessing is that you have some financial comfort," he said. The curse: "That it can change who you are." Still, Mehler insisted that in Helen's case that hadn't happened. "Not in the least," he said, noting the unpretentious, simple lifestyle Helen had embraced. Her gift, he said, was her sensitivity to her community's most vulnerable. Her goal: "to show them that there [were] people out in the world who still cared about who they are and where they're going with their lives."

CHAPTER NINE

AN INSURMOUNTABLE CHALLENGE

L ike Barbara Lavette, Helen also took on new challenges later in life. She stepped out of her comfort zone, for example, to serve as a member of Lawrence University's Board of Trustees from 1986 to 1989, a time when it was still rare for women to serve in such a capacity. And in June 1987, she co-chaired the Shapiro Jubilee Dinner held at the Jewish Community Center in honor of the fiftieth wedding anniversary of Rabbi David Shapiro and his wife, Etta, and Shapiro's fiftieth year in the rabbinate. Helen opened the event, welcoming five hundred attendees to the party, which included a pre-dinner concert and speeches from Jewish leaders and several of Shapiro's students. Over the years, Helen remained close to Shapiro, who had overseen her conversion to Judaism in 1950, and their friendship continued after her divorce. Four years before the dinner, Shapiro had suffered a severe stroke that left him able to read and under-stand what people said to him, but unable to speak or write. Nevertheless, he continued to teach a weekly religion class for several more years. In March 1989, he and Etta moved to Israel, where one of their daughters was living with her family. He died there later that year.

DEVASTATING NEWS

It was shortly after returning home from a Mexican vacation in late 1987 feeling ill that Helen was diagnosed with advanced ovarian cancer. It was

Opposite background: *The Helen Bader Foundation, Inc. was a strong supporter of the University of Wisconsin-Milwaukee's Peck School of the Arts. The concert hall at its Helene Zelazo Center is named in honor of Helen.*
UWM PHOTO SERVICES-DEREK RICKERT

Opposite foreground: *Even as her health began to fail in the last two years of her life, Helen was determined to keep up her busy, active lifestyle.*

Above: *In June 1987, Helen co-chaired the Shapiro Jubilee Dinner.*

Upon receiving a diagnosis of ovarian cancer in 1987, Helen turned to religion for comfort, sharing the news with Rabbi Peter Mehler of Beth El Congregation in Sheboygan. Mehler found Helen frightened, but also courageous.

a shocking blow to someone only sixty years old with such an active life and so many plans for the future. Turning to her religion as a source of comfort, she shared her diagnosis with Rabbi Peter Mehler, prompting a number of conversations on Judaism's moral code regarding end-of-life issues. (She also revisited her Christian Science roots, rereading Mary Baker Eddy's classic text, *Science and Health with Key to the Scriptures*.) Helen grew closer to Mehler—who, in addition to having been ordained a rabbi, also worked as a therapist specializing in the area of life-threatening diseases—and the two began meeting regularly. "She was very frightened by the cancer, as most people are, and which is reasonable," he recalled. "But she was courageous as well."

For a time, Helen also pondered the source of her cancer, taking particular interest in a study by psychologists at Johns Hopkins University that investigated the extent to which one's emotions, personality traits, and ability to handle stress correlated with the disease. The study's findings, described in a newspaper article Helen clipped and saved, were said to "add compelling evidence of the cancerous danger of repressed emotions. . . ." The researchers, although clarifying that the study's results were not definitive, went on to note that one trait common to those who developed cancer was "a tendency to hide real feelings, particularly negative ones." But what no doubt also caught Helen's attention was a quote from a cancer patient who was convinced of the link between her cancer and her inability to share her feelings with others. "I remember smiling my way through a divorce," she said. "I couldn't express my real feelings to anyone." In the end, she concluded that "Staying in a situation where there is chronic stress—like my unhappy marriage—is very weakening to the immune system."

Clearly, Helen could relate. And if there was little she could do about the decades of stress her own marriage had generated, she did take the advice of a surgeon quoted in the same newspaper article who urged his cancer patients to become fighters willing to express their needs rather than victims who accepted their fate. Determined to recover, Helen underwent surgery and two rounds of debilitating chemotherapy, telling Klitsner, "I'm not going to quit in my sixties."

Helen also took advice from Mehler, who convinced her not to let cancer manage her day-to-day life. She kept working as much as possible—at first, her only concession to her illness came in the form of longer lunch hours during which she napped. Later, in pain and exhausted, she still managed to walk to the Jewish Home to meet and dance with the residents. "Sometimes I really thought she was going to fall down," said Corré. "But she made it—she danced, and she smiled."

Helen also continued to focus on the future. One of the most vivid memories Corré had of Helen in her later years is of encountering her friend one evening in the lobby of the Newport, as Helen waited for the Gordys to pick her up for dinner. "My body's dying," she told Corré, "but my brain is not." She went on to explain to Corré that she had given money to support the work of Uriel Cohen and Gerald D. Weisman at UWM on designing living units for Alzheimer's patients, and that it remained her dream to see such a facility built. Meanwhile, Helen continued her practice of quietly coming to the rescue of individuals in need. One was a Milwaukee woman who had been honored by the mayor for the after-school program she was operating out of her home in the central city. When the *Milwaukee Sentinel* reported that the woman was unable to pay her rent, putting the program in jeopardy, Helen called Rita Gordy to say she was considering sending the woman a check. What did Rita think? Rita pointed out the program had already been vetted by the mayor, which was all the encouragement Helen needed to send a check covering the woman's rent for the next six months.

On a lighter note, Helen continued dancing, competing into the fall of 1988, and kept up with her guitar lessons. At one point, she disclosed to Peter Baime, her guitar instructor, that she was having health issues and wasn't sure how much longer she'd be able to continue. But she told him she

Despite her illness, Helen continued to dance—both in ballroom dancing competitions and with residents of the Milwaukee Jewish Home, the latter a practice that would be adopted by other of the home's staff members.
OVATION JEWISH HOME

was still taking her guitar with her to Sheboygan and was practicing as much as she could. It was all part of an effort to distract herself from the disease. "So, although the cancer frightened her, she didn't allow herself to be down for long," said Mehler. "She was one of those people who maximized her life in the face of terminal illness. And she did an incredibly good job of it."

A SUPPORTIVE NETWORK

Helen's friendship with the Gordys, which had deepened after her divorce, became an even greater comfort during her illness. Rita accompanied Helen to doctor appointments and to the hospital once every three weeks for aggressive chemotherapy treatments, each of which lasted several days and left Helen too weak to push the call button for the nurse. At their urging, Helen moved in with Rita and Fred for a time following her surgery and in between the chemotherapy sessions. There was some good news: the chemo put Helen into remission for almost six months, a period of time when she spent her days back at her apartment among her own things before returning to Rita and Fred's home for dinner and to spend the night.

The Gordys treasured the time they spent with Helen, describing their relationship as "natural, pleasant, and honest." Fred recalled the

Fred and Rita Gordy cared for Helen after her cancer surgery and during two rounds of chemotherapy. They would again be at her side as she neared death.

An Independent Spirit: The Quiet, Generous Life of Helen Daniels Bader

comfortable, companionable way he, Rita, and Helen would sit down at the breakfast table sharing the Sunday papers. He never forgot one Sunday morning when Helen looked across at him, and "with this little twinkle in her eye," told him she thought of him as a brother. Fred was touched. "If you knew how reserved she was, things like that didn't happen too often," he said.

Soon after Helen's diagnosis, Daniel—who had been living and working in upstate New York—took a job in software development in Madison, making it possible to drive to Milwaukee several times a week to see his mother. David, by then working for an architectural firm in Philadelphia, flew to Milwaukee for the weekend whenever he could. He also made sure there were flowers waiting in Helen's room when she checked in for her chemotherapy sessions. Helen returned the favor, traveling with Rita to Philadelphia to be with David during back surgery. "She was weak and frail, but it meant a lot to David, and to her, to be there," recalled Rita. The day before his surgery, David took Helen and Rita on a tour through a historic building he was rehabbing, an excursion that turned out to be a highlight of the trip. Another memorable moment took place while Helen and Rita sat in the glassed-in atrium of their hotel having tea and

Daniel (left) *moved to Wisconsin from upstate New York, taking a job in Madison to make it easier to visit Helen when she was ill. Many weekends found David* (right) *flying to Milwaukee from Philadelphia, where he was working for an architectural firm.*

sandwiches while a windstorm passed by outside, completely unaware that a tornado had touched down one block away. "We had a good laugh out of how calm, cool, and collected we had been," laughed Rita. The next day, walking around the neighborhood littered with fallen trees and damaged buildings, Helen noted that in all the years she had lived in South Dakota, where tornadoes were quite common, she'd never seen that level of damage.

Over the nearly two years Helen was ill, Marjorie DeVey visited regularly, giving the sisters who for much of their adult lives had lived in different parts of the country the chance to spend time together again. Earlier in her life, Helen had asked Dick DeVey to be one of the executors of her will, a task he told her he was glad to take on. "Of course," he recalled later, "I expected her to outlive me by twenty or thirty years." Marjorie's daughter, Deirdre Britt, was impressed with how courageously her Aunt Helen faced her struggle with cancer, and grateful for the example she set.

Marjorie visited Helen regularly during the two years Helen was ill. Spending time together again was bittersweet.

Among those who visited Helen, both at home and later at the hospital, were her dancing instructors and partners, who had become good friends. Holmquist and Mehler came as well, as did Corré—who brought flowers and get-well cards created by the Jewish Home's Alzheimer's patients. Helen found the cards especially meaningful, and repeatedly

An Independent Spirit: The Quiet, Generous Life of Helen Daniels Bader

told Corré, "As soon as I get better, I'll be back." Corré responded by keeping Helen's job open. "We just couldn't . . . no one could . . . fill her shoes," she said. "And we wanted to make sure she knew that we cared for her as much as she cared for those residents."

By late 1989, Helen had moved into the Gordy's home, where Rita nursed her until she entered the hospital for the last time. In November, to Helen's delight, Rita arranged for her daughter Molly Gordy Drew and Molly's one-month-old daughter, Chloe, to come to Milwaukee for a visit, which Molly described as "a great memory for me and my mother."

As Helen got sicker, Alfred grew more and more remorseful over the pain he had caused her, and actually made excuses to stop in and see her, first at her apartment and at the Gordys' home, and later in the hospital. Helen was gracious, understanding how important these visits were to Alfred. According to Molly Gordy Drew, it was while Helen was in the hospital that she asked David, Daniel, and Rita not to blame Isabel for Alfred's behavior over the years. "She told them, 'Please, don't take it out on Isabel. None of it was her fault. Be nice to her.'" Before long, the boys came to love Isabel, and she and Rita became friends.

Helen died on November 21, 1989. David was comforted by the fact that his mother died on her own terms, "where and when" she wanted.

Fighting the cancer as hard as she could, Helen lasted far longer—even at the very end of her life and after being admitted to St. Mary's Hospital for the last time—than her doctors had predicted. As she wished, and with death closing in, Helen was transferred by ambulance to St. Joseph's Hospital, where her oncologist practiced. A day later, and still not ready to die, she slipped into a coma, but only after her doctor and Mehler assured her that she could let go. Alfred, David, and Daniel visited her regularly, and often together, during those last weeks, reuniting as a family. "It was beautiful," recalled David. Death came two days before Thanksgiving, on November 21, 1989, at the age of sixty-two. Said David, "She decided where and when she was going to die, and there was nothing

Before her death, Helen had taken steps ensuring that Daniel (left) *and David* (right) *would be financially secure and that the bulk of her wealth would be placed into the Helen Daniels Bader Charitable Trusts, a vehicle designed to disburse the assets in her estate.*

anyone could do about it. And that was fine." Mehler found it notable that Helen was willing to share such an intimate moment with Alfred. "It was her abiding love and her forgiving nature that allowed her two boys and their father to accompany her through this passage in a very loving environment," he said. That decision, he added, allowed all three "to move on with their lives with a touching and loving memory of a woman who was most important to their lives."

Helen's death notice, published two days later, noted that she had been buried at Milwaukee's Second Home Cemetery, and suggested donations to the Milwaukee Jewish Home. A December 10 memorial service drew a relatively small group of mourners, something Corré said would have suited Helen just fine. "She was very modest, and by choice had stayed in the background her entire life. Yet I knew what a gem she was, and thought to myself, what a beautiful life to come to an end so soon."

David and Daniel spent Thanksgiving that year with the Gordys. "Rita made me come, saying 'You've got to eat,'" David recalled. "I told her I wasn't hungry, and without missing a beat, she said, 'Then you'll just have pie.'" David ended up moving in for five weeks. "What else could I do? There were five kinds of pie!"

Nita Corré (left) *and Mina Tepper* (right), *her successor as president of the Jewish Home, in 2005 with an architectural rendering of an extensive renovation of the facility that took place over the next two years.*
OVATION JEWISH HOME

THE HELEN BADER CENTER

Klitsner had begun talking with Helen about her will even before she became sick, outlining ways to put her fortune to good use. He suggested first taking steps to ensure that David and Daniel were well taken care of, and then moving the bulk of Helen's wealth into the Helen Daniels Bader Charitable Trusts through which, under the direction of her sons, the assets in her estate would be disbursed. Helen liked the idea, and as her health declined, was comforted by the knowledge that the kind of philanthropy she would have liked to have directed herself would be carried out by David and Daniel with the guidance of trusted advisors such as Klitsner.

Between 1989 and late 1991, the trusts would fund a number of ambitious projects. They included a $600,000 grant to establish the Institute on Aging and Environment at UWM to support the work of Cohen and Weisman on improving housing options for the elderly. For a number of years, the institute provided technical assistance to local caregivers on facility design and programming. Indeed, Cohen and Weisman would play a role in bringing Helen's dream of creating a facility that exemplified the highest standard of care for Alzheimer's patients to fruition, consulting on the design of what would become the Helen Bader Center at the Milwaukee Jewish Home. Funded with a $2 million grant from the

Helen Daniels Bader Charitable Trusts, the center opened in 1994, the first of its kind to offer what officials described as "a familiar home-like environment and person-centered care concept," as opposed to what was still the far more common model: clinical, custodial care served up in an institutional setting. It would go on to become internationally known for its award-winning design, innovative programming, and commitment to research on Alzheimer's.

Cohen, writing in *Aging, Autonomy, and Architecture: Advances in Assisted Living*—a resource for researchers, designers, and policy makers, as well as students in gerontology and architecture—described the twenty-four bed unit as a facility "designed to facilitate the highest level of residents' independence, to respect their privacy and dignity, and to promote activities and social interaction." He notes, in particular, the center's goal of promoting its residents' Jewish identity through culturally meaningful experiences. "The religious corner is a den filled with artifacts connected with the residents' religious heritage [and] available as a means for engagement," he writes. One example: "candlesticks that can be used by residents in Friday night services." The area is meant to

The Helen Bader Center opened in 1994 and was renovated in 2013. Today, it features a rooftop garden and a meditation center.

OVATION JEWISH HOME

An Independent Spirit: The Quiet, Generous Life of Helen Daniels Bader

be "an intimate inglenook, providing an opportunity for cozy interactions of small groups."

In 2013, as part of what was by then the Milwaukee Jewish Care Center, the center was renovated. A rooftop patio was created, and programming was expanded to include cooking classes and music therapy. Today, as part of what is now Ovation Jewish Home, the center is classified as a residential memory care facility. At a commemoration of the center's twenty-fifth anniversary in 2018, it was celebrated for its warm, welcoming environment: "Modeled to be just like a resident's home, there are no medical carts, staff wear non-clinical clothing, and residents are encouraged to use common areas for socializing and connecting," reads an official description of the center.

THE HELEN BADER FOUNDATION, INC.

If the Helen Bader Center grew out of Helen's most heartfelt desire, it was the Helen Bader Foundation, Inc. that went on to make the most lasting mark on her legacy. News of the $100 million foundation broke in the *Milwaukee Journal* in November 1991. According to the paper, it was one of the largest charitable funds in the Milwaukee area. Daniel, at the age of twenty-nine, quit his job in Madison, switched gears, and became the foundation's president and chief executive officer. David signed on as a vice president. Joining Daniel and David on the foundation's board of directors, per Helen's wishes, were Dick DeVey, Marvin Klitsner, and tax attorney Jere McGaffey.

Their goal for the foundation, Daniel told the *Milwaukee Journal,* was for it to grow into "a real grass-roots-oriented organization" that recognized the work of small agencies focused on areas of concentration that reflected Helen's interests, such as Alzheimer's disease, Jewish culture and learning in

News of the $100 million Helen Bader Foundation broke in the Milwaukee Journal *in November 1991. According to the paper, it was among the largest charitable funds in the Milwaukee area. Between 1991 and 2015, the foundation distributed roughly $250 million in ways that addressed social ills and enhanced the quality of life of in Milwaukee and beyond.*

Milwaukee, the welfare of children in Israel, and improving the lives of the impoverished and disadvantaged. In a call for grant requests, Daniel speculated that the foundation would award between $5 and $6 million dollars a year, with about 70 percent of its grants going to fund projects in the Milwaukee area. Noted Daniel, "My mother was very much concerned about the city, especially the inner city."

According to Nita Corré, shown here with her husband, Alan, Helen's financial support of the Milwaukee Jewish Home was invaluable, particularly with respect to its facilities and programs for Alzheimer's patients.

OVATION JEWISH HOME

Most people who had known Helen were shocked by the news, flabbergasted to learn that she had been a wealthy woman. But because she had lived an unpretentious and relatively simple life, it hadn't been difficult for Helen to keep her net worth a secret. Baime told of a time when Helen's tuition at the conservatory was coming due, and because it was a relatively large sum, he pointed out that if it would be helpful, he could set up a payment plan. "She must have been laughing [to herself]," he recalled. "But she just said, 'Well, no. I'll be able to take care of it.'"

Even Corré, one of Helen's closest friends, was surprised at the true extent of Helen's wealth, unaware, for example, that the grant she had made to Cohen and Weisman at UWM was so much more than she had imagined, and enough, she believed, to make a real impact. As for Helen's coworkers, they had known her as the fourth-floor social worker who had an especially keen interest in the residents. Recalled Corré, "When they saw the headlines, no one could understand why someone who had so many options and opportunities would spend her lunch hour fixing residents' glasses, feeding them, reading to them, trying to quiet them down. And the only thing I could tell them was that she really cared, that she had a lot of love to share, and that she was very special." Mehler, who had been working closely with Helen since 1984 and knew of her personal philanthropy, was nonetheless surprised to learn from Klitsner, after Helen became ill, of the considerable fortune she and Alfred had amassed. "He told me he thought I should be aware of who she was," he said, "although I'm not sure exactly why." In retrospect, Mehler came to believe that despite her strong will to live, Helen realized fairly early on that she was not going to survive her disease. That realization, he said, prompted a few conversations about her long-term financial goals, the fact that the foundation would be a direct result of her death, and some of the issues she hoped it would address.

To this day, Daniel Bader is amused when people claiming to have known Helen cite her philanthropy as her claim to fame. "That pretty much tells me they never knew her at all," he said. "Yes, she gave away money, but during her lifetime she was not known in the Milwaukee community for her philanthropy. That wasn't her style." Indeed, it was in 1991 that the Legal Aid Society of Milwaukee, which at Helen's insistence had not publicly acknowledged her donations during her lifetime, posthumously named her the recipient of its first Equal Justice Medal, an award designed to recognize individuals making outstanding contributions to social justice causes. "It seemed so natural that we could finally acknowledge to the community what an outstanding contribution she had made, not only in working with our clients but also financially," said Zander.

Daniel assumed the role of president and chief executive officer of the Helen Bader Foundation. In its earliest years, the foundation focused on three areas: the needs of families and children in Milwaukee, Alzheimer's disease, and Jewish education.

Between 1991 and 2015, the Helen Bader Foundation would go on to fund roughly $250 million in projects, most designed to address Milwaukee's social ills and enhance the quality of life of its citizens. Over the years, its efforts cemented Helen's legacy as one of Milwaukee's most prominent philanthropists. Its focus on Alzheimer's disease, for example, was a cornerstone of its mission, as was its dedication to Jewish causes, supported in part through an office in Israel from 1993 to 2010. Helen's deep concern for the marginalized led to millions of dollars in grants to hundreds of local nonprofit agencies.

Early on, the foundation embraced a collaborative process, seeking out partners who could guide its goals, such as the Wisconsin Alzheimer's

Institute, UWM's Center for Youth Work, and the Milwaukee Area Workforce Funding Alliance. Another pillar of its work is an emphasis on supporting local nonprofits, which the foundation believes "are the backbone of strong communities." The foundation has supported, for example, Marquette University's Legal Initiative for Nonprofit Corporations, which provides nonprofits with legal advice; the Nonprofit Management Fund, which provides consulting services for leaders of local nonprofit agencies; and the Wisconsin Nonprofits Association, a source of training, networking, and public policy education.

Foundation officials also placed a high premium on the quality of its own work, joining organizations such as the Council on Foundations, the Wisconsin Philanthropy Network (formerly the Donors Forum of Wisconsin), Grantmakers in Aging, Mission Investors Exchange, and the Philanthropy Roundtable to fine-tune its work in an effort to put in place best investment and funding practices. With a stable board, and a commitment to Helen's legacy and the community it serves, the foundation has been able to steer clear of obstacles that often derail family foundations such as clashes over individual vested interests or disagreement over funding priorities.

THE HELEN BADER SCHOOL OF SOCIAL WELFARE

One of the foundation's most significant investments—and, at the time, the largest in its history—was a $5 million grant to UWM's School of Social Welfare in 2001. The grant established The Helen Bader Endowed Chair in Applied Gerontology, the Helen Bader Scholarship Fund, the Helen Bader Lecture Series, and a number of age-related research studies and other initiatives. With generous, continuing support from the foundation, many of these programs continue today. At a formal ceremony on October 29, 2001, attended by 250 alumni, students, faculty, and members of the community, the school became the Helen Bader School of Social Welfare.

At the ceremony, Daniel noted that "For my family, the school holds a special place in our memories," and went on to recall his mother's time as a UWM student. "She would wake up early so she could work on papers at the kitchen table before dawn. And her MSW fieldwork often went on into the night, helping her see firsthand the needs of our most vulnerable groups—including the homeless, single mothers, and older adults. The skills she honed in the classroom helped her apply her passion for helping others throughout the rest of her life, and I couldn't be prouder that the school is named in her honor."

UWM prides itself on what the school has accomplished: serving the needs of more than ten thousand students who since 1965 have gone on to earn degrees in social work and criminal justice. Particularly noteworthy is the fact that more than 75 percent of those graduates remain in Wisconsin—and principally, in the Milwaukee area—using their skills to improve the quality of life for its most vulnerable citizens.

UWM also benefitted from the foundation's generosity in a number of other ways. Consider, for example, the Helen Bader Institute for Nonprofit Management (HBI), which speaks to Helen's business experience and her appreciation of the role of the nonprofit sector.

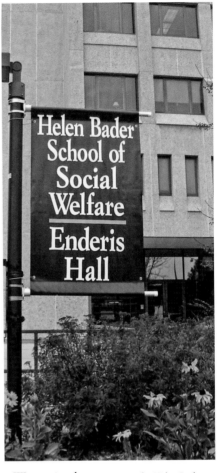

In 2001, the Helen Bader Foundation made a $5 million grant, the largest in its history, to the School of Social Welfare at the University of Wisconsin-Milwaukee. At a formal ceremony on October 29, the school was renamed in Helen's honor.

KATE HAWLEY

Established in 2001 as the first nonprofit academic center in Wisconsin, the institute seeks to connect academics with local nonprofit leaders. According to its website, "Well-managed nonprofit organizations are essential to a thriving community. The services they provide, as well as the economic benefit, civic engagement, philanthropy, and volunteerism they foster, are essential elements in our quality of life." To that end, HBI's mission is defined as an effort "to improve the leadership and effectiveness of nonprofit organizations through education, research and service." Through the College of Letters and Science and the Sheldon B. Lubar School of Business, HBI offers a master's degree in Nonprofit Management and Leadership. Also on

Local facilities named in honor of Helen include (above) *the Helen Bader Concert Hall, in the Helene Zelazo Center on the campus of the University of Wisconsin-Milwaukee, and (below) the Helen Bader Recital Hall at the Wisconsin Conservatory of Music on Milwaukee's East Side. Both commemorate Helen's love of the arts, and particularly, music.*

UWM PHOTO SERVICES–
DEREK RICKERT

WISCONSIN CONSERVATORY
OF MUSIC

An Independent Spirit: The Quiet, Generous Life of Helen Daniels Bader

campus is the 758-seat Helen Bader Concert Hall at the Peck School of the Arts' Helene Zelazo Center, a tribute to Helen's love of music. Notably, the center occupies the site of what once was Temple Emanu-El where Alfred Bader taught Sunday school for many years.

Other legacy initiatives include the Helen Bader Recital Hall at the Wisconsin Conservatory of Music where Helen studied guitar; the Helen Bader Leadership Speaker Series at the Cardinal Stritch University Leadership Center; the Helen Daniels Bader Scholarship at Lawrence University; the Helen Bader Scholarship Fund administered by the Milwaukee Jewish Federation; and Helen Bader Drive, a main thoroughfare on the federation's Karl Jewish Community campus, named in recognition of Helen's belief in the importance of a strong Jewish community, both here and abroad.

Given the quiet, unassuming, private way Helen Bader lived her life, it's not difficult to image her wincing a bit at the image of a banner on the UWM campus proclaiming "The Helen Bader School of Social Welfare" or signage welcoming music lovers to a concert at the Helen Bader Recital Hall at the Wisconsin Conservatory of Music. Yet she'd no doubt take considerable comfort—and, one hopes, a bit of pride—in what her foundation has accomplished to date and its plans for the future. Originally scheduled to close its doors in 2020, the Helen Bader Foundation was given new life in 2015 with an infusion of additional capital from Alfred and Isabel. Restructured as the Helen Daniels Bader Fund under the umbrella of what is now Bader Philanthropies, Inc., it will continue to support Helen's legacy in perpetuity—a testament to the life of a little girl with an independent spirit born on the South Dakota prairie on the eve of the Great Depression.

EPILOGUE

Helen was preceded in death by her father, Lloyd Allyn Daniels, in 1978, and her Uncle Leonard Mabbott, in 1985. Shortly after Lloyd's death, Jessie moved to Fayetteville, New York, where she lived with Marjorie and her family for many years. Jessie died in 1993 at the age of ninety-nine. Dick DeVey lived until 2008, and Marjorie, until 2013. Fred Gordy died in 2017, at the age of ninety-seven. Rita, afflicted with dementia the last few years of her life, eventually moved to the Helen Bader Center at what is now Ovation Jewish Home, where she died in 2019 at age ninety-five. "I'd wheel her over to Danny's portrait, which was hanging on the wall," recalled Rita's daughter Molly Gordy Drew. "And I'd tell her that Danny was watching over her, just like she took care of Danny."

For Alfred, the years following Helen's death were difficult. On the one hand, after pining for Isabel for decades, he found great contentment in their marriage. Yet Alfred was also plagued with guilt over his treatment of Helen. What's more, in 1992, even as he struggled to reconcile his emotions, Alfred was voted off the Sigma-Aldrich board of directors and forced out of the company, which over the next two decades saw considerable growth. By 2013, it was employing 9,000 workers, operating in 37 countries, and reporting annual sales of $2.7 billion. In 2015, it was acquired by Merck KGaA, a German multi-national chemical and pharmaceutical company, for $17 billion. Sigma-Aldrich operates today as a brand of MilliporeSigma.

Alfred spent his last years collecting art; investing in small, emerging chemical companies; speaking dozens of times a year on chemistry and art; and engaging in philanthropy. Although he suffered a stroke in 2010, he kept up his weekly Sunday night phone conversations with Ralph Emanuel for several more years, sometimes telling him, "This is my last call." Death for Alfred Bader came on December 23, 2018. He was ninety-four.

Decades after Helen's death, her relatives and close friends still express deep regret that Helen did not live to see her sons grow into adulthood, meet their wives and children, and witness all they have accomplished. Marvin Klitsner believed David and Daniel each grew into his own person while also incorporating lessons learned from Helen and Alfred to "work hard, value what they had, and not take anything for granted."

Following his mother's death, David enrolled at the Pennsylvania Academy of Fine Arts, where he studied figure drawing, sculpture, and painting; passed his Pennsylvania State architecture boards; and met his first wife, Michelle Henkin, whom he married in 1992. They moved to Upper Bucks County, Pennsylvania, and had three children: Helena (who resembles and is named after her grandmother), Isaiah, and Noa. Following his divorce from Michelle Henkin in 2003, David married Michelle (Chellie) Berrong, who gave birth to their daughter Faye in 2006. In addition to serving as vice president of what is now Bader Philanthropies, Inc., David spends his time working on architecture projects; collecting old master paintings; and, with the help of his devoted employees, running Fat Badger Bakery (FatBadgerBakery.com) in Bucks County.

In February 1991, Daniel left a career in information systems to develop the Helen Bader Foundation, Inc. Working on his own for most of 1991, he launched the foundation in January 1992, assuming the role of president and chief operating officer. In 1994, Daniel married Linda Callif, a social worker who at the time was living in Madison. Three years later, they adopted their son Carlos from Guatemala. Linda and Daniel were blessed with the birth of a biological child, Alexander, in 1999. And four years later, they adopted their daughter, Jessie (named after her great-grandmother), also from Guatemala. In addition to raising their own children, Linda and Daniel have mentored and nurtured several young men working to escape the grip of heroin addiction who have gone on to lead productive lives. Today, Daniel devotes himself to running Bader Philanthropies and spending time with Linda and their children. The family enjoys international travel and has explored many parts of the world together, including family heritage sites in South Dakota, Austria, and Hungary.

Daniel sees himself as more like his father than his mother, both physically ("sort of an Alfred Bader clone, in a way," he says) and in terms of his "hard-nosed" penchant for business. He sees his brother, "very much an artist and very creative," as more like Helen. David agrees, noting that he is cut "more from my mother's cloth in my build and bone structure, but also my aptitudes." Like Alfred, both have grown up with an appreciation for art, and thanks to Helen, a love of music. Both are strong social justice advocates, dedicated family men, and ardent philanthropists.

As for that last point, "Giving and volunteerism have been values that have been instilled in our family from when I was a little kid," notes Daniel. "When we grew up in our family home, we were always talking about who we would give money to and also how we would help other people. It was more than making that check to a nonprofit organization. It was volunteering at a local agency, or even more so, just helping people individually. We grew up in the context that helping people is just part of life."

BADER PHILANTHROPIES, INC.

The Helen Bader Foundation—which had been operating under a sunset clause that saw it due to close its doors in 2020—was given new life in 2015 when it received $10 million in additional income from a trust set up by Alfred and Isabel and was reorganized as Bader Philanthropies, Inc. As a result, the foundation's annual giving, which had been averaging $10 million, increased that year by more than 40 percent. Subsequent, annual payments from the trust continued to grow over the next four years, hitting $20 million in 2019, when Bader Philanthropies' giving totaled nearly $16.5 million. What's more, the infusion of new capital set the stage for the new foundation to continue operating in perpetuity.

As Bader Philanthropies, the organization encompasses two distinct philanthropic funds to reflect the values and interests of their respective namesakes: the Helen Daniels Bader Fund and the Isabel and Alfred Bader Fund. The Helen Daniels Bader Fund "seeks to enhance the lives of older adults in Wisconsin and Israel, to promote the arts, and to further Jewish education." To that end, it funds research in Alzheimer's disease here and in Israel; supports arts education for underserved populations locally; and, through the Helen Daniels Bader Jewish Education Fund, helps support local Jewish day schools and their students.

The Isabel and Alfred Bader Fund "seeks to strengthen Milwaukee and the world, by helping individuals realize their fullest potential through the arts, faith, and individual opportunity." Its grants focus on meeting the needs of low-income Milwaukeeans through workforce development initiatives and programs for youth, supporting Jewish education in greater Milwaukee, and underwriting projects that promote social equality among underserved populations in Israel and central Europe.

Despite the structural changes, Bader Philanthropies continues to operate today in much the same way as did the Helen Bader Foundation, with Daniel serving as president and chief executive officer, and David as vice president and a member of the board of directors. In November 2015, in a nod to Daniel's leadership of the new organization, *Milwaukee Magazine* named him one of its "Most Influential People in Milwaukee." Reads the segment on Daniel: "Passionate. Engaged. Thoughtful. That's how many describe Bader." And as one local leader noted, He's the real McCoy. He makes sure the money is spent wisely.'"

The makeup of the board remains stable. Three members of the original Helen Bader Foundation board (Daniel, David, and Jere D. McGaffey) continue to serve, as do Daniel and David's wives, Linda Bader and Michelle Berrong Bader, respectively. Dick DeVey was succeeded by his daughter, Deirdre DeVey Britt, and Marvin Klitsner, by his daughter Francie Klitsner Wolff. Klitsner's granddaughter, Adina Shapiro, and Isabel's niece Margaret Foster joined the board in 2015. That same year, Isabel began serving as an advisor to the board. Also contributing to the continuity between the two organizations is Bader Philanthropies' emphasis—like that of its forerunner—on working in collaboration with community partners and supporting the work of local nonprofits.

In 2018, in a move designed largely to commemorate what Daniel described as Helen's deeply held passion for those living in poverty in Milwaukee's central city, Bader Philanthropies relocated its headquarters from leased space in downtown Milwaukee to a renovated historic building in the city's Harambee neighborhood on its North Side. "The family is very excited about this," he said, referring to the $12 million project in an interview with the *Milwaukee Journal Sentinel.* "This is who we are." Since 1992, the Harambee neighborhood has been the recipient of nearly $20 million in grants from the Helen Bader Foundation and Bader Philanthropies. Daniel says that's only fitting, given the history of the Aldrich

Chemical Company, which was located from 1951 through 1969 on the city's North Side. "The success of the company had a lot to do with the workforce, and a big component came from the central city. We felt an obligation in honoring our history and legacy to return to our roots as a family and develop a headquarters in a similar type neighborhood." According to the *Journal Sentinel,* more than five thousand people—including many of the neighborhood's residents—visited Bader Philanthropies' new headquarters in its first year, taking part in what Daniel calls "community convenings and conversations." He noted that although he and his staff continue to meet with and learn from professionals, academics, and staff members of other nonprofits about issues related to its funding priorities, "now we can add to that . . . real conversations with the people most affected."

HELEN'S LEGACY

And so, even as Bader Philanthropies' relocation represents a nod to the financial source of the Bader family's philanthropy, its work will continue on into the future, supporting the ideals and values that shaped Helen's life. Yet, beyond that, remains Helen's personal legacy. Consider, for example, the experience of Joan Prince, who as a fifteen-year-old growing up in Milwaukee's central city crossed paths with Helen at Aldrich and came away empowered, more determined than ever to study science. "It made all the difference," said Prince, recalling their interaction. "She taught me that you never know the impact you can have on someone's life. And that's what I've tried to embrace and pass on: to always be available, no matter when or where you are, to someone who needs you or seeks you out."

Helen touched the lives of thousands over the years, including family members, friends, business associates and coworkers, fellow students, clients, and the countless individuals who benefitted from her philanthropy. Prince is just one of many who continue to model their approach to life on what they learned from Helen—whether it be her willingness to break from convention, the joy she took in raising her sons, or the way she bounced back from adversity with determination and grit. Helen Daniels Bader's life—embodied in a quiet and unassuming personality underneath which ran a fiercely independent spirit—was guided by a deep sense of generosity, social justice, and a nonjudgmental approach to life that was nothing short of enlightened. With a sense of humor, compassion, and empathy for society's most needy, and a commitment to the service of others, she lived a life of consequence. The legacy she leaves behind is one of both triumph and hope.

BIBLIOGRAPHY

Sources include materials from the Daniels, DeVey, and Bader family collections; the Helen Bader Foundation, Inc. and Bader Philanthropies, Inc. archives; personal interviews; archival editions of the *Aberdeen American-News, Aberdeen Daily American, Aberdeen Daily News, Aberdeen Evening News, Aberdeen Sunday American-News,* and the *Red Wing Journal;* US and South Dakota census records; and South Dakota Department of Health indices.

Other Sources:

"Alzheimer Disease." *Encyclopædia Britannica.* Britannica.com. https://www.britannica.com/science/Alzheimer-disease.

Bader, Alfred. *Adventures of a Chemist Collector.* London: Weidenfeld and Nicolson, 1995.

———. *Chemistry & Art: Further Adventures of a Chemist Collector.* London: Weidenfeld and Nicolson, 2008.

———. "Which Door Will You Open?" *Milwaukee Journal Sentinel,* April 10, 2016. https://www.jsonline.com/story/opinion/contributors/2016/04/10/alfred-bader-which-door-will-you-open/84900146/.

Bader, Isabel Overton. *A Canadian in Love.* Toronto: Victoria University, 2000.

Bauer, Fran. "One Woman's Dream." *Wisconsin: the Milwaukee Journal Magazine,* March 6, 1994.

Berg, Donald J. "Dusting Off the Dust Bowl: The Historical Geography of the Northern Plains during the 1930s." Paper presented at the West River History Conference, Rapid City, SD, October 2015.

"Blizzard Brings Tragedy to Northwest Plains." *This Day in History: January 12, 1888.* History.com. https://www.history.com/this-day-in-history/blizzard-brings-tragedy-to-northwest-plains.

Breunig, Charles. *A Great and Good Work: A History of Lawrence University, 1847-1964.* Appleton, WI: Lawrence University Press, 1994.

Brown County Museum and Historical Society. *Brown County History.* Aberdeen, SD: Brown County Museum and Historical Society, 1980.

Brown, Ralph J. "Economic Cataclysm: South Dakota and the Great Depression." Power Point Presentation. http://www.powershow.com/view/5d8c1-YTk4N/ECONOMIC_CATACLYSM_SOUTH_DAKOTA_AND_THE_GREAT_DEPRESSION_powerpoint_ppt_presentation.

Burns, Ken. "The Native Americans: Yankton Sioux Indians." *Lewis & Clark: The Journey of the Corps of Discovery.* PBS.org. http://www.pbs.org/lewisandclark/native/yan.html.

Chandler, Kurt, ed. "Most Influential People in Milwaukee." *Milwaukee Magazine,* November 2015.

"Club Movement." Encyclopædia Britannica. Britannica.com. https://www.britannica.com/event/club-movement.

Cohen, Uriel, and Keith Diaz Moore. "Integrating Cultural Heritage into Assisted-Living Environments." *Aging, Autonomy, and Architecture: Advances in Assisted Living*. Edited by Benyamin Schwarz and Ruth Brent. Baltimore: Johns Hopkins University Press, 1999.

Cohen, Uriel, and Gerald D. Weisman. *Holding on to Home: Designing Environments for People with Dementia*. Baltimore: Johns Hopkins University Press, 1991.

Cole, Harry Ellsworth, ed. *A Standard History of Sauk County, Wisconsin*, Vol. 1. Chicago: Lewis Publishing, 1918. http://digicoll.library.wisc.edu/cgi-bin/WI/WI-idx?type=header&id=WI.ColeStandardv1&isize=M.

Daykin, Tom, and Bill Glauber. "Bader Foundation Moving to King Dr." *Milwaukee Journal Sentinel*, August 3, 2016.

Devena.holmes. "Melgaard Park." *Aberdeen Area History* (blog). July 19, 2012. http://www.aberdeenareahistory.org/blog/2012/07/19/melgaard-park/.

Ecenbarger, William. "Cheer Up, It Could Be Worse—Yes, the Recession is Bad, But it's Nothing Like What Happened When America Was Hit by a Real Depression." *Seattle Times*, March 8, 1992. http://community.seattletimes.nwsource.com/archive/?date=19920308&slug=1479900.

Eddy, Mary Baker. *Science and Health with Key to the Scriptures*. 5th ed. Boston: Trustees under the Will of Mary Baker G. Eddy, 1906.

Edlhauser, June. "The Heritage of Milwaukee-Downer College." *Milwaukee Reader* 42, no. 16 (April 16, 1984).

Fast, Howard. *Second Generation*. Boston: Houghton Mifflin, 1978.

Ford, Alyssa. "125 Years Ago, Deadly 'Children's Blizzard' Blasted Minnesota." MINNPOST, January 11, 2013. https://www.minnpost.com/minnesota-history/2013/01/125-years-ago-deadly-children-s-blizzard-blasted-minnesota/.

Gates, Sue, ed. *Looking Back: Aberdeen's First 125 Years*. 2 vols. Aberdeen, SD: Dacotah Prairie Museum Foundation, 2006.

Glauber, Bill. "Alfred Bader Lends Name to Milwaukee Jewish School." *Milwaukee Journal Sentinel*, April 2, 2016.

———. "Bader Family Committed to Giving." *Milwaukee Journal Sentinel*, January 25, 2015.

———. "Bader Philanthropies Part of the Fabric of Milwaukee's Harambee Neighborhood." *Milwaukee Journal Sentinel*, August 19, 2019.

Golub, Rob. "Journey of a Giving Family." *Wisconsin Jewish Chronicle*, June 28, 2017.

Gould, Nathan. "Cornerstone Ceremonies Sunday, September 8." *Wisconsin Jewish Chronicle*, September 6, 1929. https://www.newspapers.com/newspage/49951397/.

Grelson, Eric F. "Blizzard Stories." *Encyclopedia of the Great Plains*. Edited by David J. Wishart. Lincoln, Nebraska: University of Nebraska Press, 2004. http://plainshumanities.unl.edu/encyclopedia/doc/egp.fol.004.

Gurda, John. *The Making of Milwaukee*. Milwaukee: Milwaukee County Historical Society, 1999.

Hamburg, James F. "Railroads and the Settlement of South Dakota During the Great Dakota Boom, 1878-1887." *South Dakota History* 5, no. 2 (Spring 1975). https://www.sdhspress.com/journal/south-dakota-history-5-2/railroads-and-the-settlement-of-south-dakota-during-the-great-dakota-boom-1878-1887/vol-05-no-2-railroads-and-the-settlement-of-south-dakota-during-the-great-dakota-boom-1878-1887.pdf.

Hearn, Michael Patrick. "The Wizard Behind the Plate: L. Frank Baum, the Hub City Nine, and Baseball on the Prairie." *Baum's Road to Oz: The Dakota Years*. Edited by Nancy Tystad Koupal. Pierre, SD: South Dakota State Historical Society Press, 2000.

Humphrey, Hubert H. *The Education of a Public Man: My Life and Politics*. Garden City, New York: Doubleday, 1976.

"Influenza Pandemic of 1918–19." *Encyclopædia Britannica*. Britannica.com. https://www.britannica.com/event/influenza-pandemic-of-1918-1919.

Journal of the House of Representatives during the Fourth Session of the Legislative Assembly of the Territory of Minnesota. St. Paul, MN: Owens & Moore, 1853. https://books.google.com/books?id=DPdBAQAAMAAJ&printsec=frontcover#v=onepage&q&f=false.

Kehoe, Karen, Kevin Abing, and Daryl Webb. "Wartime Milwaukee." *Encyclopedia of Milwaukee*. https://emke.uwm.edu/entry/wartime-milwaukee/.

Kenney, Ray. "Aldrich Firing Up All Burners." *Milwaukee Sentinel,* September 2, 1974.

Kieckhefer, Grace Norton. *The History of Milwaukee-Downer College, 1851-1951*, Centennial Publication. Selection from Lawrence University Special Collections, book 2. Milwaukee: Milwaukee-Downer College, 1951. https://lux.lawrence.edu/cgi/viewcontent.cgi?article=1001&context=selections.

Kingsbury, George Washington. *History of Dakota Territory*. 2 vols. Chicago: S. J. Clarke, 1915.

Kleinman, Lynne H. *The Milwaukee-Downer Woman*. Milwaukee-Downer College Written Histories, book 1. Appleton, WI: Lawrence University Press, 1997. https://lux.lawrence.edu/cgi/viewcontent.cgi?article=1000&context=mdc_writtenhistories.

Koupal, Nancy Tystad. "On the Road to Oz: L. Frank Baum as Western Editor." *Baum's Road to Oz: The Dakota Years*. Edited by Nancy Tystad Koupal. Pierre, SD: South Dakota State Historical Society Press, 2000.

Kramer, J. Howard. *South Dakota State University, a History: 1884 to 1975*. Brookings, SD: South Dakota State University, 1975.

Laskin, David. *The Children's Blizzard*. New York: Harper Perennial, 2004.

Lass, William E. "The Eden of the West." *Making Minnesota Territory: 1849-1858*. Edited by Kaplan, Anne R., and Marilyn Ziebarth. St. Paul, MN: Minnesota Historical Society Press, 1999.

Lee, Shebby. "The Great Dakota Boom." Unpublished manuscript, 1985. Available at https://www. journeymuseum.org/assets/docs/uploads/The%20Great%20Dakota%20Boom.pdf.

McBride, Sarah Davis, ed. *History Just Ahead: A Guide to Wisconsin's Historical Markers*. Madison: State Historical Society of Wisconsin, 1999.

"Milwaukee-Downer College Buildings." The Historical Marker Database. HMdb.org. https://www.hmdb. org/m.asp?m=59605.

New York Times. "Lucia Briggs Dies at 72." January 11, 1960. https://www.nytimes.com/1960/01/11/archives/ lucia-briggs-dies-at-72-head-of-milwaukeedowner-college-from-1921.html?searchResultPosition=1.

"1918 Flu Pandemic in South Dakota Remembered." The South Dakota State Historical Society. https:// history.sd.gov/Archives/docs/Spanish%20Flu%20Article.pdf.

Norton, Minerva Brace. *A True Teacher: Mary Mortimer, a Memoir*. New York: Fleming H. Revell, 1894.

"Orphanage Records." Archdiocese of Milwaukee. archmil.com. https://www.archmil.org/offices/archives/ Orphanage-Records.htm.

Palmer, Virginia A., ed. "Faithfully Yours, Ellen C. Sabin: Correspondence Between Ellen C. Sabin and Lucia R. Briggs from January 1921, to August 1921." *Wisconsin Magazine of History* 67, no. 1 (Autumn 1983).

Pardini, Priscilla. *Women Making a Difference: American Association of University Women in Milwaukee, 1894–2012*. Milwaukee: Milwaukee Branch of the American Association of University Women, 2012.

Peot, Rachel, and Anne Atwood Mead, eds. *Time & Traditions: Lawrence University, Lawrence College, Milwaukee-Downer College, Conservatory of Music, 1847-1988*. Appleton, WI: Lawrence University, 1988.

President's Commission on Law Enforcement and Administration of Justice. *The Challenge of Crime in a Free Society*. Washington, DC: United States Government Printing Office, 1967. https://assets.documentcloud.org/ documents/3932081/Crimecommishreport.pdf.

Rezatto, Helen Graham. *The Making of the Two Dakotas*. Lincoln, Nebraska: Media Publishing, 1989.

Rogers, Katharine. M. *L. Frank Baum, Creator of Oz: A Biography*. New York: St. Martin's, 2002.

Roster of Wisconsin Volunteers, War of the Rebellion, 1861-1865, Vol. 1. Madison: Democrat Printing, 1886. http://archive.org/stream/rosterofwisconsi01wisc#page/691/mode/1up.

Sauer, Alissa. "History of Alzheimer's: Major Milestones." *Our Blog*. Alzheimers.net, December 30, 2013. https://www.alzheimers.net/history-of-alzheimers/.

Schmiedeler, Tom. "Civic Geometry: Frontier Forms of Minnesota's County Seats." *Minnesota History* 57, no. 7 (Fall 2001). http://collections.mnhs.org/MNHistoryMagazine/articles/57/v57i07p330-345.pdf.

Schuler, Harold A. *A History of Pharmacy in South Dakota*. Sioux Falls, SD: Pine Hill Press, 2004.

Secretary of the Interior. "Annual Report of the Secretary of the Interior on the Operations of the Department for the Year Ended June 30, 1881, Volume II." Washington, DC: Government Printing Office, 1882.

Seymour, E. S. *Sketches of Minnesota: The New England of the West; With Incidents of Travel in that Territory During the Summer of 1849*. New York: Harper & Brothers, 1850. https://books.google.com/books?id=oVMzAQAAIAAJ&q=new+england#v=onepage&q=new%20englandnew%20england&f=false.

Sigma-Aldrich Corporation. "Merck KGaA, Darmstadt, Germany, to Acquire Sigma-Aldrich to Enhance Position in Attractive Life Science Industry," September 22, 2014. http://news.emdgroup.com/N/0/553D2351699994CBC1257D5B0029982E/%24File/EMD20140922.pdf.

———. "Sigma-Aldrich Corporation Announces Filing of Definitive Proxy Statement and Date of Special Meeting of Stockholders," November 3, 2014. https://web.archive.org/web/20141103210435/http://investor.sigmaaldrich.com/releasedetail.cfm?ReleaseID=879879.

Smith, Eleanor. "A Link Between Repressed Emotions and Cancer?" *San Francisco Examiner*, November 26, 1988.

"State Board Examinations." *The Pharmaceutical Era* 49, no. 2 (February 1916).

Staub, Patrick. *It Happened In South Dakota: Remarkable Events that Shaped History*. Guilford, CT: Globe Pequot Press, 2010.

Tank, Ronald. *The Consolidation of Milwaukee-Downer College and Lawrence College*. Milwaukee-Downer College Written Histories, book 3. Appleton, WI: Lawrence University, 2019. https://lux.lawrence.edu/mdc_writtenhistories/3.

Territorial Pioneers and Descendants. *Early History of Brown County, South Dakota: A Literature of the People*. Aberdeen, SD: Western Publishing Company, 1965.

Torrey, Edwin C. *Early Days in Dakota*. Glendale, CA: Arthur H. Clark, 1925.

"Understanding the Great Sioux Nation." *Akta Lakota Museum & Cultural Center*. aktalakota.stjo.org. http://aktalakota.stjo.org/site/News2?page=NewsArticle&id=9017.

US Department of Education. "High School Graduates, by Sex and Control of School: Selected Years, 1869–70 through 2019–20." *Digest of Education Statistics,* (August 2010). https://nces.ed.gov/programs/digest/d10/tables/dt10_110.asp.

US Department of Education. "Historical Summary of Faculty, Students, Degrees, and Finances in Degree-Granting Institutions: Selected Years, 1869–70 through 2008–09." *Digest of Education Statistics,* (September 2010). https://nces.ed.gov/programs/digest/d10/tables/dt10_196.asp.

United States Holocaust Memorial Museum. *"Kristallnacht."* Holocaust Encyclopedia. https://encyclopedia.ushmm.org/content/en/article/kristallnacht.

"Wooden Horses for Training Recruits." *Field Artillery Journal* 7, no. 3 (1917): 337. https://books.google.com/books?id=Z7lMAAAAYAAJ.

Zaret, Melvin S. "Klitsner Was an Architect of the Best in Our Community." *Wisconsin Jewish Chronicle*, March 31, 2008.

Index

Numbers in *italics* denote illustrations.

Aberdeen, SD, xi, 1, 5, 11-19, *14*, *15*, 45, 55, *69*, 73-74, 110, 139-144; commerce, 12, 13, 14, 16, 17 20-21, 27, 70; Hub City, 12, *12*; population, 12, 45; schools, 13, *34*, 37-40, *39*, 82; settlement, 12-13; social life, 13-14, 28-29

Adventures of a Chemist Collector (Bader), 95-96, 101, 115, 154

Aetna Insurance Company, 21, 23, 58

African Americans, 40, 85, 93, 107, 108-109, *109*, 144-146, 170-171

Aldrich Chemical Company, *94*, 95, 104-109, *105*, 113-114, 116, *117*, 127, 149, 151, 161-162, 223-224; name, 105

Alfred Bader Fine Arts, 116

Allyn, Helen, 3-4, 61

Allyn, John Sidney, 3-4, *3*, 27

Allyn, Theresa Gaylord, 3, *3*, 4, *4*

Alzheimer, Alois, 186, *186*

Alzheimer's disease, 168, 186-193, 200, 205, 211-212, 215, 223

American Indians, *8*, 74, 92, 107, 191; Chippewa, xi, 1, 2-3, 4; Sioux, xi, *xiv*, 1, 6, 7; trading, 2, 8; treaties, 6, 7

Arishe Sfard, 100-101

B & D Motor Company, 31, 32

Bader, Alexander, 222

Bader, Alfred (father), 95-96

Bader, Alfred Robert, 95-117, *124*, 144, *159*, *181*; adoption, 96-97; art collecting, xi, 103, 114-117, *116*, *117*, 121, 132, 134, 144, 149, 221; Asperger's Syndrome, 159; birth, 95; in Canada, 98-99; character, 95, 108, 110, 113-114, 127-128, 129, 133-134, 149, 158-159, 178; and children, 119, *119*, *122*, 123, 126, 128, 131-139, *132*, *148*, 151, 158, 167, 175-176, 179, *181*; citizenship, 99-100, 127; death, 221; divorce, 158, 166-167, 175-181; education, 95, 98, 99-100, *99*; employment, 95, 96-97, 100, 104, *114*, *151*, 161-162, *162*, 221 (*see also* Aldrich Chemical Company); and Helen, xi, *94*, 95, 100, 101-103, 110, *110*, 114-116, *117*, 119, 127-128, 132, 135, 149-150, 153, 157-159, 162, 165-167, *166*, 175-181, 199, *199*, 209-210, 219, 221; internment, 98-99; and Isabel, 101, 103, 153-159, 166, 177-179, 219, 221; and Judaism, 95, 97, 98, 100-101, 114, 130, *131*, 134, 135, 137, 155, 157, 223; philanthropy, 109, 117, 199, 219, 221, 222-224; travel, 98-99, 103, 105-106, 116, 119-120, 121, 131, 132, 134-135, 155-156, 180; weddings, *94*, *102*, 103, 179

Bader, Carlos, 222

Bader, Daniel Joseph, viii, 117, 122, 123, *123*, *124*, 126, 129-131, *129*, *130*, *133*, 139, *144*, *145*, *146*, 166, 167, *207*, *209, 210*, 211, 215, *215*, 216-217, 222, 223-224; birth, 119; children, 222; education, 127, 134, 144-145, 151, 152-153; employment, 147, 151, 166, 207, 213-214, 222, 223; and father, 114, *119*, 123, 131-135, *132*, *148*, 151-152, 167, 175-176, 179, 181, *181*, 195, 222; and Isabel, 179, 181, 209; and Judaism, 100, 130, 134-139; and mother, ix, xi, *118*, *119*, *120*, 121, 128-133, 135, *140*, *146*, *147*, *153*, *160*, 195, 200, 207, 209-210, 221; name, 119; reminiscences, 129, 130, 133, 135, 138, 139, 141, 145, 167, 185, 195, 222; travel, 121, 134-144, *135*, 222

Bader, David Martin, *124*, 126, 129-131, *129*, *130*, *133*, *144*, *145*, *146*, *158*, 188, *195*, *207*, *209*, *210*, 211, 221-222; birth, 119; children, 221; education, 127, 134, 144-145, 151-152, 192, 221; employment, 135, 147, 151, 152, 207, 213, 222, 223; and father, *119*, *122*, 131-134, *132*, *148*, 151-152, 158, 175-176, 179, 181, *181*; and Isabel, 179, 181, 209; and Judaism, 100, 130, 134-139; and mother, vii-viii, xi, *118*, *119*, *120*, 121, *121*, 128-133, *128*, 135, *140*, *147*, 165, *165*, 192, 194, 195, 197, 200, 207, 209-210, 222; name, 119; reminiscences, 54, 107, 127, 128, 129, 130, 131, 132, 134, 136, 139, 140, 141, 144-145, 149, 151, 158, 166, 167, 175, 185, 197, 209-210; travel, 121, 134-144, *135*

Bader, Elisabeth Serényi, 95-96, 98

Bader, Faye, 222

Bader, Helen Ann Daniels, *i*, viii, *60*, *62*, 63-68, *63*, *64*, *65*, *66*, *67*, 75, 81, 82, *82*, 83, 88, *89*, 92, *107*, *110*, 122-125, *123*, *124*, 126, *148*, *149*, *150*, *160*, *174*, *176*, *178*, *182*, *185*, *191*, *195*, *196*, 198-199, *198*, *201*, *202*, *213*, 224; and Alfred, xi, *94*, 95, 100, 101-103, 110, *110*, 114-116, *117*, 119, 122, 127-128,

131, 133, 135, 149-151, 153, 158, 159, 162, 164, 166-167, *166*, 175-181, 199, *199*, 209-210; birth, 60-61; cancer, 203-209, 215; character, vii, viii, xi, 35, 67-68, 107-108, 123, 125, 126, 141-142, 146, 150, 164, 166, 174, 191, 192, 219, 224; and children, vii-ix, *118*, 119-121, *119*, *120*, *121*, 126-127, 128-142, *128*, *140*, 144-147, *146*, *147*, *153*, *160*, 165, *165*, 194, 195, 200, 207, 209, 211; and Christian Science, ix, 65, 131, 204; and dance, 189-190, *189*, 205, *205*; death, 209-210; divorce, 164, 166-167, 175-181; education, xi, 87-88, *87*, 89, *90*, 128, 164-166, 168-171, 175, 216-217; employment, ix, xi, 88, 93, 104, 105-108, 110, 126-127, 161, 162, 165, 183-186, 205, 209; and guitar, 196-197, 205-206, 219; homes, 30, *31*, *62*, 104, 114-115, *115*, 121, 127, *130*, 133, *146*, 167, 194-195, *194*, *195*; and Isabel, 179-180, *180*, 181, 209; and Judaism, ix, 100, 101, 103, 130-131, *131*, 150, 179, 196, 203-204, 215, 219, 223; names, ix, 3-4, 61, 87, 196; philanthropy, xi, 196, 199-201, 205, 211-219, 222-224; politics, 93, 150; and social work, ix, xi, 45-46, 107, 164-165, 168-175, 183-193; travel, 64-65, *102*, 103, 107, 116, 119-120, 134-135, 137, 150-151, 203; and violin, viii, xi, 87, 103, *104*, 130, *161*, 167; wedding, *94*, *102*, 103

Bader, Helena, 167, 221

Bader, Isabel Overton, 101, 103, 153-159, *154*, *156*, 177, 178, 179-181, *180*, *181*, 209, 219, 221, 222, 223

Bader, Isaiah, 221

Bader, Jessie, 222

Bader, Linda Callif, 117, 167, 222, 223

Bader, Michelle Berrong, 222, 223

Bader, Michelle Henkin, 221-222

Bader, Noa, 222

Bader Philanthropies, Inc., xi-xii, 138, *220*, 222-224; Helen Daniels Bader Fund, 219, 223; Isabel and Alfred Bader Fund, 223

Baime, Peter, 196-197, *197*, 205-206, 214

Baum, L. Frank, 17-19, *18*, 80, 81

Baum, Maud Gage, 13, 17, 80

Beecher, Catharine, 47

Beth El Congregation, 179, 190, 196

Beth Moshav Zekanium, 183. *See also* Milwaukee Jewish Home

Breslauer, Barbara, 95

Briggs, Lucia Russell, 85, *85*, 89

Britt, Deirdre DeVey, 108, 119, 120-121, *120*, *121*, *122*, *125*, *139*, *141*, 223; reminiscences, 57, 67, 74, 81, 114, 125, 133, 142, 143, 168, 192, 208

Buttz Drug Store, 59

Canadian in Love, A (Bader), 156, 157

Cardinal Stritch University: Helen Bader Leadership Speaker Series, 219

Chicago, Milwaukee, and St. Paul Railroad Company, 12, 15, 16, 27, 28, 31, 139

Cohen, Uriel, 192-193, 205, 211-213, 214

Cooper, Marilyn, 167

Corré, Alan, 162-163, *214*

Corré, Nita, 126, *126*, 129, 131, 162-165, *163*, 166, 183, 185-186, 188, 191, 192, 194, 205, 208, 209, 210, *211*, 214, *214*

crime and criminals, 4, 15, 23, 28, 85, 96

Dakota Territory, 6-11, *6*, *7*, *9*, 68-69

Daniells, Daniels, 58

Daniels: family tree, xiv, 1

Daniels, Jessie Leonia Mabbott, viii, *21*, *22*, 25, *34*, 35-40, *35*, *36*, *41*, *43*, *44*, *50*, *53*, 55-61, *56*, *75*, 80-82, 84, 110-112, *110*, 119-120, *120*, *124*, 138, *139*, 141-144, *141*, *143*, 191, *191*; birth, 20; and children, 57, *57*, 59, *59*, 60-61, *62*, 63-68, 80-82, 87, *89*, *90*, 101, *102*, 110-112, *110*, 221; and Christian Science, 59-60, 65, 80; and Daniels Drugs, 68, 75-77, 92; death, 221; education, 35-36, 37-40, 42-44, 46, 49-53; employment, 53, 126; homes, 30, *31*, 57, *62*, *118*, 140; social life, 36, 43, 53, 55-56, 58, 221; wedding, 56

Daniels, Joseph Wilson Jr., 11-12, *26*, 27-28, 30-33, *32*, *33*, 60, 63, 65, 77, 92, *93*, 139, 141; birth, 2-3; death, 32, 92

Daniels, Joseph Wilson Sr., 2

Daniels, Kenneth Mabbott, 57, 59, *59*, 80, 81, 140

Daniels, Lloyd Allyn, *26*, 29, 30, 32, *33*, *34*, 35-41, *36*, *44*, 54-57, *54*, *56*, 58-59, 64, *74*, 80, 84, 107, 110, 119-120, *120*, *124*, 125, 139-144, *141*, *142*, *143*; birth, 27; and children, 57, 59, 60-61, 66-67, *67*, 84, 87, *89*, 101, *102*, 110; death, 158, 191, 221; education, 37-41; employment, 31, 37, 54, 55, 58-59 (*see also* Daniels Drugs); homes, 30, *31*, 57, *62*; military service, 54-55; nickname, 54, 77; wedding, 56

Daniels, Martha Uselton, 2-3

Daniels, Nathaniel, 2

Daniels, Pearl Rose Allyn, 3, 11, *26*, 27, 28-30, *29*, 31, 32-33, *33*; death, 32, 60

Daniels Drugs, xi, 68-71, *69*, *71*, 74-80, *76*, *78*, 87, 92, 140, 142, 191

dementia, 183, 186. *See also* Alzheimer's disease

DeVey: family tree, xiv, 1

DeVey, Allyn, 93, *102*, 119, *121*, *122*, *123*, *141*; reminiscences, 121, 142

DeVey, Dan, 119, *122*, *141*; reminiscences, 81, 121, 123, 125, 142, 162

DeVey, Don, 82-83, *89*

DeVey, Graham, 93, *102*, 112, 119, *121, 122, 123, 141*; reminiscences, 121, 122-123, 142-143

DeVey, Helen, 82, *89*

DeVey, Marjorie Jean Daniels, *25, 57, 59, 66*, 67, 82-84, *84*, 110, 112, 119-121, *120, 139*, 153; birth, 57; death, 221; education, 82-87, *86*; employment, 86-87, 88, 126; family tree, xiv, 1; and Helen, 63, 64-68, *64, 65*, 75, 82, *82*, 84, 88, *90*, 93, 101, *102*, 119, 122, 176, 208, *208*; nickname, 85; reminiscences, 25, 31, 60, 61, 63, 64, 66-68, 70, 71, 74, 75, 77, 78-79, 85, 86, 88, 92, 93, 95, 122, 127, 185, 195; wedding, 88-89, *89*

DeVey, Richard Wilder, 82-84, *83, 84*, 93, 101, *102*, 119, 121, *122, 139*, 153, 177, 197, 208, 213, 223; birth, 82; death, 221; reminiscences, 83, 101, 129; wedding, 88-89, *89*

DeVey, Victoria, 82, *83, 89*

Dick, Marion Overton, 154, 157, 179

Dirty Thirties, 72-75, *72, 73*, 79, 112

Downer, Jason, 48

Downer College, 48, 49. *See also* Milwaukee-Downer College

Draeger, Henry, 31, 32, 33

Draeger Land & Loan Company, 30, 31, 58

Drew, Chloe, 209

Drew, Molly Gordy, 159, 195, 209, 221

Dust Bowl, 72-75, *72, 73*, 79

Ed. Schuster & Co., 87, 88

Eddy, Mary Baker, 59-60, 204

Edelstein, Bernie, *162*

Edge, Cyril, 125, *181*

Edge, Marion, 96, *124*, 125, 155, *181*

Edge, Robert, 125, *181*

Eisendrath, Jack, 95, 104, 105

Eisenhower College, 152-153

Elkin, Rosetta Wolff, *124*, 125

Elkin, Victor, *124*

Emanuel, Alfred, 106

Emanuel, Bessy, 98, 103

Emanuel, Moritz, 98

Emanuel, Muriel, 106, 116, 177-178, *177*

Emanuel, Ralph, 103, 106, *106*, 116, 126, 127-128, *127*, 129, 134, 158-159, 167, 176, 177-179, 180, 221

Farrington, Maudie, 20, 21, *22*

Fat Badger Bakery, 222

fires, 7, 15, 68, 82

Flansburgh, Allan, 43

Flansburgh, Edgar John, 4-5, *5*, 22

Flansburgh, Eliza Sarah Farrington, 5, *5*

Flansburgh, Leon, *1, 42*, 43

Fort Lennox, *98*, 99

Foster, Margaret, 223

Gage, Dorothy Louise, 18, 81

Gage, Henry, 18

Gage, Matilda Jewell, 18, 80-81, *81*

Gage, Matilda Joslyn, 17, *17*, 18-19, 80, 81

Gage, T. Clarkson, 17

gerontology, 168-170, 171, 183-185, 216

Goodale Pharmacy, 37, 40, 54, 55, 58, 70

Gordy, Fred, 126, 176, *176*, 189, 195, 206-207, *206*, 221

Gordy, Rita, vii, 126, 127, 128, 176, *176*, 190, 191, 195, 197, 205, 206-208, *206*, 209, 210, 221

Granger, Ethel, *33, 56*

Great Depression, xi, 63, 71, 72, 89, 96, 191

Gugel, Rita Nacken, 188

Gut, Ellen, *86*

Harvard University, 95, 100, 101

Harvey, David, 127

Helen Bader Center, 211-213, *212*, 221

Helen Bader Concert Hall, *202, 218*, 219

Helen Bader Drive, 219

Helen Bader Endowed Chair in Applied Gerontology, 216

Helen Bader Foundation, Inc., 138, 213-219, 222-223

Helen Bader Institute for Nonprofit Management, 217

Helen Bader Leadership Speaker Series, 219

Helen Bader Lecture Series, 216

Helen Bader Recital Hall, *218*, 219

Helen Bader Scholarship Fund (Milwaukee Jewish Federation), 219

Helen Bader Scholarship Fund (UWM), 216

Helen Bader School of Social Welfare, xi-xii, 216-217, *217*

Helen Daniels Bader Charitable Trusts, 210, 211-212

Helen Daniels Bader Fund, 219, 223

Helen Bader Jewish Education Fund, 223

Helen Daniels Bader Scholarship (Lawrence University), 219

Hergoz, Robert, 96-97

Hill, Lorraine, *196*

Hillel Academy, 127, 134

Holding on to Home (Cohen & Weisman), 193, *193*

Holmquist, Carson, 167

Holmquist, Nina, 128, *128*, 165, 166, 167, 175, 208

Holmquist, Tom, 167

Home for the Aged, 183. *See also* Milwaukee Jewish Home

Humphrey, Hubert H., 79, *79*

Hunt, Ruth, 155

Isabel and Alfred Bader Fund, 223

Jewish Community Foundation, 199

Jewish Home for the Aged, 183. *See also* Milwaukee Jewish Home

Johnson, John Bockover, 89

Kindertransport, 97-98, *97*

Kirk, Carol, *86*

Kirkland Lake, Ontario, 154, *154*

Klitsner, Jane, 112, *112*, 176, 179

Klitsner, Marvin, 112-113, *112, 113*, 116, 129, 134, 145, 162, 165, 175, 176, *176*, 178, 179, 192, 199, 205, 211, 213, 214-215, 221, 223

Kozak, Hilda, 96, 98

Kristallnacht, 97, 159

Lawrence University, 52, 91, 199-200, 203; Helen Daniels Bader Scholarship, 219

Legal Aid Society of Milwaukee, 168, 172-174, 199, 200; Equal Justice Medal, 215

Levy & Daniels, 2, 3

Lohr, C. H., 70

Long Fox (Yankton Sioux), *xiv*, 1

Mabbott, Blanche Dusseau, 61, *102*

Mabbott, Edward James, 4, *5*

Mabbott, George Amos, 11, 12, 20-23, *22*, *24*, 25, 36, *60*, 61; birth, 4, 49; death, 68; homes, 21, *21*, 25, 49

Mabbott, Leonard, 20, 24-25, 35, 36, 41-42, *41*, 46, 59, 61, *61*, *102*, 221

Mabbott, Leonia Annie Flansburgh, 11, 20, *21*, *22*, 23-25, *24*, *25*, 29, *29*, 63, 66, 67, 68, 82, 87; birth, 5, 20; death, 88; homes, *20*, 21, *21*, 25, 49, 64

Mabbott, Margaret Bernard, 4, *5*

Mabbott, Marilyn, 61, *102*

Mabbott, Parke, *5*

Marquette University: Legal Initiative for Nonprofit Corporations, 216

Marshall Field & Company, 21, 88

Mayer, David, 97, 119, 135

McGaffey, Jere D., 213, 223

Mehler, Peter, 179, 190, *190*, 196, 201, 204, *204*, 205, 206, 208, 209, 210, 214-215

Meir, Ruth, 135-137

Melgaard, Oscar, *56*

Merck KGaA, 221

MilliporeSigma, 221

Milwaukee, WI, 44-46, *45*, 84-85, 104, 141; population, 45; social problems, 45-46, 85, 175, 214, 215, 223

Milwaukee Area Workforce Funding Alliance, 216

Milwaukee College, 47, 48

Milwaukee-Downer College, 43, 46-53, *47*, 82, 84, 85-86, 87-88, 89-92, *169*

Milwaukee Female College, 47

Milwaukee Female Seminary, 46-47, 49

Milwaukee Jewish Care Center, 213. *See also* Milwaukee Jewish Home

Milwaukee Jewish Federation: Helen Bader Drive, 219; Helen Bader Scholarship Fund, 219

Milwaukee Jewish Home, 163-165, 183-193, *183*, *184*, *188*, 205, 208-209, 210; Helen Bader Center, 211-213, *212*, 221

Milwaukee Jewish Welfare Fund, 113

Milwaukee Normal Institute and High School, 47

Milwaukee State Normal School, 48, *49*, 86

Milwaukee State Teachers College, 86, 90

Mork, Clyde, 142

Mortimer, Mary, 47

Mount Sinai Green Tree Health Care Center, 168

Murphy Paint Company, 100

Narregang, Vera, 39

Nonprofit Management Fund, 216

Northern Normal and Industrial School, 38, 42-43, *43*, 53, 82

Northern Pacific Railroad, 8, 10

Northern State Teachers College, 82

Northern States Power Company, 42, 61

Olwin Dry Goods Company, 20-21, 23, 25

Oostburg, WI, 146, 167, 194

Orkin, Sarah Wolff, 98, *124*, 125

Ovation Jewish Home, 213, 221. *See also* Milwaukee Jewish Home

Overton, Clifford, 154

Overton, Herbert, 154

Overton, Stella Sirr, 154, 157, 179

Page, Warren J., 68-69

pharmacies, 68-71, 75, 80; Buttz Drug Store, 59; Goodale, 37, 40, 54, 55, 58, 70; Humphrey's Drug Store, 79. *See also* Daniels Drugs

philanthropy: Alfred, 109, 117, 199, 219, 221, 222-224; Helen, xi, 196, 199-201, 205, 211-219, 222-224

Pittsburgh Plate Glass Company, 95, 100, 104, 105

Portch, Christine, *156*

Portch, Harry, *156*

Portch, Stephen, *156*

Portch, Yvonne, *156*

Prince, Joan, 108-109, *109*, 224

Queen's University, 99, 116-117, 152

racism, 40, 51, 175

railroads, 8, 10-11, 12, 16-17, *16*, 27-28, 139

Ralph N. Emanuel Ltd., 106

Reich, Gisela Bader, 96-98, 125, 149

Reich, Sigmund, 96

Renner, Dorothy, 51

Riverside High School, 123, 144-145, 175

Rochester Institute of Technology, 153

Sabin, Ellen Clara, 48, *48*, 49-51, 85

St. Rose Orphanage, xi, 175, *175*

Scharff, Ethel, 98, 99

Scharff, Sidney, 98, 99

Shapiro, Adina, 223

Shapiro, David, 100-101, *100*, 103, 134, 176, 203, *203*

Shapiro, Etta, 203, *203*

Sheboygan, WI, 194-196

Sigma-Aldrich Corporation, 161-162, 221

Sigma Chemical Company, 161

Smith, Samuel, 39-40

South Dakota, 1-2; Children's Blizzard, 9-10, 9; Dakota Territory, 6-11, *6*, *7*, *9*, 68-69; exploration, 1; gold rush, 8; grasshoppers, 7, 8, 72, 73-74; Homestead Act, 6; name, 1, 6; population, 10, 72; settlement, 6-11; social problems, 45, 71-75, *72*, *73*; statehood, 11; weather, 1, 7, 9-10, *9*, 15, *15*, 19, *19*, 21, 72-73, 111, 208. *See also* Aberdeen, SD

South Dakota State College of Agriculture and Mechanic Arts, 40-41, *40*

South Dakota State Pharmaceutical Association, 58-59, 70, 71, 75, 80

South Dakota State University, 200

Stojkovic, Stan, xi

Taft, William Howard, 38, *38*

Temple Emanu-El B'ne Jeshurun, 95, 100, *100*, 112, 219

Tepper, Mina, *211*

Thorpe, Harry, 100

University of Wisconsin-Madison, 152

University of Wisconsin-Milwaukee, 49, *49*, 90-92, 109, 152, 163, 165, 168-171, *169*, 192-193; Center for Youth Work, 216; Helen Bader Concert Hall, *202, 218*, 219; Helen Bader

Endowed Chair in Applied Gerontology, 216; Helen Bader Institute for Nonprofit Management, 217; Helen Bader Lecture Series, 216; Helen Bader Scholarship Fund, 216; Helen Bader School of Social Welfare, xi-xii, 216-217, *217*; Institute on Aging and Environment, 211

Van Houten, Jane Evelyn, 88
Victor, Emil, 15

Walfoort, Jerline E., 88, 199
Ward, Stella, *196*
Weis, Fran, *150*
Weisman, Gerald D., 192-193, 205, 211-212, 214
Wisconsin Alzheimer's Institute, 215-216
Wisconsin Conservatory of Music, 196-197, 199, 214; Helen Bader Recital Hall, *218*, 219

Wisconsin Female College, 47-48
Wisconsin Nonprofits Association, 216
Wisconsin State College, Milwaukee, 90
Wisconsin State Public Defender's Office, 167, 170
Wolff, Francie Klitsner, 113, 129, 130-131, 149-150, 159, 178-179, 192, 223
Wolff, Martin, 99, 119, 125
women, 47; education, 39, 42, 46-48, 49-50, 84; employment, 85
Women's Medical College of Philadelphia, 46, *46*
World War I, 36, 53, 54-55
World War II, 84-85

Zander, Thomas, 172-174, *173*, 200-201, *200*, 215
Zietlow, John L. W., 14
Zupnik, Steffie, 126-127, *126*, 128, 165, 187